Ringside
at the
Fireworks

The air battle of World War II as experienced by a lead pilot in a B-17 bomber, Governor of Iowa, and Federal Executive

By
Governor Norman A. Erbe

I

© 1997, First Printing

Published by
Toreador Press
P.O. Box 25218, Des Moines, IA 50265

Printed by
Sigler Printing & Publishing, Inc.
Ames, Iowa 50010-0887

Library of Congress Catalog Card Number: 97-090118
ISBN Number: 1-888223-10-3

TABLE OF CONTENTS

DEDICATION

This book is dedicated to my wonderful wife, Jackie, who has sustained me in my long life, and to our three great daughters, De Elda, Jennifer, and Kevin. They have cheered me on and encouraged me down through the years. Also to our five wonderful grandchildren, Justine, Ellen, Charlie, Henry, and Jacqueline, who now have my answer to the questions about the experiences and life of their grandparents. It was exciting!

ACKNOWLEDGEMENTS

Thanks to Graham Cook, without whom this book would not have been possible either in its concept, its beginning, or its conclusion. Deep appreciation to Rod Stafford and Heidi and Jeff Rains who made it possible to share it with the readers, and to my editors: Edward Sisson, Julia Bergman, Dee Wittmack, Jennifer Wilson, and Catherine Cook. And many thanks to Jack Day who made it all happen in an orderly fashion.

FORWARD

A preacher's youngest son from a small town in Iowa didn't know it couldn't be done, so he just went ahead and did it: he worked his way through college, was commissioned a 2nd. Lt. in the Infantry, became a pilot of a B-17 Flying Fortress, and flew 32 bombing missions over Nazi Germany. He went on to become a lawyer, the Attorney General of Iowa and the Governor of Iowa. He was later appointed by the President of the United States of America to the highest, non-elected, administrative position in the United States Government. In the meantime, he and his wife raised three terrific daughters, and they now enjoy five wonderful grandchildren.

Here is his story...

ONE: PREACHER'S SON TO FIGHTING MAN

I grew up in the parsonage of the Trinity Lutheran Church in Boone, engaging in the usual pursuits of children my age: running errands to the nearby grocery store for my mother, watching the blacksmith practice his art on various horses that had been brought to the neighborhood farrier for new shoes, and chasing the horse-drawn ice wagon on a hot day as it delivered ice, hoping to nab chips of ice to suck. I hiked with neighborhood boys along abandoned railroad tracks in search of excitement, watched the Ringling Brothers, Barnum & Bailey Circus unload their train on a nearby street as they prepared to parade through downtown Boone on the way to the circus grounds, and witnessed the erection of the big top with the help of the elephants.

Sundays would find me in the next door church listening to my father preach a German sermon and taking up the collection. Following the service, I replaced the German language hymn books with the English version in preparation for his second service of the day in the English language.

From 1934 to 1937, Boone High School, with its various activities, readily attracted my attention. An exciting new world opened up. I challenged the baritone horn until I could play the tune "America." I soon discarded that effort, and swam the 20' x 50' high school pool in the buff, and learned the magic of checking out library books that carried me to faraway places. I performed roles in school plays and joined the school football team, over the mild objections of my parents who feared injuries, and then as a Senior, I experienced the initiation to infatuation.

The object of my affection was Jacqueline Doran, who practiced the cello in the high school orchestra every morning before classes. I went to school early so that I might stand in back of the auditorium and admire her as she practiced with the orchestra. Finally, a mutual friend, Bruce Corl, acceded to my request for an introduction and the connection was made.

Dates consisted of movies in downtown Boone. This meant a fifteen block walk to her home, another nine blocks to the movie house, and then back to her home and then back to my home again. When the snowstorms were roaring over Iowa, this was a cold walk for Jackie clad in a short raccoon jacket and high heels. Jackie and I saw each other infrequently, our time taken up with other interests and my constant search for jobs. Summers were filled with part-time employment for a general contractor, or over in Illinois, packing peas for Del Monte. In winter, work was more scarce. I prayed for blizzards. The railroad hired high school boys to clear the tracks of huge snowdrifts. We earned forty cents per hour.

High school graduation approached and the need to earn money for a college education became imminent. We all had to work our way through college since my father's compensation in those days was $2,500 per year. My parents were second generation German-Americans and of very conservative Lutheran stock. They practiced the work ethic, instilled this in their children, and believed that higher education was for the men in the family only.

My sister, Ellen, was encouraged to go to business school and get a job as a secretary, which she did reluctantly. She ultimately left the secretarial field and went to the University of Iowa to study nursing.

My two brothers and I were expected to work and secure board jobs to provide food while at the university. We sent our dirty laundry home in boxes to be washed each week. Working as a common laborer for a contractor in Boone, my brother Herbert and I were able to amass the tuition of $45 per semester at the University of Iowa.

There were four Erbe children at the University at the same time— all of us carrying a full load of classes and working part time. Below are listed the educational achievements of my siblings.

Olga - BA in French and Education, BS and MS in Library Science

Fred - BA in Greek and Latin, MA in Sociology, Ph.D. in Criminology

Ellen - BS in Nursing, MS in Nursing Education

Herbert - BS in Science, DDS in Dentistry

I went off to the University of Iowa and a year later Jackie went to Iowa State. We didn't see much of each other those next two years until she transferred to my school. My education was much like any young man who attended the State University of Iowa. I expected a career to develop as a result of my schooling. I roomed in the Quadrangle Dormitory with Mike Enich, a fellow student from Boone with whom I had played football at Boone High. I had a job a block away at the University Hospital which provided one meal for each of

2

the three hours worked. This was above and beyond the $25 received every six weeks from blood donations at the hospital.

Mike was the son of Serbian parents. At six feet, 225 pounds, he was a football and basketball athlete on full school scholarship. The press called Mike and his teammates Ironmen because they played the full 60 minutes of most football games, Mike went on to become Captain of the team and was voted All Big Ten and All American, amid other football honors. Other Ironmen were Nile Kinnick, Al Coupee, Erwin Prasse and Bill Green.

Norm Erbe and roommate Mike Enich

Mike took his meals in the Quadrangle cafeteria and frequently complained that they didn't give him enough to eat. I worked in the kitchen of the hospital during our second year, cleaning pots and pans from the hot-carts used on the wards. One evening some fine pork chops arrived as left-overs on the hot-cart and there was considerable doubt as to their future use. I set them aside and at the end of my shift wrapped five chops in a towel and stuffed them under my jacket. I exited out the rear hospital door where the kitchen people waited for the bus, remarking to a friend of mine, "I have quite a bust, don't I?" A hand appeared out of the crowd and took my arm.

"Yes, you do. Come to my office." It was Dr. Kate Daum, the head of Nutritional Services for the hospital. She asked for an explanation and I told her that my roommate never had enough to eat. She demanded my meal ticket and I of course surrendered it along with my eating privileges at the hospital which ended with the pork chops.

For ten days my normally balanced eating habits abruptly shifted to a diet of grapefruit until I secured a job at the Iowa Memorial Union, the best move I ever made. The Iowa Memorial Union was a student and public gathering place on the campus used for student and faculty activities, as well as dining and recreational purposes. It was built as a memorial to the students who fought in World War I. I had to be up at four each morning to scrub floors on the janitor crew with Bill Bell, an engineering student. My fellow workers were from every college of the University, and some of the finest people I have ever known. We were all poor, high spirited and enjoyed a camaraderie of shared experiences. I worked my way up to dish-crew, cafeteria line, and finally private dining room service, which was considered by some to be the best of the board jobs.

Ben Buckingham was the Director. Chet Lyman, Dick Eaton, and Ivan Goddard were our student superiors in the cafeteria. Bernie Hermann, John Cumming and I were proud to be "Union Boys," and 60 years later we still try to get together.

I asked Jackie who was then a student at Iowa State College at Ames to the Iowa State Military Ball, a formal affair, before she transferred to Iowa City in 1939. Her gown was purple velvet and she was stunning. I wore my ROTC dress white mess jacket with blue trousers. Tom Hannum from Boone and his date, Catherine Kidd, whom he was later to marry, made it possible for me to go. He was in advanced ROTC at Iowa State College and we had a great time.

The biggest formal dance of the year at the University of Iowa at Iowa City was the "Club Cabaret"- a dinner and dance at the Memorial Union. Tommy Dorsey's band played. Of course, I invited Jackie who had by that time transferred to the University of Iowa at Iowa City. Although we had not dated while she was at the university, my fellow Union workers knew my date and what she meant to me. They hovered over us and catered to our every whim. We had a great time that evening.

War clouds were growing over Europe in the spring of 1939, yet there was little thought then that the U.S. would become involved. At this time a decision was required whether or not I wanted to pursue the advanced ROTC program. For young men, the freshman and sophomore years at the University included the mandatory course of Reserve Officers Training Corps (ROTC). At the conclusion of two years of basic training in ROTC we were offered the opportunity to take advanced ROTC. This meant we would be paid $21 per month, attend a six-week summer training camp at Ft. Snelling, Minnesota, and two years later, following completion of the advanced ROTC course be commissioned as 2nd Lieutenants (Lt.) in the Infantry Reserve. The

4

College of Law offered a combined course wherein one could take three years of pre-law in Liberal Arts and then transfer to Law School for the balance of three years to obtain a law degree.

I decided to take the combined liberal arts: Law and Advanced ROTC. My consideration of law school was met with less than enthusiasm by my parents. To them I was taking a step backwards. They did not feel that the law was an honorable profession. Lawyers obtained divorces and represented people who committed crimes, and were generally involved in shady practices, including politics. In their view, it was an unsavory profession that involved crooked deals, smoke filled rooms, and practiced illegalities dreamed up by the top rascals.

By the end of my senior year, which was also the combined freshman year in Law, I did not have enough hours to graduate in Liberal Arts. The rumblings of war were appearing in the news more often, and classmates who held reserve commissions were being called out of school to report for active duty. I was commissioned a 2nd Lt. in the Infantry Reserve in May of 1941 and alerted that I would soon be called. My education would have to be postponed. The beginning of summer brought about a period of waiting for the mailman to deliver orders of active military duty to my door.

Two: Foxholes To Flight Decks

In late June of 1941, I decided to go to Army Headquarters in Omaha to discover the reason for the delay. My name was on the list and I was informed that I would receive orders to Ft. Huachuca, Texas, by the first of July. I hitchhiked back to Boone, the normal mode of transportation used by college students. While awaiting my official notification I decided to do a little research on Ft. Huachuca. I discovered that it was not in Texas, but in Arizona, and was also the principal training post for Negro soldiers.

On July 1st I finally received orders to report, not to Ft. Huachuca, but to the 2nd Infantry Division at Ft. Sam Houston, San Antonio, Texas. At the end of the longest train ride I had ever had I reported to Ft. Sam Houston, 2nd Division Headquarters, where I was assigned to the 23rd Infantry Regiment. Immediately I was directed, along with about 100 other shavetails (2nd Lts.), to report to the training site of Ft. Sam, Camp Bullis, for indoctrination training.

Camp Bullis was located about 20 miles away and was used by the entire Division for field training. The temperature was Texas hot with deer and mosquitoes plentiful; ticks made a thrice daily tick inspection mandatory. Following completion of indoctrination training we returned to Ft. Sam for duty with the troops. I was assigned to Company B of the 23rd Infantry Regiment. I must have had some spare time for I sent a "first impression" letter home:

July 29, 1941

Dear Folks:

Well, it has been some time since I have written my last missile (sic) and the time has come again when I think that I have something to talk about. So here goes. I don't remember when I wrote last but I will try to cover some of my actions of the past week.

As you know I finished my course of training at Camp Bullis last Saturday morning. They worked us up to the last minute. We were really going strong all day. Since it was our last night in camp, they arranged a party for that evening with money left over from the mess fund.

Well, when we got back to camp about 17:00 hours, we discovered that since we were having that party at night, we would have to miss our daily study time of an hour and a half. We had it from 17:00 hours until 18:30 hours that night. Then we all ran for the shower, cleaned up and returned to one of the halls where they had a 32-gallon keg of beer, canned beer, Cokes, cigarettes, cigars, potato chips, pretzels, etc., on the tables. Naturally, I took Coke. We were there for about an hour and then we retired to the mess hall for a swell T-bone steak dinner with all the trimmings. I really didn't think that the army cooks could do such a good job on the food, but that meal convinced me that if they have the material to work with, they can do plenty.

Following the meal we returned to the other hall to drink a few more "Cokes" and then went to bed. It was all-in-all a very nice affair. General Walker was there and several colonels were in evidence. The next morning we checked in our stuff and went to town to report to our companies.

The unit I am assigned to, Company B, was firing out on the range at Camp Bullis, the place which I had just left that morning. Well, we got orders from the Regimental Adjutant to report out there and serve as range officers for the firing. We got there about 15:00 hours and checked range cards the rest of the afternoon and then went to bed. To get on with the story, we were awakened by an orderly about 04:00 hours. It was a battle but we made it. We were on the range by 06:00 hours and I sat on my fanny and checked safety precautions for the automatic rifle and men firing until 11:00 hours.

At that time we (or rather they) started to fire for record and some officers including me went down to the pits to check and sign score cards. We finally got done with that about 13:30 hours and ate at 14:00 hours. We then checked more range cards until supper at 17:00 hours. Around 19:00 hours I went into town with some fellow officers and took a shower, cleaned up, and had two bottles of "Bud" before returning to camp about 23:00 hours.

Anyway, the next morning, up again at 04:00 hours and a convoy of trucks brought us back to Ft. Sam at about 09:00 hours. We then reported to our Company Commander where I was informed that I was to be in command of the Light Machine Gun section of the Weapons Platoon of Rifle Company B. I was also told to instruct *a class of non-commissioned officers (non-coms or NCO's) at 13:00 hours on the Browning Automatic Rifle. That was about four hours notice but I got along all right. General Strong was due to visit the class this afternoon but he didn't show.*

Following that, I inspected rifles, light machine guns, etc., listened to some more of the Company Commander's wisdom, and was finally home at 17:30 hours. Tomorrow the officers of the company conduct athletic exercises for one-half hour, then close order drill for one hour, then extended order drill for two hours. After lunch we have another class from 13:00 hours until 17:30 hours for the non-coms and another for the backward men in the outfit, athletics until 16:00 hours, and then inspections, etc.. That is just about a typical day.

If you are reading this letter carefully you probably wonder why I reported to the Company Commander when he should have come in with the troops from Bullis. Well, it's like this: The regular Company Commander is a 1st Lt. and has held the position for about a year. He took a week off to take an exam for his regular commission. In the meantime they replaced him with a 1st Lt. from the officers training camp out at Bullis whose experience with troops can be considered as negligible.

You have no idea what a responsibility it is to be a Company Commander. They have to look out for approximately 210 men, be their mother and father, see that they are properly fed, housed, drilled, and schooled. In fact, see that just about every hour of their life is taken care of. If he has subordinates he is still personally responsible for their work. His rank is supposed to be a Captain but that is an illustration of just how short this army is of higher ranking officers. As far as the present officer situation, there are more 2nd Lts. than anything else.

Previous to July 1, there was a 1st Lt. and a 2nd Lt. running the company when the table of organization calls for six commissioned officers for a company. Since we have returned from Bullis there are four 1st Lts. and six 2nd Lts. in the outfit. There are so many of us the Company Commander doesn't know what to do with us all. I think that just about takes care of the Officer situation.

Now for the men. The company to which I am assigned is

composed, for the most part, of draftees from the eastern seaboard. They comprise 90% of the total company strength. They have been in service anywhere from two to five months. I find them on the whole to be a much lower intelligence group than expected. I think I expected them to be somewhere near the caliber of high school or college kids I knew or ran around with. They need lots of training.

The non-coms have relatively short terms of service, also. The way they work it is to train a group of men for a certain period of time and then select the best to form the base of new units. The qualified privates are busted up to non-coms for the new draftees that come in. In that way you have twice as many outfits yet both of them really need training. I guess that is what these new officers are for.

The Light Machine Gun section, for example, has one sergeant who knows something about the gun but is unable to instruct the men. It will be my job to teach them something about it in the week and a half before we leave for maneuvers. That may illustrate what kind of a job has to be done.

I have obviously discovered that I will be an "instructor" in the army. All of us are. I can't say that I don't like it. From my meager experience today, I believe that I am going to enjoy it immensely. I will have to study at night to keep up or ahead of my outfit but that won't hurt me. As I mentioned we are leaving for maneuvers on the 5th of August. They are to last until September and we expect to be back on the post on or about the 1st of October. We start about 150 miles Northwest of Alexandria, Louisiana, and work SE, then proceed back up to the starting position and home.

I am looking forward to some valuable training on these maneuvers and I know that I won't be disappointed. They say that if you aren't a soldier when you get back from them, you never will be. I believe it. Naturally it will be impossible for me to get home before the 1st of October. At that time I think that I shall apply for leave and if I get it, come home for about a week, buy a car, etc.

As yet I do not know my address but shall send it to you as soon as they put out more information on these maneuvers. Don't look for any regular letters from me from now on. I expect to be one busy man. I'll try to get another one off before we leave but after that...???

That is about all I know for the present.
NORM

While at Camp Bullis we were busy training. Our Company Commander was William Hinsch, a Captain and a native of Fort Dodge, Iowa, and a graduate of the University of Iowa. About eight to ten years older than I, his rank of Captain was based on the fact that he had gone into the Civilian Conservation Corps when it was most active in the mid-to-late thirties. That time counted towards his promotion prospects.

He was a very good leader, firm but fair. Fellow shavetails in the regiment and indeed in the Division, were products of various advanced ROTC programs around the country. Most of them were from Nebraska, the Dakotas and Texas A&M. Several friendships included John M. Stephens, Texas A&M, from Tyler, Texas, and Frank E. Roth, University of Nebraska, from Omaha. Stephens won decorations for valor, especially during the Battle of the Bulge. Roth did not survive the war.

Dating was not a high priority but we had fun when we could. There was a nightspot on Broadway Avenue called The Tower. It was a good place to party, drink, and dance. Without a car, I usually double-dated. Lt. Jones *(alias)* fixed me up one night with a blind date and the four of us hit The Tower. Jones enjoyed his rum and began belting it away without the Coke mixer. We had a great time, but pulling out of the parking lot the rest of us in the car realized that Jones had gone over his drinking limit. Pretty soon he was driving too fast and running red lights. From the back seat, I was tugging on his shirt and yelling for him to slow down when he suddenly turned to careen through a parking lot and clipped a parked car. The vehicle Jones struck was a police car.

The chase was on, Jones trying to escape and the rest of us dismayed at the action. With the sirens and the girls screaming he eventually pulled over. Jumping out, he did the unbelievable. He ran. One policeman took off after him while the other stood guard over us. "Where did you steal the car?" he asked. We told him that it was Jones' car, and none of us could answer why he had run. The other policeman returned with Jones in handcuffs. They allowed me to drive the girls home but I was required to show up at the station the next day.

I returned to Camp Bullis and had to report the incident to the M.P.s and his unit Commander.

The next morning Jones had numerous charges filed against him. I saw little of him after that. Months later he called and asked me to testify on his behalf at a General Court Martial (military trial). He was in big trouble this time, writing bad checks and other charges. I was little help and he was found guilty. Rumor had it that he was sent overseas to the fighting, the usual military way of handling misfits.

At Ft. Sam Houston, we lived in the Bachelor Officer Quarters (BOQ's) which were located on one side of the parade ground while Regimental Headquarters and enlisted barracks were directly opposite on the other side of the parade ground. BOQ's were standard wooden barracks divided to give each of us a private room. The mess hall was located in the center of the buildings. Close by was the officers club, a nice diversion for the junior officers who congregated there on Saturday nights for drinks and formal dances. Yes, formal, which rather surprised me. I didn't have a tux. If I was to "party" at Ft. Sam Houston, it was necessary that I get a tux. So I bought one.

The enlisted quarters had open bays with two private cubicles for the NCO's. At the end of the parade ground was the large Brooke Army Hospital. When the Infantry Division moved to Camp McCoy, Wisconsin, in 1942, the post became home for the Adjutant General School and the hospital was rededicated as a Burn Center for the Army.

A small cottage existed on the opposite end of the parade ground, with outside pigeon lofts attached to it. This was a left-over from WW I and the home of Sergeant Bronkhorst, who was also a veteran of WW I. As the senior instructor on post, he taught all units the fine art of using the bayonet and he really knew how to use it. By the time the troops finished his class, they had also become fairly proficient. This included the necessary shouting and growling when making the thrust. Sergeant Bronkhorst had another responsibility. He kept and trained the carrier pigeons stationed on the post, another remnant of W.W.I.

Near Sergeant Bronkhorst's quarters was the Post Exchange (PX), the famous and well patronized store for the military which had better prices than anywhere else at that time. More importantly, they advanced credit to military officers. This was the first time that I'd ever had credit. I could purchase what I needed and pay the bill at the end of the month.

The first week of August before departure for maneuvers went swiftly amid 1000 other details. Preparations included making sure that all needed equipment was issued. We traveled to East Texas by two and a half ton trucks and personnel carriers. The popular jeep vehicle had not yet been developed. Our weapons were WWI Springfield .03 rifles, while howitzers were represented by stove pipes. The executive officers wore tan uniforms for all duty and the enlisted men wore fatigues. Both officers and enlisted men wore canvas leggings over their boots and a beige, rimmed, cotton fisherman's hat while in the field. The steel helmets were 1918 vintage since the WWII helmet with plastic liner had not yet been invented.

Our route to the exercise area was through East Texas, noted for its timber rattlesnakes, which are about the size of a pencil. The streams were watched carefully for copperhead snakes that were also reputed to be poisonous. We made a night-crossing of the Sabine River along towards the end of the maneuver. Locals informed us afterwards that they never went into that river, even in the daytime, because of its abundance of snakes and alligators.

The maneuver exercise in which we were engaged consisted of 2 armies. The Blue Army made-up of the military units of the Second Infantry Division from Ft. Sam Houston, Texas. The Red Army, an infantry division from Tennessee. We were involved in simulated combat exercises which usually lasted about a week. They involved the simulated capture of a hill, a bridge, a critical area, or a town with actual movement controlled by umpires. Upon completion of the particular exercise the movement would be halted. The officers of each side would be gathered for a critique of the moves, and decisions by the commanders, and suggestions for improvements in the next exercise. There maneuvers were the longest military training efforts to be held in the U S since World War I.

While on the 1941 maneuvers in the middle of rugged Louisiana, I was requested to report to regiment. Colonel Woodruff, the regimental commander would like to see me in his tent, a call from the Almighty! I reviewed my activities and couldn't figure why I was receiving the unsolicited attention of the regimental commander. It so happened that he had gotten word from the PX that my monthly bill remained unpaid. I assured him that I had done so, with a check stub and canceled check back at Ft. Sam to prove it. The PX had made a mistake. I learned something from this experience: be sure to pay my bills while in the army or the Regimental CO would make sure that I did. Colonel Woodruff, incidentally, was a native of Oskaloosa, Iowa, and after Pearl Harbor was promoted to Brigadier General.

These maneuvers were where Lt. Col. Dwight Eisenhower made his reputation. He was a planning officer and went from the maneuver area to the Plans Division in Headquarters of the Army, Washington, D.C. The rest is history. I never saw the man while I was there. Regular soldiers were so distanced from Headquarters that we only saw big wheels when there was a problem. I did spot General Krueger when there was a terrific traffic jam of military vehicles at a country road intersection in Louisiana. When our vehicle reached the point of confusion, there he was, directing traffic — the air was blue from his remarks. He was a three-star general, and later finished the war in the South Pacific. A real warrior.

One night I was exhausted. Climbing into my bedroll, my foot slid down inside it and ran into a territorial scorpion who delivered his sting. Too tired to worry about it, I decided that should I be fortunate enough to wake up in the morning, they were probably not poisonous. If I didn't wake up, they probably were poisonous. I didn't care either way.

Moving down highways in convoy, we stopped periodically for the troops to jump out and enter nearby stores, which they cleaned out of candy bars and food. The store owners were wise to these soldier appetites from past experience and really stocked up. They sold candy bars by the box. The soldiers made good customers.

Our main routes were along Highway 171 and through the towns of western Louisiana—Many, Zwolle, Converse and others. Most of the houses had a dog-run in the center for pets. We waved to all the elderly folks as they sat in rocking chairs. Children excitedly ran alongside, shouting to us as the convoy rolled past.

My platoon and I were part of the Blue Forces and were captured on one of the tactical exercises. Taken as prisoners to Camp Polk, we were held for a few hours by the Red Forces. We also had a Major from the British Army with our unit who acted as an observer. The maneuvers were excellent in spite of the fact that equipment was not really as good as it should have been, but that was remedied on the

1942 maneuvers.

It was good to return home to Ft. Sam. after 6 weeks in Louisiana Our training was not unlike that described in my "first impression" letter home. It included 20- and 25-mile marches with full field-pack for physical conditioning. In the hot Texas weather we took salt tablets to counteract heavy sweating on the march, and sometimes placed a few drops of ammonia in our canteens. We felt that this would help give us energy. I'm not sure whether it worked or not, but it didn't seem to hurt us any.

San Antonio surrounded the post, an army town for more than 100 years. The Post included an original quadrangle dating back to the Civil War where they kept peacocks and deer. Upon our return from Louisiana, I was surprised that my unit followed some of the customs of the "Old" Army. A notice appeared on the regimental bulletin board that the Regimental Commander would be "receiving" at his quarters on the following Sunday, from 14:00 hours until 17:00 hours. Junior officers were invited to "call." I had heard about this "old school" custom in ROTC but didn't believe it really occurred. Of course this was an order and not an invitation. We, the junior officers, did indeed perform that duty at the Colonel's quarters and left our calling cards, hoping that he had an eligible daughter.

The Division Commander thought it would be a good idea for the junior officers to form a chorus and sing at events on and off post. We believed this was a very poor idea, but the Division Commander wore the stars. Someone on his staff must have gotten to him since we never had to sing for anyone. It was also suggested the junior officers purchase white summer dress uniforms, another task with which we grudgingly complied. But now that we had this unwanted dress uniform, we looked for places to wear it besides the dance at the officers club on Saturday nights.

Several of us discussed the matter and agreed that the Navy always treated their junior officers better than we were treated. My buddy Lt. Roth came up with an idea. We would go on an " inspection" trip to a Navy base, at nearby Corpus Christi, Texas.

Our chosen weekend there happened to be a dance at the Navy officers club. We ate at their club and danced with their girls, only mildly offended when Navy personnel asked us, "What's the name of

15

your band?" They had not seen the infamous summer white dress uniform of the army before. We left town deflated but not defeated from lack of respect.

We thoroughly enjoyed the soldiering at Ft. Sam in the fall of 1941, learning while working and playing hard. Some Saturday afternoons we went downtown to a hotel and had mint juleps. They came in pewter mugs with sprigs of mint. Frequent refills from our bottle kept frost on the outside.

October 1st was drawing near and draftees in the units began disappearing. In 1940 Congress had passed the Draft Act which mandated one year service following draft and induction. Later, the Draft Act was extended, which was deemed unfair by those whose year was almost up. They had fulfilled their commitment and referred to themselves as "OHIO" (Over the Hill in October), meaning they would go absent without leave, and some of them did. It was encouraging that, following December 7th and the Japanese sneak attack on Pearl Harbor, former soldiers who belonged to the unit but were absent without leave (AWOL), or had deserted, returned on their own, knowing they would be punished. Some of them had been gone for years. If they were going to be in the war, they wanted to ensure that they would be with their own units.

I received orders to report to Infantry School at Ft. Benning, Georgia, from November 30th of 1941 until March 10th of 1942. Several of my fellow officers and I drove, detouring to New Orleans for a mandatory tourist stop to see if all of the stories were true. The joints of Bourbon and Royal Streets more than lived up to our expectations.

Ft. Benning had been "The Infantry School" for many years. Among its most updated equipment were jump-towers for parachute infantry training. Located on the Chattahoochee River, the Fort encompassed vast thousands of acres. In fact, we took a narrow gauge train out to some of our more distant training areas. The wood-burning locomotive which pulled our train on the narrow gauge track is now out of service but not out of sight. Placed on a concrete pedestal, it is properly identified as the moving force for thousands of Ft. Benning students.

There were 120 junior officers in the Rifle and Heavy Weapons Course of Company Officer Basic class 21. We formed into four platoons, ranked from Captain to 2nd Lt., and lived in open barracks such as the enlisted men used at Ft. Sam. The best instructional aids were used by outstanding instructors and we were expected to learn proper operation and teaching of the latest equipment. We groused that we didn't have those sophisticated pieces of equipment back home, but at least we had seen them and now knew how they were to be taught and used if we ever got them.

I had been on post for one week when a buddy and I decided to go to a movie on Sunday afternoon in Columbus, Georgia, a nearby army town. There was a notorious town, Phenix City, just across the river in Alabama. It was off-limits to soldiers at night because of rampant gambling, prostitution, thievery, and drugs. In fact, years later it was the town which the Attorney General of Alabama promised to "clean up." He was murdered in the process.

It was December 7, 1941, when we took in the movie. About 14:00 hours they interrupted the show and came on stage to announce that Pearl Harbor had been bombed. A number of women screamed at the horror of this news and ran out of the theater. With our minds churning, we remained to "see" the rest of the movie, although, truth be told, none of us were paying the slightest attention to the movie. The enormity of the situation was felt by everyone. We were at war.

Now our training was for real although no less than before Pearl Harbor. A half-dozen Puerto Rican Lts. had been in our class and shared our floor in the barracks. We had enjoyed them immensely. At the end of each day they gathered at the far end of the floor and gave their own review of recent happenings and teachings in class, laughing and shouting at each other in Spanish, which made us laugh, too. They were ordered home at once with the news of Pearl Harbor.

This was about the time that army tanks were recognized as a separate branch of the military, with its special training base at Ft. Knox, Kentucky. General Patton went there from Ft. Benning to command the training operation. I saw him one day while riding on the post. He was riding a beautiful horse and looked just like his photographs.

We company grade officers were not the only rank of officers being trained at Ft. Benning. We saw a convoy of staff cars on post and discovered that the occupants of these vehicles were one-star Generals who had just been promoted from Colonel. They were there for their indoctrination. I was so impressed by seeing so many generals all in

Lt. Stephens pins on my promotion bars — to 1st Lt.

one place.

Christmas came and we were granted leave over the holidays. We didn't know whether there would be another opportunity before the war was over, so everyone took it. I went home to Boone and took my brand new tuxedo along for my brother who was in dental school since I wouldn't be using it until after the war. Since the beginning of December, they no longer held black tie dances in the officer's club at Ft. Benning or Ft. Sam. Since my leave was so short, I did not see Jackie.

There was a class dinner party at the end of course work in March. We sang a tune we had made up on the long train rides out to the training area. The words included some of the rules we had followed and some that we hadn't. It was great fun but the evening air brought with it a sense of nostalgia. These were our colleagues we knew so well after being together for three monthes, and there was a good chance that we would never be together again.

We returned home to the 23rd Infantry Regiment at Ft. Sam Houston. It was good to be back on familiar turf with its regular training exercises. Some of us became intrigued by the sight of airplanes flying overhead. San Antonio had a well known air base, Randoph Field, which was located just a few miles outside of the city. It was called by some, "The West Point of the Air."

In our free time we satisfied our curiosity by going to check out the air base. It confirmed our suspicions that the Navy was not the only branch which treated their people well. The Air Corps did also. This is not to say that we were suffering, but there was a shade of difference between the branches. Those 25-mile marches with full field pack, ticks, mosquitoes, and foxhole digging could be improved upon. Another advantage which had a great deal of appeal was the fact that pilot and air crews received hazardous duty pay of an extra 50% if they flew at least four hours per month.

The airplanes continued to fly overhead while we carried on our "ground pounder" training that spring and summer. One day a message appeared on our bulletin board that the Air Corps needed personnel for pilot training. Transfers from other branches of the Army were encouraged and commanders were prohibited from refusing to forward applications of officers who showed an interest. This caught my eye, and I immediately made application for transfer to the Air Corps for pilot training.

THREE: NEWLYWEDS WITH SILVER WINGS

I took a week leave of absence and went back to Boone to see the family before the 1942 Maneuvers were to start in August in Louisiana. While home I asked out Jacqueline Doran. She had collected five fraternity pins while I was gone. At that time I realized I couldn't be without her. I asked Jackie to marry me. I was as surprised as she was. My romantic words of proposal went something like this:

"I'm in a good position to get married."

"How good?"

"Real good."

"Talk to my father."

But this spontaneous plan had some attached conditions on a number of unknowns. The first was the most traumatic: asking her father, mother and two younger brothers, John and Bill, if I could have her hand in marriage. I passed that test. The next problem was whether I could get time off from the Army to get married after maneuvers.

I went back to Ft. Sam to confer with my company commander about the possibility of getting time off for that purpose. He was a bit noncommittal about the whole thing. During maneuvers however, I heard from Jackie that my commanding officer (CO), Captain William Hinsch, had sent a telegram to the Kappa Alpha Theta housemother in Iowa city which was reported years later in the newspaper as follows.

"One day in September, 1942, the Kappa Alpha Theta housemother at the State University of Iowa rose at dinner to read a telegram from a U.S. Army Captain, William Hinsch a former houseboy at the sorority house: "Tell your little Theta girl that Norm will be home the last week in September."

Norm and Jackie Engagement - Boone, July, 1942

Jackie, on campus, was to assist with rush week activities, knew what that meant

Cutting the Cake — Wedding September 27, 1942

if none of the others did. The company commander had pulled strings for her fiancé to get leave. And on that leave we were to be married.

The wedding date was fixed for September 27. I was oblivious to the preparations going on in Boone but I did get there in time to participate in some of the pre-wedding events. Since my father was a Lutheran minister, it was agreed that in deference to him and his position, we would be married in his Trinity Lutheran Church in Boone, even though Jackie and her family were members of the Episcopal Church. Her discussions with him about the wedding confirmed that the two denominations were not so far apart anyhow. But there were personal preferences. Jackie wanted the Ave Maria played or sung during the service. He wouldn't budge, giving her an emphatic NO. He also insisted that there would be no kissing at the end of the ceremony. When the time came we did it anyway, and he seemed to get over it okay.

Very few of my relatives were present at the wedding. Jackie's father, however, was one of thirteen children who all lived within 50 miles of the church. They brought their families. I was overwhelmed at the reception by the sheer number of people named Doran who went through the receiving line.

Afterwards we drove through a three inch snowfall to spend our wedding night at a hotel in Omaha. From there we drove our new car, a wedding present from Jackie's parents, to Denver, where we stayed for two days with Lt. Paul Thorngren and his wife, Mary Jo Bostwick. Paul and Mary Jo had been high-school classmates of ours and were stationed there. Then we hit the long trail to Texas, where I took my bride to live.

Our new home was a unit in Grande Courts, adjacent to Brackenridge Park of San Antonio. It was close living, about three hundred and fifty square feet consisting of a bedroom, sitting room, kitchen, dining area and bath. Located about ten minutes by car from Ft. Sam Houston, it was accessible enough for me to be home for lunch. I arrived one evening to find my cook almost in tears. She had repeatedly tried to light the gas oven with a match, and it had finally erupted into a hair-singing fireball. We went out for dinner that night.

My reporting orders for Air Corps training at Kelley Field in San Antonio were just a week or so before my former unit of the 2nd Division left for winter training at Ft. McCoy in Wisconsin. It was an emotional experience to view my Division in parade. I had served with them for more than a year and a half and made many friends. I had enjoyed every minute of my assignment there. But that was behind me now. I had made the decision to fly one of those birds and I channeled my focus in that direction.

Kelley Field was the principal starting point for cadets and students assigned from the midwest. When I arrived, there were 1,000 or more cadets at Kelley Field undergoing pre-flight training. These cadets were of a different category from us since they would receive commissions only after their successful training. Student officers already wore their bars. For example I had received my promotion to 1st Lt. during maneuvers. There were about thirty-five men ranging in rank from 2nd Lt. to Captain. We were the student officer class of 43-G, the seventh class to graduate in August of 1943 if we didn't wash out. This was a significant threat to each of us. We underwent rigorous physical and psychological exams to determine our qualifications, this in itself resulting in a significant wash out rate. An unlucky cadet who was passed over was relegated either to the navigator or bombardier program, or to the gunner or ground crew training program.

The company commander, also known as the tactical officer, was a 1st Lt. assigned there full-time. He enjoyed this position, treating us as underlings, totally ignoring the fact that we were also officers with extensive training in military rules and customs. As can be imagined, by the time we finished our course work, he had become our most despised man at Kelley Field. But we were going to show that guy a thing or two. We were not going to let HIM wash us out of pilot training. Some of the student officers did indeed wash out at the pre-flight level,

At Primary Flying School, Bonham, Texas - 1943.

but the rest of us completed the course in spite of our nasty tactical officer, and we moved on to our next phase of training, Primary Flight Training with real airplanes.

Our course work included map and aerial chart reading, aircraft recognition, and other related subjects. One day we had a visit from General H. H. 'Hap' Arnold, Chief of the Army Air Corps. All of the students marched onto the field and waited in the hot Texas sun for him to appear, and then listened to his 30 minute speech about how important we were. The Army Air Corps was a branch of the Army. Following World War II, it broke away to become the Air Force with its own identity: uniforms, programs, academy, and everything that goes with it.

Since we were barracks-bound during pre-flight training, Jackie went back to Boone to be with her parents while I was at Kelley Field. I later was sent to a contract flying field at Bonham, Texas, the home town of U.S. House of Representatives Speaker Sam Rayburn. This phase of training meant that I could have my bride with me for the balance of my flight training. We rented the top floor of a house which the owners had modified to provide an apartment for the 'fly' boys who had invaded Bonham. It was cozy with a very low ceiling. Our bed was under a low gable, a collision point for our heads. We had to be careful upon rising or our heads would collide with the ceiling. We returned to Bonham after the war to see if we could find our house, but it had been demolished and replaced by a Veterans Administration Hospital.

The phrase "Contract Flying Field" refers to the fact that the Air Corps was growing so fast, there were not enough fields to take care of all of the cadets who were in training. To solve the problem of numbers, the Air Corps contracted out the "Primary" flying fields to civilian operators. Following a thirteen-week period, pilots then went on to "Basic" and "Advanced" fields, both of which were regular army installations.

One fellow became a close friend while in Bonham and we stayed together all during training, as well as over in England, where he was killed in a crash while test flying a B-17 Bomber. Bill Doherty was a National Guard 1st Lt. from Tacoma, Washington, in a Tank Destroyer battalion. He and I were about the same size and coloring and people sometimes guessed that we were brothers. He and his wife Inez had recently married while at Ft. Benning. Jackie and Inez became good friends and it worked out well for them to be able to commiserate together while Bill and I were training.

Lt. Erbe & Lt. Doherty

On weekends we explored nearby sights like the Red River where the Corps of Engineers were constructing a huge dam. Bill and I with our wives inspected the project and discussed its progress. Dallas and Ft. Worth were not far away. Toward the end of our tour in Bonham we were in Dallas and ran into the owner of our training field while sightseeing. He took us to the Adolphus Hotel for a meal and drinks. That was pretty tall cotton for a couple from Boone, Iowa.

Our days consisted of ground school and flight training, with civilian instruments. Our aircraft was the PT-17, a single engine, low wing, fabric-covered airplane with a wooden propeller and two open cockpits. In my youth I had been on several $5 flights by barnstormers at Boone, but that was about the extent of my previous flying experience.

I donned my leather helmet, goggles, leather flying jacket and flight suit, and climbed into the front seat of the plane while the instructor climbed in the back. It was a grass field and I was going to learn to fly. Well, maybe. Everything looked fine after we got up in the air. I could see Bonham and where we lived, and the engineers building the dam up on the Red River.

When we approached the field at the end of our 45 minute spin, I began feeling queasy and vomited as we were coming in for a landing.

25

I was not going to wash out of flying school, nor was I going to let it go into the face of my instructor, so the only thing left was to swallow it. This saved my career in flying. Although I may have looked a little bit green, I don't think the instructor knew the difference that day nor after the following two days, when I was able to conquer the nausea.

The plane had no intercom or other way of communicating while in the air. My instructor tapped my knees with the control stick and yelled to converse with me. Proficiency gradually improved, and I can still remember the instructor asking me how I was going to get back to the field.

"I don't know," I responded.

I can still hear him say, "Plan your work and then work your plan."

After nine hours and 20 minutes in the air with my instructor mothering me along, he trusted me to take the plane for my first solo flight including the toughest part of the process, landing the plane by myself. I did it.

While one group of students was flying, another group took ground instruction in the classroom. The various subjects included airplane recognition, study of aerial charts, Morse code, and other subjects relating to being in the air. The Morse code class was interesting because it reminded me of my high-school typing course. Soon those dit-da-dit signals became automatic.

One of the cadets who took his training at Bonham at the same time I did was Bob Forney of Pilot Mound, Iowa, a small town in Boone County. He went on, also to fly a B-17 Flying Fortress, training at bases other than those I attended. Shot down by Nazi fighters while flying with the 8th Air Corps from England, he spent several years in a prisoner-of-war camp in Europe. His father had flown in World War I and was a member of the famous "Hat In The Ring" squadron in those World War I years. Bob returned to live in Boone after the war.

By the time I finished the primary flight training in March of 1942 at Jones Field, Bonham, Texas, I had completed 62 hours of flight time, 30 hours of which were solo. March came and we moved onto the next phase of our training at Perrin Field at Sherman, Texas, an Army Air Corps field manned by military officers as instructors and supporting staff.

Jackie and Inez investigated the availability of housing and found a two-bedroom house with bare but adequate furnishings at nearby Denison, Texas. The four of us moved in together to share expenses. Bill and I reported for duty on March 26 and became acquainted with our next flying machine. The open cockpit Vultee BT-13A had a Pratt & Whitney engine of 450 horsepower, metal skin and a low wing.

A number of variations were added during our basic training at Perrin Field. We were introduced to the Link Trainer, an instrument training machine which simulated actual conditions in the air. It required the pilot to fly into and through all kinds of weather and flight conditions with no view out of the cockpit. The trauma and tension of flying the Link Trainer was enormous when one ran into trouble. We used it often and were required to have a designated number of hours in this instrument training-aid as part of our training experience.

Night flying was another innovation in Basic Training, as was cross-country flying. As we flew around a designated area we used Morse code for the first time in our night flying. The small airfields we approached after dark were identified by revolving light beacons, and on their back sides, with a blinking-green Morse code signal identifying the name of the field. When seeing this, a student pilot would emit a long sigh of relief, knowing he was indeed on the right path. It was easy to become lost in the night, which was as black as the inside of a cow, especially during the national wartime blackout.

Our joint living arrangements worked out well. At night we had great bridge games enhanced with rum and Cokes. Inez became pregnant. Our wives took turns cooking, which gave Jackie and me the opportunity to enjoy some of Inez's biscuits and other southern cooking. Jackie treated them to Iowa cooking.

Our incomes were supplemented by the extra 50% hazardous duty pay for flyers. Some Air Corps instructors that were 2nd Lts. resented that we were being paid more than they were. Since they had the power to wash us out of the program, we had to exercise a great deal of tact in our relationships.

While I was training at Perrin Field, Jackie became bored with so little to do. She enrolled in a secretarial course which included shorthand, typing and other skills. Unfortunately, she could not complete the course since Bill and I finished our training and were told to move on to our next air base for advanced training. It was no picnic to be a student pilot's wife.

We were offered our choice of Multi-Engine Advanced or Single-Engine Advanced training. Obviously single-engine school meant the pilot would be going to a fighter role, while multi-engine school meant a future in heavier bombers. Bill Doherty and I selected multi-engine training. With ten hours of Link training and 70 hours of actual flying experience at basic behind us, we moved on at the end of May to Frederick, Oklahoma.

Frederick was a town with a population of about 5,000 in Southwestern Oklahoma, with the air base constituting its major industry. We arrived there without pre-arranged living accommodations. The Chamber of Commerce and the Air Corps offered lists of possible arrangements, from which we eventually rented a bedroom in a house that had no kitchen. The landlady was single and over 60 years of age. She spent a great deal of time in a rocker on the front porch outside our bedroom window as she chewed tobacco. She used a large coffee-can sitting next to her as a spittoon. She was a good shot, making a noise every time she hit the can, often late into the night.

We took meals either at the five-story hotel with the largest cockroaches we had ever seen, or in one of several cafes. Yet the best food was the Officers Club on base; the chef was from the Waldorf Astoria in New York. What a shock it must have been for him to come to Oklahoma, and what a break it was for us.

Midway through our training, Inez hemorrhaged and had a miscarriage. Of course Bill and I were flying so Jackie ran the six blocks to town for help.

Our flight training was interesting and challenging. Now we had two engines to deal with. The Cessna UC-78 was a fabric covered twin-engine plane with 450 horsepower in each engine. It carried a pilot, co-pilot and five passengers. It was also referred to as a C-45. We trainees called it "the butter paddle bomber." Gone were the leather helmets and goggles of our early training days. The instructor sat right beside us in the enclosed plane.

For the first time there was a radio which enabled us to converse with the tower at the field. We also had retractable landing gear. Landing the aircraft was a continual challenge for all pilots and is so to this day, even for commercial pilots who do it for a living. The goal is to "grease it in" each time you land. This takes a great deal of practice and judgment tied to acute depth perception of the distance between the pilot's eyes in the cockpit, the wheels of the plane, and the runway.

Cross country trips became common, sometimes as far as Oklahoma City. Seldom if ever did we carry passengers in the back of the plane. A fellow student came along in the right seat and we changed places in the course of the flight. Each of us would then record the time we spent as pilot or co-pilot.

As we approached the time to graduate and get our wings from the flying program, we were advised that as student officers we would have our choice as to where we wanted to pursue further training for combat duty. The usual path for graduates of Advanced Training was to be sent to a transition school for training in the plane of that school and then report to a combat group for assignment to a squadron. Bill Doherty and I both wanted to fly the B-17 Flying Fortress. In July 1943 the action was in Great Britain and that's where we wanted to go.

We didn't want to waste time with transition training, but go directly

Jackie pinning wings on Lt. Erbe, Frederick, Oklahoma, July 19, 1943.

to a group which was scheduled for overseas. Bill saw that one of the options was Moses Lake, Washington. He was from Tacoma, Washington and urged that we go there. He indicated that Moses Lake was a beautiful place not far from Tacoma, and a vacation spot for people from the Puget Sound area. Jackie and I had never been in the Northwest and we followed his suggestion.

In July 1943 with 68 hours solo, 19.8 hours dual, and 12.8 hours in the Link Trainer, I graduated from Frederick Field in Oklahoma, and Jackie pinned silver wings on my chest with a kiss. Now I was a certified pilot. With a three-week leave of absence before us, we drove home to Boone and made preparations for making our next move to Moses Lake. We were, of course, going to drive the route and visit some interesting spots on the way.

I took my footlocker down to the Railway Express office in Boone for shipment. The clerk said that they didn't have a Moses Lake on their list and routed my gear to an alternate destination nearby. The trip was good. On military orders, we had sufficient gasoline ration points to make it possible to drive through Yellowstone Park. Because of the war we were among the very few who were there to enjoy Old Faithful Inn and Old Faithful Geyser.

During our drive through Coeur D'Alene, Idaho, we promised ourselves that sometime after the war we would return and enjoy that beautiful part of the country. Approaching Moses Lake we discovered why there was no Railway Express office in the village. It was more of a crossroads than a town. Moses Lake consisted of a service station, general store, liquor store and several houses. That was all! "Bill Doherty, where is this lake and vacation spa for the Puget Sounders?" Vacation spa? It was nothing but desert as far as the eye could see.

Of course the air base was nearby. It consisted of two 10,000 foot runways and tar-paper buildings to shelter the human habitation and training quarters for the airbase. I removed my gear from the car and suggested that Jackie go somewhere, anywhere. "Find a place for us to live." Wenatchee seemed like a likely place to start since they have apples there (although that has nothing to do with finding quarters for the wife of a bomber pilot). I asked her to call me when she found a place to stay.

Inquiring at a home in Wenatchee (about 60 miles west of Moses Lake), she met a woman with a room. The woman believed in transcendental meditation and wanted to teach Jackie how to transport herself anywhere in the world, including India. Jackie decided that she didn't want to go to India. After about a week in her room in Wenatchee, she drove across the mountains south of Wenatchee to Ellensburg, Washington, and she found a room with a firefighter couple.

Ellensburg was more conveniently located, since we planned to drive over to Seattle a number of weekends while at Moses Lake. My sister, Ellen, was teaching nursing in one of the Seattle hospitals. Our landlady was engaged in canning vegetables for the war effort and Jackie joined her, working at the canning factory during the week.

Bill Doherty was surprised when I caught up with him. He thought the whole thing was a great hilarious joke. He had dreamed up all that resort nonsense. But we really didn't mind. We were young and everything was an adventure.

Bill and I went out to the flight line to get our first good look at the famous B-17. It was the largest plane we had ever seen, and were we going to fly this monster? I soon had an orientation flight with an experienced pilot. We first went through an extensive check list to see that all of the switches and controls were in order. Then we started each of the four 1,200 horsepower Curtiss Wright engines to taxi out onto the runway. The plane took off with an enlisted engineer at our shoulder who spent his time watching the performance of the plane and instruments. Landing was even more daunting than usual, with the cement runway so far down below the nose of the plane.

We had been assigned to the 396th Bomb Group with training scheduled around the clock. The routine flights averaged about five to seven hours each and Link Trainer training was scheduled on a 24 hour basis as well. Indoctrination and familiarization flights continued for about 15 hours flying time and then they turned me loose to fly with my crew. My first several landings were awful, just like a rabbit hop-hopping down the runway. The abuse I gave the plane was a testimony to the quality of the B-17.

In time I learned to land that plane and "grease it in." Handling something that size was not a one-man operation. Full combat staffing of my training plane consisted of ten men. I was the pilot and, as the commander of the plane, sat in the left seat of the cockpit. My co-pilot, Lt. Joe Shaffer, sat on the right. The crew-chief/engineer, Tech Sergeant Richard Cochrane, stood between and behind us. He also manned the two 50-caliber machine guns in the top gun-turret. The bombardier, Lt. Harry Will, was located in the nose of the plane near the famous Norden bombsight, and the navigator, Lt. Bob Marquis sat close by at a navigation table where he spread out his charts. The twin 50-caliber machine guns located near him could be used by either the bombardier or the navigator when in combat. In newer planes, they installed a chin gun turret with twin 50-caliber machine guns at the nose. These were introduced in the B-17G which appeared in the late spring of 1944.

Immediately behind the cockpit and engineer's position was the bomb bay. The bomb bay doors were opened hydraulically by a flip of a switch at the pilot station. If the hydraulics malfunctioned, they could be opened manually by using a crank. A bulkhead enclosed the bomb bay both fore and aft. Behind the bomb bay bulkhead was the radio equipment and stool for the radio operator, Private First-Class (PFC) James Kirkland.

Just to the rear of the radio operator, in the middle of the floor, was the entrance to a ball-turret, which was manned by Sgt. Wayne A. Taylor. The ball-turret gunner was ideally small of stature. He had the loneliest position in the entire plane, a hellish, stinking position in battle. The gunner must draw up his knees, crunching up his body into a half-ball to match the curving lines of the turret. The guns are to each side of his head and they stab from the turret eyeball like two long splinters.

Jailed in his little spherical powerhouse, the turret gunner literally aims his own body at enemy fighters. It took both hands and feet in deft coordination, spinning and tilting while depressing switches atop the gun grip handles to fire the .50's. The man most unlikely to escape from a blazing fortress was that lonely soul in the ball. He must climb out of the ball to put on his parachute since there is not enough room inside to wear it.

Behind the ball-turret gunner were the two waist gunners, PFC Noma Norman and Sgt. Paul Frank, one on each side of the plane manning a single .50-caliber machine gun. At the very rear was the tail gunner, Sgt. W.L. Egri. He had to lie on his belly and creep forward to his position behind the twin .50's in the tail. On some missions the co-pilot of the crew rode in this spot to advise the Group Commander of the position and condition of other planes behind us in our formation as we fought our way through flak and fighters.

The enlisted men on the crew were generally staff sergeants. They had their own specialized training in gunnery. Every man had to be an expert, as the B-17 was a very complex machine. The plane's formidable firepower was the basis for calling it the Flying Fortress.

As pilot and commander of the plane and crew, I looked forward to the assignment of each new crew member. Some stayed with us throughout the European campaign. The ground crew were no less important. They were assigned to a specific aircraft, not to a particular crew. We were extremely fortunate to have experts performing their work on the planes we flew. Our maintenance problems were minimal on our missions, attributed to the quality of their work. Our crew chief, Sgt. Richard Cochrane, was highly efficient and reliable in his oversight of the work done on our planes.

We often were assigned to another plane that had its own ground crew. Our crew chief and I were the watch-dogs insofar as the ground crew was concerned. We were all kept very busy with our own responsibilities and it was comforting to have him double-check my inspection and everything about the plane.

Training at Moses Lake continued to improve our skills with each other and the aircraft. The training missions were generally five hours long, flying near 7,500 feet altitude. Once in a while we would fly formation with other craft, generally at an altitude below 10,000 feet. We spent time on the practice bombing range, dropping sand filled bombs. When the bombardier, Lt. Harry Will, hit the target, we cheered and called it "hitting the shack."

Our cross country flying included a box-shaped flight from Moses Lake to Pullman, Walla Walla, Pasco, Ephrata, and back to Moses Lake. Navigation was accomplished from the cockpit by using a radio compass and other navigational aids before our crew navigator arrived. After a while our crew could almost fly the box with our eyes closed because it was so familiar in both daylight and dark.

Our navigator, Lt. Bob Marquis, reported to the crew from navigators school and we all greeted him with pleasure. We had assembled our crew:

2nd Lt. Co-Pilot, Robert J. Shaffer, 0816602, Alliance, Ohio

2nd Lt. Navigator, Robert C. Marquis, 0748079, Arizona

Bombardier, 2nd Lt. Harry E. Will Jr., 0689566, Pittsburgh

Crew Chief Engineer, Sgt. Richard H. Cochrane,
    16046773, Wisconsin

Waist Gunner, Pvt. Noma R. Norman, 14063503, New York

Front - Left to Right - Lt. Harry Will, Bombadier; Sgt. Paul Frank, Waist Gunner; Sgt. James Kirkland, Radio Operator; Sgt. Richard Cochrane, Crew Chief; Sgt. W.L. Egri, Waist Gunner; Lt. Robert Marquis, Navigator; Sgt. Noma Norman, Tail Gunner; Standing - Left to Right - Lt. Robert J. Shaffer, Co-Pilot; Sgt. Wayne Taylor, Ball Turret Gunner.

Waist Gunner, Sgt. Paul Frank, 32704713, New York
Radio Operator, Pfc. James M. Kirkland, 14174689, Alabama
Ball Turret, Sgt. Wayne A. Taylor, 31281360, Connecticut
Tail Gunner, Sgt. W. L. Egri, 13088881, Pennsylvania

I invited Lt. Marquis on a training flight his first night with us. Asking him to do the navigation, I did not say that we were familiar with the route and radio compass. I flew his headings as he gave them to me, and on one leg we flew and flew and flew. Feeling that it was past time to make a change in course, I looked up and saw a mountain approaching rapidly in the night. I pulled back the stick and pushed forward on the throttle with a hard right turn, just in time to avoid crashing the plane into the side of a mountain. A lesson learned. Never take anything for granted. Never assume anything.

Training continued at a regular, rapid pace 24 hours per day. Inez was at Bill's parents' home for a while in Tacoma. Several weekends, Bill and I took off to pick up Jackie in Ellensburg for a trip to Puget Sound.

One day startling news appeared on the bulletin board. The entire group was moving to Drew Field near Tampa, Florida. Some group members would be flying their aircraft, while others would be taking the train. My crew was assigned to the train trip.

Jackie and Inez had to drive down to Florida. They did so after some difficulty acquiring gasoline ration stamps. But they prevailed by sweet-talking the local boards into making ration stamps available. When they stopped in Boone on the way, Jackie's father took the car to the local garage for a once over. The owner said that the girls were lucky to have made it to Boone. The bearings were in bad shape. The delay was temporary: the car was repaired and they reached Tampa without mishap.

Army Regulations authorized travel pay for dependents just once, and then only for permanent change of station. This was a permanent change of station and you just couldn't go much further in the United States than from Moses Lake, Washington, to Tampa, Florida. Upon arrival I immediately put in for her $81 travel pay.

The train trip across the country in late fall was a great experience. I'll never forget the flocks of pheasants winging across the land in North Dakota, the beautiful landscapes, the great cities of Minneapolis, St. Paul, and Chicago, and other towns I'd never before seen.

There was the usual quest for living quarters when arriving in Tampa. Jackie was successful in finding a nice furnished apartment for us about a block from the beach in Clearwater, Florida. It was so nice that at Christmas we had the crew over for a pasta and red wine Christmas dinner. To Jackie's chagrin, the pasta cooked too long and turned into a bowl of wallpaper paste. One can't expect to be a premier cook overnight.

Our wives biked and enjoyed the warm weather of Florida while we were busy training at Drew Field. The air field was across Tampa Bay from Clearwater and we pilots shared rides each day. This is the site of the present commercial airport for Tampa. There was a causeway leading from Clearwater over to an island just off shore and we often wondered about the partially completed buildings which we could see from our beach. It looked like an interesting place to visit and investigate further but we never found the time.

MacDill Field was also located on Tampa Bay and was the location for B-26 Martin Marauder training. There was a long standing joke stating one could walk across Tampa Bay on the B-26's littered on its bottom. We called the B-26 the "flying prostitute." There was no visible means of support since it had a large body and small wings. The B-26 was hot and fast. None of us were interested in flying one of them.

Flying in Florida was different than flying in the northwest. In Washington, we had the mountains on both sides of us. Florida was a long, low peninsula. If we flew above the clouds and too far East or West over water, we might run out of fuel by going past the point of no return. In fact, this was not uncommon and whole crews were lost that way. The bombing range was at Sebring, Florida, and daily training flights included practice there. More time was spent on formation flying, generally near 12,000 feet. We always used oxygen when going above 10,000 feet. The Link Trainer became an old friend for continued instrument training, and cross-country flying was now routine.

A new challange was added when our assignment was to fly round-trip over water to San Antonio, Texas. The Gulf of Mexico was pretty big and there were no navigation check-points along the way. We left mid-morning with an indicated air speed of 150 miles per hour, it took us until mid or late afternoon to begin circling the airport in San Antonio.

When landing the pilot always looks for the lead jeep with the sign that says "Follow Me" to determine where the plane is to be parked. In this case the jeep driver must have been day dreaming or something, for my left wing-tip stopped just above a grease shed. Had I gone any further, the craft would have scraped the building and caused damage to the airfoil of the wing.

We jumped out and examined the situation. I decided that the plane could probably be moved to a safe position, we just had to figure out how. Tomorrow. We'd sleep on it and worry about it tomorrow.

I didn't want to fly over water in darkness and I had received authorization to spend the night in San Antonio. I took a lot of ribbing, because the crew believed I had planned it that way so I could see my brother and his wife, Fred and Ednamae, who were stationed there. Nevertheless I slept that night worrying about my plane.

The problem did not go away overnight. The next morning we inspected the situation again and decided that letting the air out of the tire on the right side of the plane which might raise the left wing enough to proceed. This did not quite do it so some of the crew climbed on top of the right wing and, voila, the left wing cleared the shed and it worked. We cranked up the engines and made it back to Drew Field without further incident.

When training was complete we received orders to travel by train to Langley Field, Hampton, Virginia, to report to the 1st Sea Rescue Search Attack Unit. There were a number of crews that were thrown together throughout training and we were together again for the transfer to Langley Field. They included the crews of 2nd Lt. Edward Taylor, 1st Lt. Bill Doherty and 1st Lt. Jim Scheller.

Four: Flying To The Front

We were very upset with this particular assignment. We had joined the Air Corps to drop bombs on Nazi Germany. Working as a Sea Rescue unit in a B-17 looking for submarines and enemy ships off the coast of Virginia seemed pretty lame in comparison.

It was time for our wives to be on the move again and to search for housing. I had promised Jackie when we were married that there wouldn't be a lot of money, but we would lead an interesting life with our travels. This was our fourth move in a half year of marriage, and we had just started our Air Corps career.

The crews took the train north while Jackie and Inez drove the cars to Virginia. Hampton, Virginia, was a bustling town of about 15,000 population and the home of Hampton Institute, a famous Negro college. Their search for housing started there and continued in the other communities nearby.

They settled on Buckroe Beach, a vacation village on the Atlantic Ocean. Public bus and streetcar transportation were available from there to Langley Field. They found a three-story apartment house which the owner had been in the process of remodeling when the war began.

An amusement park, closed down for the winter and the war, was just across the street. The new quarters consisted of a bed, combination sitting room, bathroom, and a small kitchen with an ice box and a kerosene-burner cook stove. The furnishings were basic. Our bed was directly beneath the ice box in the apartment above us. When our neighbors upstairs forgot to empty the pan holding the meltings from their ice box, the water came through the ceiling onto our bed. Then we pounded on our ceiling.

As training progressed Jackie and Inez came to Langley Field for meals and dances at the officers club. The title of the outfit to which we were assigned was a camouflage, designed to confuse people

At the Officers Club at Langley Field just before departure for England. April, 1943.

37

Erbe at Propeller of B17 - 1943

as to our mission. We were relieved. The 1st Sea Search Rescue & Attack Unit was a phony. We were to undergo secret training with a new weapon which was still highly classified. "Radar" had been invented and refined to fit in such a small package that a disk inside a dome was placed into the B-17 as a replacement for the ball turret.

The radar unit itself was referred to as "Mickey" or PFF. The Mickey operator was the navigator and was referred to as the Mickey Navigator from then on. Mickey equipped aircraft were stationed at Langley because it was the research field for the Air Corps. The base engineer personnel were equipped to carry out any design changes necessary for its operation.

The use of radar while on bombing runs would be a great advantage since the presence of unexpected cloud cover over the target would no longer mean scrubbing or canceling the mission. The Mickey navigator could look right through the clouds and identify the target for the bombardier.

Not all planes were so equipped. Generally the Mickey plane was flown by the Lead Pilot and Group Commander, with no more than two radar ships being allocated to an entire squadron formation. We would be flying a more sophisticted aerial machine in which we were proud to be chosen as Lead Pilots. We knew what we were doing was important.

Our high-tech training emphasized skill improvement and tightening of the coordination between the pilot, navigator and bombardier. The navigator had to make an important adjustment from working with aerial charts which show every rail-line, church and building on clear days. A radar chart pictured rivers and manmade objects in relief as they appeared through his radar scope on cloudy days.

This special training at Langley continued until the beginning of April 1944. During our time there, Jackie and I took a boat trip up the

Chesapeake Bay and the Potomac River from Old Point Comfort to Washington D.C. Our room for the overnight trip was about the size of a small bathroom and claustrophobia reigned. We did not often stray to Norfolk. That was a sailor's town and one went there in an Air Corps uniform at his own risk. The sailors were everywhere in Norfolk, which was just across the bay, and they didn't care for the Air Corps.

I had gotten word that I would be leaving before Jackie's birthday, which was on the sixth of April. We dropped in at Woodward & Lothrop

Climbing aboard the Flying Fortress, September, 1944

and I bought her an olive-green suit. She was stunning, and wore it to dinner in the Langley officers club when we returned from Washington. Woodword & Lothrop since then has failed, sold in bankruptcy proceedings, and is destined, after considerable fundraising and renovation, to become the new Opera Building in Washington, D.C.

My parents and Jackie's parents came out to see us during the last month we were in Virginia. It must have been a rigorous rail trip for them during wartime. I can still hear Jackie's father saying, "Tommy, (his pet name for his daughter), what are you doing living in a place like this?" He was not impressed.

Actually, Jackie did a wonderful job making the best of shortages and inconveniences in the primitive living conditions. She became an expert at baking cakes in the box-like oven which she placed on top of the kerosene burners stove. She could not get sugar for frosting to put on her chocolate cake. Adapting, my wife purchased several Hershey chocolate bars and melted them for frosting.

Jackie pleaded with the landlord to paint our rooms. But he refused. His name was Hull, so we called it not the Hull House, but Hell House. Jackie spent a good deal of time listening to radio music and claimed the cockroaches were so big and plentiful that they changed the stations on the radio.

We had a party for our friends and crew members several nights before we left for overseas. Jackie decided that she would fix the owner, and turned our quarters into an art gallery. We used a table lamp and she drew the silhouettes of our guests on the white wall with a black marker. The subjects then signed their names beneath the silhouette. It was a striking improvement.

We received orders to leave in the first week of April, 1944. They were sealed to be opened only after take-off. The first stage was to Bangor, Maine, and we would await further orders there. The plane was a brand new aluminum clad B-17F. It looked great.

We left Langley Field at about 08:00 hours and had told our wives that we would fly over Buckroe Beach on our way north. Jackie and Inez were out on the beach waving goodbye. As Bill's plane flew over, Jackie told me afterwards, Inez broke into tears. He never made it back.

The flight was uneventful yet interesting. Our path took us over Manhattan and every skyscraper on the island. Upon arrival in Bangor we had more processing and papers for our next stage, as well as another physical exam. We stayed there overnight and the next morning took off for Goose Bay, Labrador.

Once we left the continental United States the aerial charts we carried became unreliable. There were hundreds of lakes down below, frozen ponds and areas of water which didn't appear on any of our charts. It was at times like this that our Navigator, Lt. Marquis, earned his keep. He was very important to all of us.

We spied the air base at Goose Bay nestled in the snow amid the trees. There were ten-foot high snow drifts along the runway. We landed in good shape with the usual "Follow Me" jeep parking us. We reported in and they showed us to our quarters where we ate and spent the night. There was also a theater where we could see a free movie.

In our quarters the walls of toilet cubicles were covered with messages from former occupants including one that said, "Clark Gable Was Here." Throughout this period in the Air Corps, "Kilroy" too, preceded us wherever we went. He left his messages on every available space. I still wonder if there really was a person named Kilroy.

Our original plan was to stay at Goose Bay for only one night, but the weatherman increased it to two nights. This was not uncommon.

A much longer stay at Goose Bay had been in store for our group commander, West Point graduate Lt. Colonel Luper who had traveled the same route earlier, in February, 1944.

His pilot, Lt. Milton Jaraszlow of New York, went out to prepare Luper's plane for takeoff. He warmed up the engines in the severe cold and the oil pressure would not come up on two of the four engines. He called the tower and advised them of the problem. The tower responded that the pressure would eventually rise, just go ahead and run the engines. He continued to run them for 30 minutes until they destroyed themselves. Jaraszlow remained there several months waiting for new engines to be flown up from the States and installed, while Col. Luper caught the next plane to England. That was not exactly the best way to get brownie points from your commanding officer.

I received a good briefing for the next leg of my flight, across the southern tip of Greenland to Iceland. The weather was accurately predicted and it was an exciting event for me to be flying my own plane over the North Atlantic. As we left the coast of Labrador at 16:00 hours, I thought of my cousin the dentist, Dr. Kurt Kuehnert, who was part of the Sir Wilfred Grenfell mission to the Labrador natives in 1932. One day someone reported icebergs off-shore and they decided to fly out to see them. The plane never returned.

We watched for icebergs but saw none and didn't go out of our way looking for them. The Aurora Borealis put on a spectacular show as we neared a land mass. We were able to see the southernmost tip of Greenland as we passed that huge continent.

We arrived in Iceland at 8:00 A.M. our expected time without incident. When opening my cockpit window, there seemed to be a pervasive musky odor in the atmosphere. We later learned that the natives dried fish heads in their back yards for fertilizer, but doubted that was the sole source of the odor. We became used to it after awhile.

We expected to stay for only one night, but again the weather added another day for us in Iceland. It was Easter Sunday as well as Jackie's birthday, April sixth. Although I didn't leave the base, I certainly wanted to explore Iceland. There was no transportation, nor had I any idea where to go if I did find a ride. My brief impression was that Iceland was a barren country with very few trees. I had seen a few mountains to the north of the airbase on our way in and that was it.

Our landing in Iceland provided the first chance we had to enhance, indeed to build on our Short Snorter Club. The club consisted of those people, military and civilian alike, who traveled to foreign countries, and as a matter of pride and pleasure, collected paper currency of each country they visited. The paper was Scotch-Taped together in a long string and their friends signed their names on them.

The string of currency was then folded and kept in your billfold. When the next meeting at a bar or drinking occasion, anyone discovered without having his Short Snorter had to buy the next round. When overseas one carried the Short Snorter with you at all times or it would become very expensive.

My Short Snorter consisted of a British ten-shilling note, Algerian five Frank, French Fifty Franc, one Krona Icelandic, five Kamar, Landskonki Islands, and a $1 silver certificate of the U.S. Treasury. These were covered with the names of my crew and friends.

I started to keep a diary in a small notebook of my expenses after I left the U.S. And kept it up for each of my combat days. I described briefly the target for the day, the bomb load, our altitude, and our position in the formation with the time for takeoff and landing. I also briefly described the intensity of the mission including the enemy flak and fighter opposition. My descriptions were brief and matter of fact about the entire operation. In some cases I supplemented the diary entries with the "offical"description of our efforts in the sky over enemy territory. Since our days on the ground were usually filled with sleep or poker games, I entered my winnings and losses at that game. Fortunately I broke about even over the long run neither winning or losing very much.

I received a briefing for our next leg of the trip which was to end at Nutts Corner Air Base in Ireland. We were especially cautioned to follow our compass headings and not our radio compass. The Nazis knew about allied traffic from Iceland to Ireland and had installed a radio beacon on the same frequency. Instead of leading us to Ireland, it would have taken us directly into Nazi Germany and they would get a brand new B-17 for free. And more importantly, they would imprison an entire crew. This did happen a number of times.

We took off at mid-morning, passing over Stornaway, Scotland, to land during the mid-afternoon in Ireland. It was a major Royal Air

Force facility next to a large lake in Northern Ireland, and our introduction to the British way of doing things. It wasn't much different than our way. They were very businesslike and knew what they were doing. We expected that. I wandered the grounds of the base and found the forsythia in full bloom. Of course, we were not to mention in our letters home where we were located and all outgoing mail was censored. I decided that I would pick some forsythia blooms, include them in a letter to Jackie and she would then know immediately where I was. Snip-snip. It didn't work. She had no idea where I had been.

In the short time spent at the British base, I ate several meals at their mess. The British thought we Americans were crazy for wanting water with our meals and said so. I didn't care very much for their food preparation.

While at Nutts Corner I discovered that my old 2nd Infantry Division was stationed at a training camp nearby. I thought I would try to get over to see some of my friends from the 23rd Infantry but that was not possible in the short time allotted.

My next stop was to be Alconbury, England. It was a short but beautiful hop from Ireland to south central England. The sun was out and white fleecy clouds enhanced the view as we flew in an easterly direction to England. On that clear spring day, I could see that the farm and pasture plots were separated by rock fences. There were none of those square lines like we had dividing our farm fields in Iowa.

Alconbury was a major depot for the U.S. Air Corps in England. Not surprisingly, we had to give up our aircraft there. We hated to say goodbye to this great plane which had carried us so well across the Atlantic Ocean.

Of course we had some more training to do before we could join in the war that was going on. Our next trip was by train to an Air Corps training facility in the Midlands of England. On this the 12th of April, we noted in the military newspaper, *STARS AND STRIPES*, a first reference to the long-awaited D-Day allied attack over the channel to the continent. It said that all passes, leaves and furloughs were canceled at midnight, and when the shooting starts we would be busy as part of the American Expeditionary Force.

In London we changed trains for the North country. We were intrigued with the British railroad passenger cars that had an individual door for each compartment. It looked dangerous for occupants to be able to jump in or out of compartments at the station while the train was still moving. On the other hand, it certainly was convenient. The conductor didn't give us any specific instructions as to when to get off so we missed our stop and ended up at Stoke on Trent, which is near Newcastle-under-Lyme. An exasperated railroad official redirected us so that we finally arrived in the proper village, Stone.

Our training consisted of classroom work during which we reviewed enemy aircraft identification, Morse code, formation flying positions, aircraft problems, gunnery, bombing, and related matters. They inquired how many hours of high altitude formation training I had flown. I responded and then was asked, "How high?" I gave them the altitude of 12,000 feet. This elicited an exclamation of dismay. In their vocabulary, high altitude meant over 20,000 feet. The characteristics and handling of aircraft are much different flying at and above that altitude. When combining that with flying close formation, it was an entirely different ball game.

Poker was a large part of our life. So was the mail. Another pilot, with whom I went through training at Moses Lake, Drew Field, and Langley Field, James W. Scheller, kept a diary and compiled his letters home forty years later. His words back then summed up how we all felt:

April, 10, 1944. (Keflavik, Iceland) Darling, I've been almost too busy and tired to really get blue for you, but am expecting a severe onslaught any day now.

April 13, 1944. (Nutts Corner, Ireland) Speaking of Spring, Darling, I should like to spend this and every one with you. I'm beginning to get terribly lonely and hence anxious to get started and get it over with.

April 17, 1944. (Stone, England) Still here, Sweetheart, seeing sights and riding bicycles and learning things. No excitement of any kind except poker games with Bill, Norm, Shaffer, Bob and (of all people) Ed Taylor. I'm absolutely starved for news and words from you, not standing this separation as well as I thought I would, but then I never do, do I?

April 20, 1944. Everything much the same as before with big 'A' poker games taking up the leisure.

April 21, 1944. Received your first letter today and your V-mail letter. Boy! Did I ever need them and love them. Also, other thoughts of you crop up this evening as we are finishing up the last of the 'wonderful' cookies you made on the eve of my departure. 'Sweets,' as the English say, are scarce. I opened the box before on a train from 'hyar to thar' and offered them to some Britishers. They refused politely as they could, with all the drool blocking their vocal passages, so I insisted and am firmly convinced that your cooking has done more than lend-lease to cement Anglo-American friendship.

April 22, 1944. Just to show you how absolutely chaste I am and intend to be, I bought two pair of flannel pajamas. Of course the cold nights and the pricky RAF wool blankets have nothing to do with the decision.

Keely bought a bicycle the other day at a terrific bargain. Naturally it was 'hot' and the bobbies had to retrieve it from him. They have the culprit but as yet Bob hasn't seen his dough.

April 26, 1944. Received three letters from you today, one V-mail and two airmail. The airmail jobs are lots faster. The time involved bantering back and forth by letter is almost too great for me to comment on anything of interest you write. One thing you may recall is a remark about 'delightful torture,' but it makes me feel close to you again. Mmmm, such goings on in my mind.

April 28, 1944. Got your letter of April 17 today, a day after one mailed the 21st, so sequence means nothing. And the first thing that comes to mind is the last remark you wrote, something about chandeliers...anyway it's FUN to think about, isn't it? I've just been sucked into a big poker game so will write this in snatches...

May 8, 1944. Let's see. Saturday night was dance night at the old 95th, lots and lots of men, very few gals, mostly culls who seem to be occupied by 'permanent personnel' —Bob and Mac and I proceeded to get quietly but efficiently drunk during a snooker game. We just had a wonderful time by ourselves. Scotch is wunnerful(sic) stuff.

Bob and I each bought a bike and took a three or four mile trip to one of the nearby villages. The English garden is an institution, really gorgeous. No formal planting at all, just large clusters of snap-dragons, stocks, and always a plot of vari-colored tulips. All the fruit trees are in bloom, the apple blossoms being prettiest and most prominent. There are lots of big fat partridge, about as large as our hen pheasants.

—be a good girl for me on account of I'm getting tired of getting behind in my duties and....

May 11, 1944. Today is a beautiful day with little to do. I would go for a bike ride but would have to wear a blouse and that would be too hot. I could read a book but I don't feel like it. I could go to the club but it's too early for beer, and anyway I'm tired of beer. Or perhaps a game of ping pong... nope, too strenuous. Could this be Spring? Yup, it is. And the only thing I do want to do, I can't, because you're not here...

Following our crew training at Stone, I was assigned as a replacement crew to the 457th Bombardment Group (Heavy) of which my squadron, the 751st was a part. The long training period which began in San Antonio, Texas, in October of 1942, was now completed. It was late April of 1944, and we were considered ready and qualified to undertake the combat missions for which we had been trained.

At this time a little background about combat flying might be useful to understand the situation in which we operated. In 1943 and 1944 the average life of an 8th Air Corps bomber and crew was fifteen missions. The first few missions were an unreality, a movie like you would see in a theater. But by the 10th mission one becomes an expert, cool, and responsible fighter. We acquired a sense of importance, knowing the personal effort we executed made a difference in the war as we carried our bombs to critical targets. We dropped them and saw the clouds of black smoke coming from the suppliers of Nazi's fighting machine.

The air war was a volunteer operation by our American flight crew members. A transfer request from flying status to ground duty was instantly granted with no resenting stigma on the record of the crewmen. Some performed not only their required 25, 30, or 35 missions but volunteered to fly as many as 60 missions over the continent. I was not among them. Too many of my friends had gone down as a result of enemy action. I did not.

46

By the time I arrived in England in the spring of 1944, there were more than 130 military airfields in southeastern England, in an area no larger than the state of Vermont and smaller than some counties in Texas and California. Forty-two of these fields were home for the 8th Air Corps, B-17 and B-24 Divisions, and 14 were occupied by their fighter escorts, P-47 and P-51s. The fighters were referred to as "little friends" by the bomber groups.

These bases were not located in wastelands, for there was no place like that in Eastern England. They were set down amid prime farmland and villages, all of which continued to operate while the airmen did their job.

The only straight lines in our airfield at Glatton were the two runways. Everything else was melded into existing landscape. The airfield and combat unit to which I were assigned was midway between Cambridge and Peterborough in Huntingdonshire, England. I learned in 1970 that the name Glatton was a subterfuge. There was a town named Glatton on the east coast and they were trying to confuse the Nazis. It was an unsuccessful ruse since our crews that had been shot down and taken as prisoners reported that the Nazi interrogators knew nearly everything about our bases, where the POWs (Prisoners of War) came from, the names of staff officers and other supposedly secret information.

The closest village to our base was Conington, where there is now a granite memorial erected in a churchyard dedicated to our outfit, the 457th Bomb group. Our base was located on the Great North Road, the highway from London to Edinburgh which was orginally laid out by the Romans in ancient times. It was a quite narrow two-lane road by American standards. A railroad track existed parallel to the Great North Road and they both were just beyond the end of our principal runway.

Six officers of the squadron were assigned living quarters, in each Nissen Hut during my stay at Glatton. The other officers in my hut were:

1st Lt. Jack Owens, a pilot from California
2nd Lt. Chuck Berta, a co-pilot from Illinois
2nd Lt. Shaffer, my co-pilot from Ohio
2nd Lt. Francis Minturn, a navigator.
2nd Lt. Armen Topakian, a navigator from Rhode Island.

Our beds were flat steel-spring frames on which we arranged three, thirty-inch square straw mattress pads in a mattress cover. We topped that with a sheet, blankets and a straw-filled pillow. When the weather was cold, the center of attention was the stove in the middle of the room. It was about 30 inches high and 15 inches in diameter; it burned coal and/or coke and sent fumes and smoke through a stove pipe in the ceiling. We were allocated a certain amount of fuel for the stove, but when the temperature got chilly outside we needed more. We soon engaged in "midnight requisitioning" at the forbidden coal pile.

Other Nissen Hut furnishings consisted of a board table and wooden arm chair made by a previous occupant. We played poker when we were not otherwise engaged, using a bed for a card table. We discovered that that game was the most efficient way to learn the British monetary system.

Bicycles were issued to get around the base. Toilet and shower facilities were 30 steps away in a bath house. The food was good in the consolidated group mess nearby. There was very little Spam served, a meat product made famous/infamous during the war, and I became well acquainted with powdered eggs.

Any food that would cause gas in the intestines was avoided, since gas expanded at high altitudes. Brussels sprouts and beans were nowhere to be seen. The mess account was under the control of the Mess Officer. Our particular Mess Officer was later found to have skimmed funds, and was caught and was subsequently court-martialed for his indiscretion.

Not far away was the Officers Club with a bar that opened each day at 16:00 hours. A large fireplace at one end of the club was decorated by the group insignia, our group motto, *FAIT ACCOMPLI*, and names of the target missions flown by the group. Easy chairs and pool tables were scattered around, and a portrait of the group commander Col. Luper's live-in British girlfriend was another wall decoration for all of us to admire or simply wonder about. It was an odd thing to hang in a public place, even for Col. Luper. He was shot down in August of 1944, spent the balance of the war in a POW camp, and was killed in a plane accident in the States after the war.

The club was converted into a dance hall on Saturday evenings, when Special Services brought British girls from nearby towns. I have read that U.S. show business people entertained troops on air bases in England, but I never saw a headliner at our base.

The Post Exchange Nissen hut was an important building in our complex where PX rations were issued every Wednesday. A week's ration included beer, soft drinks, tobacco, candy, candy roll or gum, cookies, matches (book or box), soap, and toilet paper. Every two weeks we were authorized peanuts, four ounces of laundry soap, razor and razor blades. Each four-week period we could also have fruit juice, tooth powder or paste, shaving cream or stick, writing tablet, envelopes or portfolio, pipe cleaners and two women's handkerchiefs. With our PX card we purchased the limit of everything on the ration card whether we liked it or not. If we did not want what they had to sell, we bought it to use for trading stock with others.

FIVE: B-17 COMBAT MISSION PROCESS

Each mission was conceived at Supreme Headquarters Allied Expeditionary Forces (SHAEF), which established a priority list of targets for the 8th Air Corps bombers. There was a difference of opinion when the Americans first arrived in England. Prime Minister Churchill felt that the American bombers should join the British bombers in night bombing of enemy targets. The American generals disagreed, and convinced him that "around the clock" bombing, with the British on night missions and the American bombers on day missions, would be more effective in keeping the enemy awake and hasten the war effort.

The priority list established by Supreme Headquarters in conjunction with the British bombing strategies included oil fields, synthetic oil factory sites, aircraft and munitions plants, railroad marshaling yards, submarine pens on the Atlantic coast, V-1 and V-2 launching sites, rocket research installations on the Baltic Sea, and large cities in Nazi Germany.

Regardless of the nature of the target or its location, each mission required good weather to enable the bombers to take off and assemble in formation at 12,000 feet, and to land upon their return in the afternoon. We also hoped for good weather over the continent so we could steer clear of clouds at 18,000 feet or higher, and at least broken clouds at 25,000 feet over the target. Although these atmospheric criteria were desirable, they were not always met because of other factors. When less than ideal weather occurred, we went anyway.

We worried about concentration trails, "contrails," made by ice crystals which formed at very high altitudes. They are the characteristic white cloudy streaks often seen trailing behind high-flying aircraft. Contrails made formation flying much more difficult and they enabled the enemy on the ground to see us more clearly. One pilot described contrails in the book, *One Last Look* by Philip Kaplan and Rex Alan Smith:

> *They look so beautiful from the ground, but in the air, both in assembly and otherwise, they strike fear into every man's heart. They appear behind the ships ahead, looking so much like spun glass that you fear they will become entangled with the propellers and stop them. Then suddenly you're in them, in a blanketing fuzz that makes your heart pound. Then the*

51

formation can be seen only occasionally through the holes, at times flying totally blind, and you know that in one of those blind moments you may crash into a friend,...so you squirm and pray.

The weather man sometimes predicted the presence of thick London-type fog at our landing base on our return. I have been in London and experienced such fog where one could not see more than four feet to his front. When such an event happened at the air base, an emergency landing strip would be used, where aircraft fuel would be run through pipes in ditches on each side of the runway and then set afire. I never had to land in that situation.

Once the weather forecaster gave a favorable report to headquarters, everything moved into motion. Specific targets were selected, flying units designated, and bomb loads specified. There was a choice of ordinance, 1000 lb., 500 lb., and 250 lb. bombs, all of which were general purpose, incendiary sticks, or fragmentation (anti-personnel) or grenade bombs. The fuel load was determined, as well as routes to and from the target.

With these decisions completed, orders were issued and ground crews worked through the night to prepare the aircraft. Since blackout was in effect, dim blue lights flitted about the airfield like fireflies. At the same time, the office staff and clerks were typing information to be distributed to pilots, navigators, bombardiers and crew members at the briefing.

The day of the mission usually began about 01:00 hours, with an insistent tap on the shoulder or foot by the "charge-of-quarters" (CQ) saying it was time to get up and ready yourself for your mission. The preparation included a close shave since a snug fit of the oxygen mask on your face required a smooth jaw. We donned the long underwear, fleece-lined boots, flight suit

Erbe at Home

and fleece-lined flight jacket.

We hopped into two-and-one-half ton trucks for the ride to the mess hall and had hot cakes or powdered eggs and a lot of coffee. Then we headed for the Group Briefing Room to learn about the mission for the day. This was the most significant building on the

Roommates in the Nissen Hut behind us — L to R back - Jack Owen, Chuck Berta, Norm Erbe, Joe Schaffer, Francis Minturn, Seated-Armen Topakian - June 1944

base for those of us who were flying missions.

The briefing room was a large Nissen hut with 100 or so chairs facing the end wall to view a sheet covering the large map of Europe. The crews entered and took their seats. The Operations Officer would arrive and pull the sheet aside. There on the wall would be the exposed map of Europe with a red tape running from our field to and from the target for the day. Brief remarks were made by the Group Commander about the nature of the target and the reason for hitting it. In addition he gave expectations of enemy fighters, flak and other obstacles to the mission, as well as planned friendly fighter cover.

If the assignment was going to be tough or far distant, there was sometimes a general groan. A comparatively short mission brought a sigh of relief because we envisioned a simple milk-run, (an expectation which might not necessarily hold true.) We were then given assigned times for take-off, assembly, over target, and return. Each staff specialist would then brief us on what to expect in his area of expertise.

Following the briefing, we were given the opportunity to spend time with the chaplain before being taken out to the planes scattered around the field. We took our gear with us to the planes. This consisted of helmet, flak jacket, a Mae West, and a parachute. The Mae West was an inflatable life preserver for use in case we had to ditch in the cold North Sea. The word "flak" was a descriptive word referring to "anti-aircraft artillery" which was put up by the Nazis to shoot down our planes. The flak guns usually surrounded by cities and probable targets. The projectile was an iron shell with a fuse on the end of the projectile which was set by the gunner to explode at a fixed distance from the gun-usually 20,000 to 30,000 feet. These were known as "fixed fuse" projectiles. In the later part of the war, the U.S. developed a secret weapon — the proximity fuse which exploded the shell when it came close to the target. It was very effective and made the "flak" shell very accurate and dangerous. The flak jacket was in two parts: upper and lower part clipped together. In the cockpit, I usually sat on the lower part to protect my crotch from flak. The pilot and co-pilot were also protected by a 1/4-inch steel plate at their backs that went from the floor almost to the ceiling of the cockpit.

Our throat microphone for on-board and outside radio communication was the next bit of equipment to don. The two mikes were each the size of a nickel coin, attached by an elastic neck band so that they were positioned on each side of the throat. The oxygen mask snapped onto the helmet. Some of the crew wore electrically heated flying suits which they plugged into the aircraft. The outside temperature at high altitudes often reached 58 degrees Fahrenheit below zero.

We also carried an escape packet which was issued prior to each mission. It consisted of four photos of us dressed in civilian clothes to be used on a phony passport in an escape attempt. The packet also contained a four language phrase card, German and French money, a detailed map of Europe printed on silk and a brass-button compass.

After arriving at our planes from briefing, crew members checked and tested their assigned areas of responsibility to insure the craft was in proper working order. Since it was usually dark when preparing to take off, and radio contact with instructions were forbidden, the signaling process for action consisted of flare pistols fired from the control tower. Its shells gave off different colors, each having its own meaning: Yellow-yellow for start engines, red-yellow for taxi, green-green for take off.

Each plane was supplied with one flare pistol. It was used for signaling other planes in the formation when necessary. Upon approaching the field for landing, a red-red signal was fired if injured or dead were aboard. The plane was then met by ambulances called "meat-wagons."

One thousand bombers with 10 crewmen in each plane comprised the 42 heavy bomber groups, all located within eight or nine miles of each other at their air bases on the ground. The goal was to get them off the ground and assembled in a long line without colliding. Instructions were given for the take-off heading, rate of climb, and compass headings with exact minutes and seconds in order for the bomber stream to assemble properly over England. This was done by flying a circle over a radio compass called a "buncher." After assembly, it was time to head for the continent in a straight line, climbing continuously to cross the coast at an altitude of about 20,000 feet.

We referred to our squadron formation as a "box." The lead ship, the planes flying on each wing of the lead ship, and another identical set right behind and below that trio would be the lead "Box." Then another formation behind and above the lead would be the "High Box," and below that the "Low Box." This constituted the Group Effort for the day's mission.

The lead ship had responsibility of leading the group, squadron or box. I usually flew lead or deputy lead. The Squadron or Group Commander or his designated substitute flew in the right seat of the lead ship. The regular co-pilot rode in the tail gunner's position to report to the Commander the status and location of planes in his formation.

The lead also had the radar dome replacing the ball turret, which was distended during flight. The Mickey navigator took over Bombardier duties along with his own. He was responsible for getting to the target through the overcast, giving the signal to drop the bombs, and plotting the course returning everyone safely back home. At other times they were interchangeable: a bombardier substituting for the navigator on Mickey planes. The radar was keyed with the bombsight so that the navigator would drop through the undercast, and bombardiers on other ships in the formation would use the toggle switch to drop their loads at the same time as the radar plane.

The lead airplane was the only one to use automatic pilot, providing stability for planes flying his formation. Sometimes the lead plane would experience a pendulum effect, swaying back and forth in the air currents and propeller wash from planes ahead of him. Those flying tightly behind him exaggerated this motion. Although not disastrous, it was still very difficult for the aircraft following the lead plane. The formation would be all over the sky with curses.

In addition to our equipment, ammunition and other paraphernalia, we carried "chaff," bundles of strips of metallic paper about one-quarter inch wide and 15 inches long. We tossed this out of the plane in bundles when approaching targets or known enemy anti-aircraft positions. This was designed to impede the accuracy of enemy radar. It was said that the streets of some German cities were covered with our chaff.

Targets were very difficult to hit. We didn't have rocket propelled bombs or laser guided missiles; only gravity and a talent for aiming. The following excerpt from *One Last Look* by Philip Kaplan and Rex Alan Smith illustrates the problem nicely:

> *"During the first half of 1943, the men of the Eighth (Air Corps) managed to place only 14 percent of their bombs within a 1,000 feet of the target center (MPI), and placed only 32 percent within 2,000 ft. After that they gradually brought those percentages up to 44 percent and 73 percent. During the entire war, according to photographic record, they placed 37 percent within 1,000 feet and 64 percent within 2,000 feet of the centers of their targets. When you consider that trying to drop bombs into a 2,000 foot circle while speeding past at an altitude of 25,000 feet in a bomber under fire was much like trying to drop grains of rice into a teacup while riding past on a bicycle under fire, that was a very good record indeed."*

My brother, Fred, was a member of the U.S. Strategic Bombing Survey of the Air Corps, which, toward the end of the war, helped to develop these reports on "my" bombing accuracy.

We almost always returned to base with flak holes in the plane. Berlin, Munich, Bremen, Hamburg and Schweinfurt are some of the cities which put up an apparently impenetrable carpet of flak. We crossed our fingers and prayed each time we flew in that maelstrom, knowing our chances of survival were very low.

Nazi fighters were formidable opponents for bombers. They attacked for brief intervals of two to 15 seconds, but their toll was devastating. It was an extremely frightening feeling to have them flying inbound, red golf balls (cannon fire) coming out of their wings directly at us. I sat in the pilot seat using a great deal of body english to avoid being struck by one or more of those fatal golf balls. We couldn't imagine how they could miss. Many times they did hit the next plane. My crew watched and reported any parachutes, all the while firing at the Nazi planes with their 50 caliber machine guns, or describing the craft going down in a ball of fire. I was too busy flying to watch the results. Our B-17 shuddered from the combined recoil of our 20 machine guns all firing at the enemy at the same time.

Many of the flights were ten to 12 hours long. Body functions had to be properly disciplined to handle this although we did have a pilot relief tube. Fortunately, I was like a camel. I didn't move from the time I strapped myself into the seat until I returned to base. Returning from missions, we were debriefed. The debriefing covered the subjects of Nazi fighters and flak, the target, accuracy of the bombing, and anything new and different about the mission, and then to bed.

Dependable information on bombing results was hard to obtain. As recalled by a fellow pilot, "They'd pick you up in a truck and haul you to this little building, and you'd go in and sit at one of the long tables inside and somebody would say, 'OK, they're opening the bar, so go get your drink,' and everyone was given a glass of whiskey — a small glass, a double shot. Then you'd sit there chattering about what we saw and you saw, and so forth."

Every crew was interrogated as a group by the Group Intelligence officer. The mission was reported by each crew member from his own perspective. Discrepancies were identified by the interrogators as they probed for information about the Nazi reaction to the raid. Efforts were made to determine if the Luftwaffe was trying any new tactical wrinkles in its response to the American's attack. Questions were asked about the accuracy of the USAAC predictions regarding flak and fighter response. Immediate analysis of the Flash Reports (tabulations of the raw data from the interrogations) was then done by the headquarters staff.

But this system, even though it helped mission planners keep abreast of Nazi defensive developments, was not too helpful in revealing the actual accomplishments of a mission. In the heat of action and plowing through flak, it was hard for men to be accurate and dispassionate observers—a fact apparent in every debriefing.

"I'd hear what some of the other guys were saying," recalled

Keith Newhouse, "and wonder if we'd been on the same mission." As remembered by Paul Sink: "You'd been on oxygen for six or seven hours, you were tired, so stiff you could hardly stand up, and still half-frozen from having been so damn cold. Then they'd give you shots of whiskey, and by the time you got into the interrogation, hell!, you didn't know yourself what you'd seen." (from One Last Look by Philip Kaplan and Rex Alan Smith, Abbeville Press, New York)

There were occasions that our own coastal anti-aircraft guns decided to shoot at us as we were returning from a mission to the continent over the North Sea. We had an electronic gadget aboard which was called IFF (Information-Friend-or-Foe) which was supposed to emit a radio signal identifying us as friendly. When they ignored this signal we became very angry. Who couldn't recognize a B-17?

Six: Bomber Pilot Mission Diary, Part I

May 7 - June 25, 1944

My crew was reassembled at Glatton following the three-week training break at Stone and Alconbury. We were not assigned missions right away. I was a certified B-17 bomber pilot with all kinds of training behind me, while my Nissen hut mates were going out frequently and flying missions. Actually they didn't issue any certificates—we knew we were ready and they knew we were ready as we could be to fly our first mission. I was going stir crazy waiting. I finally went down to Squadron Headquarters and asked the Commander to please assign me a combat mission. The military likes eager beavers so he approved my request.

May 7, 1944. Berlin, Nazi Germany.
Target: City Center.

My first mission on May 7, 1944, was as co-pilot to an experienced pilot. We drew a maximum effort mission, with hundreds of Flying Fortresses (B-17's) and Liberators (B-24's) which meant 1000 plus airplanes. The target was downtown Berlin, dead center on the Friederichstrasse railroad station. The assigned bombing altitude was 25,000 feet and sighting was by PFF (Radar).

Our position was number four in the Lead Box. We kept our nose directly under the tail of the number one plane. Number five flew on our left wing and number six on our right. We assembled at 12,000 feet over the radio "buncher" (a radio signal serving as a collection post in the air for the planes) and then headed out over the North Sea for the continent. As we headed east I had a chance to look around me. It was a beautiful morning, the air sparkling clear as I admired the stunning sight of the long line of silver and olive colored bombers. I was thrilled to be a part of it all.

My pilot noticed that I was sight-seeing and punched me. He pointed at the instruments and gestured that they were my responsibility when I was not actually piloting the plane. Of course, attention to the instruments discloses not only malfunctions in one or more engines, but also damage from flak or enemy fighter cannon shot.

After an hour or so I took over piloting the Fortress and discovered that being in the number four position was not an easy task. You looked right up the tail of number one plane, about 10 feet away. Any slight move to the right or the left caused the "pendulum effect" for yourself and the planes flying formation on your plane. The effort to stay in formation became nearly hypnotic until discipline and experience enabled me to focus on the task.

We encountered flak as we came in over the coast and saw a little bit of Holland through growing cloud cover. We passed over Dummer Lake in Nazi Germany and learned to expect flak located there on subsequent missions. The Nazis knew this was our visual check point and placed flak guns on the lake itself. Their aim was excellent and just at our altitude.

North of Berlin we saw land below, but ahead was a cover of low clouds over the city itself. We did not need to be told where the target of Berlin was located; there was a massive layer of protective flak covering the city. All of it seemed to be exploding in giant black puffs at exactly our altitude.

We were trained to fly tight formations to insure that our bombs landed in a close pattern on the target and for mutual protection against enemy fighter attack. I knew however that it was statistically impossible for all of us to fly into that maelstrom of explosions and survive. Yet most of us did. This was the time for prayers to the Almighty, and the Almighty received a lot of them.

We held steady in formation through the exploding anti-aircraft shell bursts and dropped our bombs on our PFF signal on the target. My on-board aerial cameras took pictures of the bombing pattern, and to the extent that the clouds beneath us, permitted, my crew members watched for signs that we had hit the target. Pilots and co-pilots were entirely too busy with flying formation and leaving the target area flak to spend time looking five miles below.

John Steinbeck, from his vantage point as a passenger on the "Mary Ruth," describes a B-17 bail-out during the mission in his book *Once There Was A War*:

> *They all agree that what happened seemed to happen very slowly. The Fortress slowly nosed up and up until she tried to*

climb vertically and, of course, she couldn't do that. Then she slipped in slow motion, backing like a falling leaf, and she balanced for awhile and then her nose edged over and she started down, nose down, for the ground.

The blue sky and white clouds made a picture of it. The crew could see the gunner trying to get out and then he did, and his parachute fluffed open. And the ball-turret gunner- they could see him flopping about. The bombardier and navigator blossomed out the nose and the waist gunners followed them, Mary Ruth's crew yelling, "Get out, you pilots." The ship was far down when the ball-turret gunner cleared. They thought the skipper and co-pilot were lost. They stayed with the ship too long and then the ship was so far down that they could hardly see it. It must have been almost to the ground when two little puffs of white, first one and then the second, shot out of her. And the crew yelled with relief. And then the ship hit the ground and exploded. Only the tail gunner and the ball-turret gunner had seen the end. They explained it over the intercom.

David Perry, a pilot of the 390th Bomb Group, wrote, in *One Last Look:*

The noise is the soft flak. You can't hear it hit the airplane. I remember it vividly on a raid…it wasn't Schweinfurt, it wasn't that rough on our crew, but it was terrible. We lost about half a dozen planes, and one of them was right in front of me in the formation, and he just absolutely exploded....just a big ball of debris and you could feel that debris hit the airplane, and that was a very unpleasant sensation.

Once away from Berlin I breathed a sigh of relief. A check with members of the crew revealed that none had been injured and the plane was apparently flyable. They had seen a number of our friends go down in flames, explosions and tailspins. The crew watched for parachutes with the hope that some of the imperiled crew members had been able to get out of the doomed planes and "hit the silk." If they survived they would spend the balance of the war in a Nazi POW camp, but that was better than dying.

We maintained an altitude of 25,000 feet over Nazi Germany. As we reached the North Sea, speed was decreased to begin losing altitude and allow damaged planes to keep up. Sometimes the planes that were so badly damaged they were ditched in the water. It was an icy experience waiting for British and American rescue boats, to get them back to our base.

We landed at Glatton on schedule at 14:30 hours. Upon reaching the hardstand we jumped out to inspect our plane, finding holes and damage. It felt great to be back in one piece after bombing one of the most formidable and well protected targets in Europe. In exchange, my plane had dropped three 1000 lb. general purpose (GP) bombs and three 500 lb. incendiary bombs. Our group had lost eight B-17's and 80 American airmen.

MAY 12, 1944. LUTZKENDORF-MERSEBURG, NAZI GERMANY.
TARGET: OIL REFINERY POWER STATION.

My second mission, the first with my own crew and plane, marked the opening punch in the long awaited blitz against the Nazi synthetic oil refineries. Our specific target was the power station at a plant 12 miles south of Leipzig. We were up at 03:00 hours for breakfast and were briefed at 04:00 hours. Then to the planes. It was probably no surprise that everyone on the crew forgot some essential item, discovered only after using the check list. I pled guilty too. In spite of preparation errors we took off at the scheduled hour of 09:00 hours.

The Initial Point (IP) is a predetermined position where we began our straight-in bomb run on the target. Thirty minutes before the IP, number two engine began having trouble. The manifold pressure dropped to 20 inches (29 inches is normal) with a consequent loss of power. What with a full load of bombs and propeller wash from planes ahead, the poor engine kept me very busy. However we did make the target and dropped our load with the rest of the formation.

Heavy flak over Leipzig and the coast reminded us that we were still over Nazi territory. Rockets with long white tails were fired at us, but they did no damage. I feathered the number two engine (turned off the engine and turned the propellers so they wouldn't windmill) over England and landed on three engines at 16:30 hours. This was a very costly mission: the Eighth lost 44 B-17's, 440 American crewmen; 32 of the downed planes were casualties of Nazi fighters. My plane dropped ten 500 lb. bombs.

An excerpt from *One Last Look* by Phillip Kapland and Rex Alan Smith:

> *The bombers on their long, straight bombing run, were always like ducks in a shooting gallery. Under other circumstances, flak gunners, shooting at 25,000 feet, say, had to shoot at where they thought it would be twenty seconds later. But in the case of a bombing run, they knew where the ships were going to be. Accordingly, they simply chose a section or 'box' of air through which the bombers would have to pass on their way to the target, and, with what was called a 'box barrage,' kept that section full of bursting shells. The barrage when seen from below looked like a cluster of polka dots, but as seen by the bomber crews, it looked like a solid cloud—a cloud they grimly referred to as iron cumulus—and it was a frightening thing. You could take no evasive action against a box barrage, said Ray Wild. There was only one way to counteract it, and it began, 'Our Father who art in heaven..'*

MAY 19, 1944. BERLIN, NAZI GERMANY.
TARGET: CITY CENTER.

This time we flew accross the North Sea and crossed Denmark at 25000 ft in the vicinity of the Kiel Canal. Then over the Baltic Sea and straight south to Berlin. The anti-aircraft defenses at Kiel were strong and accurate and we received heavy flak. Three minutes before the Initial Point, 40 or so Messerschmidt (ME) 109 Nazi fighters attacked us head on, firing wing-cannon right through our formation. I sat in my seat flinching, moving my head and body to dodge the shells. Obviously this had no effect other than making me feel a little less vulnerable. They knocked down one ship in the lead element and the navigator aboard was from my Nissen hut, Lt. Martinjak. He became a prisoner of war.

We dropped ten 500 lb. GP bombs by radar control even though we could see the target. The Mickey Navigator had control at the start of the bomb-run, so he kept it until bombs away. Somehow we avoided the flak over the target and returned by the same route to Britain. I was flying number five position in the formation and really got a workout because of the pendulum effect. Upon finally landing I was exhausted from the physical and mental stress. Cannon shells from enemy fighters had knocked out our right landing light and put six large holes in our horizontal stabilizer (the horizontal portion of the tail). We returned to base at about 17:00 hours, and had flown at an altitude of 25,000 ft. Not a bad mission. Comments from my diary made at that time suggest that I was becoming accustomed to this very lethal war. We lost one B-17 and its crew of ten (more went down but no record exists).

MAY 22, 1944. KIEL CANAL, DENMARK.
TARGET: SHIPYARD AND SUBMARINE REPAIR BASE.

Departure at 09:00 hours with ten 500 lb. GP Bombs. We flew over the North Sea in the number one lead position, low squadron in a 12 ship formation, and crossed the enemy coast at 12:40 hours. We dropped bombs at 12:55 hours, three miles short of target. The drop was done on PFF because of cloud overcast sky. We saw a little flak behind us over the target but not much. Good mission, we survived. Back to the base at 15:45 hours. We lost two planes with their 20 American air crew. Dropping short or missing altogether happened more than either we or the base liked to admit.

When we left the English coast on a mission, our gunners tested their weapons. This was an expensive operation. A one-second burst from each of the guns in a medium-sized formation would throw out as much as three tons of lead to fall into the sea. It is said that by the end of the war the North Sea must have had a solid lead bottom.

MAY 27, 1944. LUDWIGSHAVEN, NAZI GERMANY.
TARGET: INDUSTRIAL AREA.

This was a no-credit mission. In order to put up the required number of planes for a mission, the planners always included several extra planes to fill in for those that might need to abort. An abort was usually caused by failure of one or more engines before the plane left English airspace, or some other failure in the plane or crew which made it necessary for the pilot to drop out of the formation and return to the base.

The decision to abort was a judgment call for the pilot. He was responsible for the mission and crew. If he decided to abort his spot in the formation, it was filled by one of the "spares" which went along for that purpose. If no one aborted, then the "spares" had to return to base without credit for a mission because they hadn't crossed the coast of the continent or been subjected to enemy fire. The pilot deciding to abort was given an intense questioning by the Group Commander to determine the reason for his decision, and the justification had better have been a good one.

We were not needed and didn't go to Ludwigshaven. I was later told that it was really a rough mission. They had no friendly fighter support over the target and were attacked by many Nazi fighters. They dropped their bombs but didn't hit the target either.

May 28, 1944. Dessau, Nazi Germany.
Target: Folke-Wolfe Manufacturing, Jet Aircraft and Engines.

We ran into a little flak and, as sometimes happened, our friendly supporting fighters left when we got near the target. They had to pick and choose what portion of the trip they would keep us company and hope that they were correct in planning. They simply didn't have enough fuel to join us for the entire round trip.

Just as our fighters left, the Nazi fighters came up and really gave it to us. We lost one ship before we even arrived on target. The pilot of the plane was from my Nissen hut and on his 24th mission.

During aerial combat with the enemy fighters, the plane was an intense, shuddering and vibrating platform in the air, deafening with hundreds of .50-caliber bullets spewing out in all directions. The cessation of the attack inspired a prayer of thanksgiving that we were still up in the air. An intercom check confirmed that the crew was not injured.

If needed, the crew-chief would slide on his belly over spent cartridges to attend to the wounded. If the ship was mortally damaged, I was prepared to ring a warning bell which sounded like a school bell for changing classes, letting the crew know that it was time for them to jump out and use their parachutes. Fortunately, I never had to use the bell.

The target in Dessau was obscured on the first run so we made a circle and took a second run at the target. This was a very dangerous thing to do. The ground defenders had our altitude and direction and an accurate aiming point as we came around for the second try. Since we were flying in a close formation, it was essential that we stick together for this dangerous exercise. Everything we did was perilous, but a second run at the target was asking for it. Such a procedure uses up an awful lot of "luck" points, while at the same time it might give the Group Commander a Silver Star or Distinguished Flying Cross for his bravery.

As it turned out, even on the second run at the target some of the bombers in the formation didn't unload their bombs. Malfunctions with the bomb-bay doors occurred occasionally. Those who didn't drop their bombs on the intended target took them to Leipzig where the bombs were dumped on the city. We received heavy flak up to and over the target area, but we didn't get any holes in our plane.

I saw enormous flak barrages over Hanover on our return. Some of our boys must have been bombing over there that day. Another one of our planes went down over the English Channel. We returned to the base at 18:00 hours and logged a long nine hours on the mission. It was a tough day. We lost 32 heavy bomber aircraft that day, which meant 320 American airmen would not come back.

MAY 29, 1944. SORAU, NAZI GERMANY.
TARGET: INDUSTRIAL PLANT.

This was a return trip by the 457th Bomb group to the largest and most important Folke-Wolfe (FW) 190 assembly plant existing in Nazi Germany. It was situated on the edge of the town of Sorau, one hundred miles southeast of Berlin. Our B-17's had visited the site on April 11th but had not destroyed the target because of a thick cloud undercast.

We took off from our field at 08:00 hours. I soon had turbosupercharger problems on my number three engine. For all intents and purposes I had a non-functioning engine, but since I was flying in the number three position of the lead squadron I didn't abort.

If I had been flying further back in the formation, I would have been required to surge the engines in order to stay aligned. In those circumstances I would have had to abort the mission. Because of our position in the formation, although it was risky, I felt that we could make it to the target and back.

We climbed to 21,000 feet to cross the coast at the Zuider Zee, Holland, and our old foe, Dummer Lake, Nazi Germany, used its reliable flak guns to shoot at us. We let down to 14,000 feet from our crossing altitude of 21,000 feet after we entered the continental territory. This was very dangerous; it brought us closer to the flak guns as well as Nazi planes that might have had difficulty reaching us at a higher altitude. We ran into Nazi fighters and they stayed with us all the way to the target, doing their best to knock us down.

As we neared Sorau, our own P-51 Mustangs and P-38 Lightings showed up and we found ourselves in the middle of aerial dogfights. I remembered movies I had seen as a boy in Boone of World War I fighter aircraft. Now, I was sitting ringside in a great big plane instead of a theater seat, watching the fireworks of another aerial showdown in the movie "Wings."

One P-51 sneaked up on five Nazi Junker 88's and knocked them all down. I could hear cheering from my crew. The Nazis shot down four B-17's. One of them almost disrupted our formation as he went down through us in a fireball of flames. We bombed at 13,000 feet, then returned to England by traveling east of Berlin and swinging around Stettin on the Baltic Sea, then west over Denmark and thence to the south over the North Sea.

The Politz synthetic oil refinery was burning furiously from fires started by three other combat wings. Our crews watched the smoke for 150 miles. We thought we had taken a lot of flak going into Denmark and on the way out again, as well as over the target, but it had been an excellent formation and bomb pattern with 100% of the bombs landing inside a 1000 foot circle. We pounded the Nazis with ten 500 lb. GP bombs. We lost five B-17's to enemy fighters and 50 crewmen.

We landed at 18:12 hours. My ship inspection on the ground showed that we had 20mm cannon holes in our right wing and no flak holes. It was a B-17G aircraft. The "G" designation meant it was the seventh variation of the B-17. It was identifiable by its new "chin" turret guns which the older B-17 models did not have. This additional firepower from the two .50 caliber machine guns in the nose provided more protection and confidence for the crew.

Although I flew different planes in combat, it appeared that I would finally have a plane assigned to me and my crew. I named it after my wife, BEAU JAC, Beautiful Jackie, and had the name painted on the nose of the plane. Six-inch yellow bombs were painted below it for each combat mission the plane had flown.

Everyone in the Air Corps was issued brown leather flight jackets which we wore most of the time. We decorated them with painted symbols of our name, including the crest of our Bomb and Squadron, the name of our plane, and painted figures of bombs each about one and a half inches high designating the number of missions flown.

May 31,1944.
Weather Ship Mission.

Major Watson, who was assigned to fly with me as co-pilot as part of his introduction to combat missions, had just arrived from the States. Two weather ship missions were part of his indoctrination with the 8th Air Corps. We went out alone, ahead of the regular formation to report back on the weather over the continent. Upon providing the pertinent information by radio in coded radio transmission, the plane returned to base with no credit for a mission.

The weather was fine over England but there were high cumulus clouds over the continent. Our Division was recalled.

June 2, 1944. Hardelot, France.
Target: Coastal Guns Across The English Channel.

This was the first 457th bomb group mission in the final pre-invasion D-Day assault of June 6th. The target consisted of six 155 mm French General Purpose medium field guns fired by the Nazi troops situated on the beach front at Hardelot, half way between Boulogne and Le Tourquet.

I flew number one, taking off at 10:00 hours for the French coast, dropping ten 500 lb. bombs from 19,000 feet at 12:28 hours, and returned to the base by 14:20 hours. No flak or fighters were observed and no planes were lost. We had our own P-38 fighters as cover during the mission. All bombing was done by PFF since there was complete ground cover by clouds, and we had no confirmation as to whether or not we had hit the target.

June 3, 1944 Boulogne, France.
TARGET: Four Coastal Guns Located In A Field Near Boulogne, France.

We were alerted at 10:30 hours and engines started at 11:30 hours with takeoff scheduled at 11:45 hours and no regular briefing. SNAFU. (Situation Normal—All Fouled Up.) The formation was a mess so I attached myself to number seven position low box of the 40th Combat Wing. You couldn't get more untraditional than that. There really is no number seven position, I had made it up so that I could go on the mission. We returned at 16:30 hours after dropping six 1000 lb. bombs on the target. Fortunately we saw no flak or fighters and had P-38 cover over the target at our bombing altitude of 19,000 feet. Again, cloud cover prevented us from seeing the result of our work.

June 4, L944. Paris, France.
TARGET: Railroad Marshaling Yard south of Paris.

This was going to be a milk run and I didn't want to miss it. Departure at 16:30 hours. Our group put up three twelve-ship boxes. I led the low squadron, number two box. We saw a little flak over the coast as well as over the target. Fortunately we had a P-38 and P-51 escort on this mission. We returned to a dark England in the rain at 22:30 hours. The weather was atrocious so we landed at an air base near London. The bomb load was six 1,000 lb. bombs dropped from an altitude of 20,000 feet. No bombers were lost. We returned to our home base at Glatton the next morning.

June 6, 1944. Caen, France.
"D-Day" or "Invasion Special."
Target: City Center.

We were awakened at 01:00 hours and briefed at 03:00 hours. As the briefing officer pulled the sheet away from the map we broke into a cheer. This was the day the Western World had been waiting for, D-Day, the Allied Invasion of Europe.

We were headed for a crossroads in Caen, France, to disrupt Nazi supply lines to the invasion beaches. I started my engines at 04:00 hours with a take-off at 04:50 hours. We assembled by climbing through the clouds to an altitude of 15,000 feet over the radio buncher. We used a squadron formation led by a PFF ship. I flew number two on the PFF ship. There was a cloud undercast on the English coast at 10,000 feet so I sighted on the target by PFF at 07:30 hours. I saw many rockets but no flak or enemy fighters.

There were hundreds of B-17's in a parade going back and forth to the French coast. On our return, the skies beneath us opened to about 5/10ths clouds. I could then see an astounding number of ships and boats covering the water, all of which were headed to the French Coast. It was, of course, the immense invasion fleet. What a spectacular sight! One for which the free world had waited for years, and I was a part of it.

We arrived back at the base at 10:00 hours. I flew a new plane and received no flak. In many ways it was a very easy mission for my crew and me. We carried 38 100 lb. GP bombs and dropped them from 15,000 feet. We lost five planes that day, 50 American airmen.

We were alerted for a possible additional mission at 15:00 hours and went to the briefing room to get our orders. On that day it was fine with us to fly two missions in one day. We were aching to help the boys in the invasion and have two easy missions in one day. But it was not to be. Finally at 17:30 hours the alert was canceled. We went to bed in preparation for the next mission.

LT. ERBE

Date of Mission 6 June 1944

1. Breakfast   1145   Briefing   0100
2. Check Roll for Pilots and Officer Cre...
3. C.O.'s Address.
4. S-2.   #5 Sqdn—   *White.*
5. Weather.
6. Communications.
7. Navigator's Tick.
8. Flying Control Officer.
9. Time Schedule: 1st Force   XXX   3rd Force   Bo

	Time	Code		Time	Code
Stations	0300		Stations		
Start Eng.	0400	X X Wasp	Start Eng.		N
Taxi	0410	R X Hornet	Taxi		O
Take-Off	0430	G G Bat	Take-off	0454	X
Stand By		R G Wing	Stand By		X
Scrubbed		R R R Bat			

10.   Take-off and Assembly Plan   Wendsum — GY

	1st Force XXX			3rd Force XX	
Runway	28 in 2 min	280°	Runway	XX 28 2 min	240° far
	450 M for	5 min Min.		M for	5 min Min.
	203 M for	27 min Min.		M for	22 Min.
	359 M for	21 min Min.		359 M for	17 Min.
Homing on Splasher 16 at 19000 feet			Homing on Splasher 16 at 15000 feet		

11. Zero Hour: 0725   Bomb Int. minimum XXX for all forces Box

12.

	1st Force		Box	3rd Force		Box
Climb at	MPH	FPM	Climb at	MPH	FPM
Cruise at	MPH	S FT	Cruise at	MPH	S 1 FT
Bomb at	MPH	O FT	Bomb at	MPH	O FT
Descend	MPH	P FPM	Descend	MPH	FPM

13. Altimeters: 29.92   Remember QFE on Return

14. Gasoline Loading: XXX Normal All Box   Bomb Loading: XX 38 x 100 G P Box

15. Wing Formation - 94th C.B.W.   None   in 1st Div.

Lead Box	none	High Box	none	Low Box	none
Lead Box		High Box		Low Box	

16. Task Force - 19 Sq., 1st CBW - 18 Sq., 40th CBW - 19 Sq., 41st CBW - 19 Sq., 94th CBW.

(4 Sq., 457th - 4 Sq., 351st - 3 Sq., 457th - 4 Sq., 401st - 2 Sq., 401st - 2 Sq., 351

17. Air Comm   Lt Col. LUPER   Air Comm   Major SPENCER
    Group C.O.   Group C.O.
    Group Deputy   Group Deputy

18. Fighter Cover: See Pilots flimsy.

19. Time leave Pt. XXX 1st 0605   3rd 0611   Time enemy coast
    Time over Target 1st 0700   3rd 0710   Time on oxygen   3 HRS
    ETR   1st 0930, 2nd 0988

This is the combat order for our group for the D Day invasion mission on June 6, 1944.

20. Special Instructions: No test firing of guns. Emergency A/D is Tangmere (5051N - 0042W). Do not drop bombs short. Visual bombing by squadrons echeloned down with 1 minute interval. PFF bombing, all squadrons move forward as far as possible and drop on leaders. Force leader announce in clear what type bombing. All K 20 cameras will be used. No bombing of assigned targets after latest specified times - after these times bomb secondary or last resort. If bombs released short or after specified time may hit friendly troops or landing craft. No second runs on any target. Abortive aircraft try to remain above 1000' over water - naval craft will fire on A/C below 1000'. If possible fly west and cross English coast at Portland Bill. No flares fired after leaving English coast except by A/C in distress - stragglers not in distress red or any combination red flare for distress. Normal A/S rescue procedure. Only boats headed toward England will stop to pick up ditched crews. White star on all friendly vessels.

21. Remarks from C.O.

22. Dismiss all but Pilots and Co-Pilots.

23. Spare Aircraft:

	1st Force Lead			3rd Force Lead	
Number	998	;	551 ;	001 ;	591 ;
Letter	V	;	P ;	E ;	E ;
Disp		;	;	;	;
Sqdn	751	;	750 ;	751 ;	748 ;

24. Let Down   (xxxxxxx-Buncher) Deenethorpe   Box ALL

Let Down Headings xxxx1st & 4th force   360   Degrees Mag.
" " " xxxx2nd & 5th Force   020
" " " xxxx3rd & 6th Force   035

25. Other Efforts: To be given verbally at briefing.

26. Remarks from C.O. and/or S-3.

27. All lead teams and deputy lead teams report to S-2.

We received a combat order for each mission we flew. It gave specific instructions on how we were to fly the mission.

The above is the combat order for me to fly my plane on D-Day June 6, 1944. Of special interest is item #20 on page 2 of the order. This is a very historic document which dictated how I was to fly the mission on this historic day.

72

1D THE STARS AND STRIPES 1D
Daily Newspaper of U.S. Armed Forces in the European Theater of Operations
Vol. 4 No. 185 New York, N.Y.—London, England Wednesday, June 7, 1944

Allies Driving Into France

Greatest Umbrella for Landing

Armadas of Allied Planes Hammer Nazi Targets

Unleashing the full fury of Anglo-American air power, Allied aircraft yesterday bombed and strafed mile after mile of French beaches, seizing undisputed mastery of the air and heaping record-breaking tons of explosives on Nazi coastal installations in providing the greatest umbrella in history for the invasion forces.

Between midnight and 8 AM yesterday alone, 10,000 tons of steel went cascading down on German targets on the coast of Normandy. In the same period more than 31,000 Allied airmen, not including airborne troops, dominated the sky over France.

It was estimated that in a final recapitulation the number of sorties flown yesterday would soar to more than 20,000.

Luftwaffe Stays Down

So sparse was Luftwaffe opposition that many airmen did not encounter a single German fighter. Few of the 1,750 fighter planes which it is estimated the Nazis can muster to oppose the invasion put in an appearance.

High-ranking officers of Supreme Headquarters emphasized, however, that there was no reason to believe the Luftwaffe had been defeated.

"Fighting of the greatest severity is in store before the Luftwaffe is wiped out," according to one air officer.

Bombing, strafing and patroling fighter aircraft of the Ninth Air Force were in the air continuously yesterday from 4.30 AM, covering the movement of the Allied Expeditionary Force over sea and on to the beaches, and probing ahead of the landing parties for tactical objectives beyond the operations zone.

The first ten waves of Ninth Air Force fighter-bombers to go into action reported no serious opposition anywhere over the Channel or the beachheads.

Between 11.30 PM Monday and sunrise yesterday more than 1,000 RAAF heavy bombers, divided into ten task forces, battered German batteries along the French coast to clear the way for the ground troops.

Taking up the attack where the RAF left off more than 350 Marauders swept across the Channel to pound enemy coastal guns in a sharp three-hour raid.

Almost simultaneously more than 1,000 Fortresses and Liberators rocked German fortifications in France's coastal area.

As the Allied craft filled the sky over France, strafing German troops and smashing at enemy transportation and communication lines, only 50 German planes were counted.

'This Was the Invasion'

Flying S & S Writer Files First Eyewitness Story

By Bud Hutton
Stars and Stripes Staff Writer

Six thousand feet below, troops surged over the beaches of France and against Hitler's Atlantic Wall, and as the first black dots moved over the white sand a gunner said over the interphone: "Jesus Christ! At last."

On the dirty dark green of the Channel waters, battleships, cruisers, destroyers and more man-carrying craft than you could count rolled steadily toward the green fields and the white towns the Nazis had taken from France. Through a smoke screen the wraith-like shapes of warships loomed a moment, chameleoned into blobs of flame as another broadside roared off to find some Wehrmacht strongpoint beyond the coast.

This was the invasion.

North and south, all across the Channel and deep into the reaches beyond the concrete-bound coasts of the Continent, some 7,000 American and Allied warplanes flew in the greatest aerial armada in history. They drove the Luftwaffe from the skies with guns, and with bombs the German gunners and infantry from their camouflaged strongpoints beneath. Marauders and Havocs, Fortresses and Liberators, Mustangs, Thunderbolts, Lightnings and all the myriad craft of the RAF filled the sky until there was no room for more.

From a Marauder medium bomber of

(Continued on page 4)

Cheering Crowds Greet Invasion News in Moscow

Moscow, which has long pressed for a western front to relieve the burden on the Red Army, greeted the invasion with cheering crowds, and the news "went round the city like wildfire," a CBS broadcaster said.

Moscow radio broadcast the full texts of Gen. Eisenhower's order of the day and Prime Minister Churchill's speech in Commons.

German Army Halts All Leave

Basle, Switzerland, June 6 (Reuter)—All military leaves have been stopped in Germany and even convalescent wounded have been recalled, a report from the frontier said today.

Eisenhower's Order of Day

The following order of the day was issued yesterday by Gen. Eisenhower to each individual of the Allied Expeditionary Force:—

"Soldiers, sailors and airmen of the Allied Expeditionary Force!

"You are about to embark upon the great crusade, toward which we have striven these many months. The eyes of the world are upon you. The hopes and prayers of liberty-loving people everywhere march with you.

"In company with our brave allies and brothers in arms on other fronts, you will bring about the destruction of the German war machine, the elimination of Nazi tyranny over the oppressed peoples of Europe, and security for ourselves in a free world.

"Your task will not be an easy one. Your enemy is well trained, well equipped and battle hardened. He will fight savagely.

"But this is the year 1944! Much has happened since the Nazi triumphs of 1940-41. The United Nations have inflicted upon the Germans great defeats in open battle, man to man. Our air offensive has seriously reduced their strength in the air and their capacity to wage war on the ground.

"Our home fronts have given us an overwhelming superiority in weapons and munitions of war, and placed at our disposal great reserves of trained fighting men. The tide has turned! The free men of the world are marching together to victory!

"I have full confidence in your courage, devotion to duty and skill in battle. We will accept nothing less than full victory!

"Good luck! And let us beseech the blessing of Almighty God upon this great and noble undertaking."

The order was distributed to assault elements after their embarkation. It was read by commanders to all other troops in the Allied Expeditionary Force.

Sea-Air-Ground Opposition Less Than Expected

Allied armies, supported by more than 4,000 ships and 11,000 warplanes, stormed the northern coast of France in the dark hours of yesterday morning to open the decisive battle for the liberation of Europe, and by nightfall Nazi-controlled radios were admitting penetrations "several miles" deep and predicting still other landings at any hour.

The opposition from the Germans in all quarters—sea, air and land—was less than expected, according to information at supreme headquarters late last night. Losses of troop-carrying aircraft were "extremely small," although the airborne attack was on "a very large scale," it was said. Earlier Prime Minister Churchill had said that the airborne troops themselves were "well established."

Along a front described by the Germans as 80 miles long—from the mouth of the Seine River at Le Havre to the tip of the Cherbourg peninsula—American, British and Canadian troops landed on French soil from the choppy waters of the English Channel and from the storm-studded skies.

From 600 naval guns, ranging from four to 16 inches, and from massive fleets of supporting planes, ton upon ton of high explosives thundered into the concrete and steel of the West Wall which Hitler erected to guard his conquered countries.

The mightiest air and sea armadas ever assembled paved the way for the successful landings. American warships participating included battleships, cruisers and destroyers, as well as hundreds of smaller craft and troopships.

Thirty-one thousand Allied airmen, not counting airborne troops, made a continuous road through the night in the skies over France. Between midnight and 8 AM more than 10,000 tons of high explosives were hurled upon the Normandy invasion area by Allied aircraft, which flew 7,500 sorties.

Luftwaffe: Only 50 Flights

Against this aerial might the Luftwaffe was able to mount only 50 sorties, despite an order of the day from Goering that "invasion must be beaten off even if the Luftwaffe perishes." Allied fighters swept 75 miles inland without opposition.

After an initial communique made the momentous announcement of the landings, Prime Minister Churchill gave the first word that the assault had been successful. To a cheering House of Commons he announced shortly after noon that landings were proceeding according to plan, that sea obstacles planted by the Nazis had been less serious than had been feared, that the fire of shore batteries had been largely quelled, and that airborne landings had been effected successfully behind the enemy lines.

Later, after visiting Gen. Eisenhower's headquarters with King George VI, Churchill said that "many dangers and difficulties which appeared at this time last night to be extremely formidable are behind us. The passage of the sea has been made with far less loss than we apprehended."

A spokesman at Supreme Headquarters Allied Expeditionary Forces (SHAEF) declared last night that the "first four or five hurdles" in establishing Allied forces on the Continent had been overcome, and that the positions of the Allied troops definitely gave "no cause for pessimism." No specific information was given on the landing points or the progress made.

The invasion had been delayed 24 hours because of weather, the spokesman said.

It was left to the Germans to give most of the details, and all day long came a steady stream of reports from German agencies of new airborne and sea landings, most of them between Le Havre and Cherbourg and some airborne landings southwest of Boulogne.

German radio also announced that Allied airborne troops, supported by the softening-up firepower of naval units, had landed in the Channel Islands of Jersey and Guernsey, British possessions in the hands of the Germans since 1940.

'Cherbourg Battle Grows'—Paris

Despite fierce German resistance, Paris radio—less than 100 miles from the fighting—said that the battle for the Cherbourg peninsula was "widening in depth."

A steady stream of Allied troops continued to pour onto the beaches in the vicinity of the bathing resort at Arromanches at noon, Berlin reported, with light tank formations also ashore.

The invasion force was the greatest ever used in amphibious operations. Commanding it, under the supreme leadership of Gen. Eisenhower, was Gen. Sir Bernard L. Montgomery. There were unconfirmed reports that Hitler himself was rushing to France to take charge of Axis forces.

Spurred by a final Order of the Day from Gen. Eisenhower, expressing his confidence in the courage, devotion to duty and battle skill of the troops and pledging acceptance of nothing less than full victory, the American, British and Canadian forces who long had trained for the crucial task struck their initial blow during the five short hours of darkness which the summer provides in these latitudes.

The weather, which had caused postponement of the invasion for 24 hours, ruffled the Channel and caused "awful anxiety," said a spokesman at SHAEF. But the landings were made, although some of the troops undoubtedly were seasick.

For hours without interruption the vast armada of planes charged with softening up the defenses roared over the coast, while in the water more than 200 minesweepers cleared obstructions before the invasion fleet.

As a result comparatively light opposition was met from enemy naval forces and shore batteries. Coast defense guns were not nearly as effective as they might have been, and despite German claims of heavy damage inflicted by Nazi E-boats, the Allies' naval losses were "very, very small," a SHAEF spokesman said.

The Allied Command said nothing about the great battle being on at last until the Germans found it out for themselves. At 6.35AM the German Overseas News Agency broadcast a bulletin: "The invasion has begun. German naval forces have engaged enemy landing craft. Paratroops have

(Continued on page 4)

U.S. Hears News Soberly; FDR Pens a Prayer

President Sits Up Late to Follow Action; Lights Blaze in Pentagon

NEW YORK, June 6—Prayers were said in churches and homes throughout America today as the nation grimly and soberly heard the news at last that its sons were embarked on the great invasion.

President Roosevelt, closeted alone in his bedroom, spent the early hours before dawn composing a national prayer for the victory of the Allied liberation forces. Time was reserved on all the radio networks at 10 o'clock tonight (4 AM in the ETO) for the Commander-in-Chief to read his prayer and for listeners all over the land to join in it.

Other prayers were offered during the day in the various states in accordance with D-Day proclamations issued by the governors. In New York, Mayor Fiorello H. LaGuardia arranged a mass prayer meeting at Madison Square Garden.

Times Square Nearly Deserted

It was half-past midnight in New York and the theater crowds had departed from Times Square when the first German announcements came, and the endless belt of lights around the Times building spelled out the news and the radios of the taxicabs along the curbs broadcast cautious bulletins. SHAEF's confirmation did not come until three hours later, when most of the East was asleep.

It was still Monday in Hollywood—the day before D-Day—when the first news reached the movie colony. Bands stopped playing in the night clubs and dance halls while the glib MCs, not so glib for once, announced the opening of the invasion. The gaiety went on—but somehow it was not as gay as it had been. At the Clover Club many prominent film stars bowed their heads while an Army chaplain offered a prayer.

In war plants from coast to coast, men and women on the night shift heard the news over public address systems. In some plants they cheered, in others they listened silently—in all of them they went right on working.

Lights Blaze in Pentagon

There was no sign of anything unusual in Washington before the news broke but soon after 1 AM lights flared up in windows all over the War Department's sprawling Pentagon Building and officials began arriving at other Government offices by taxi and private car.

At the White House, President Roosevelt sat up with a few intimates listening to the radio and receiving direct reports from the War Department. Gen. George C. Marshall, Chief of Staff, had remained at his desk all night but other officials, including Secretary of War Henry L. Stimson, were at home.

Moscow Salutes With Music

In Moscow, long eager for a "second front," the ace radio announcer named Levitan who usually delivers only Marshal Stalin's orders of the day read Gen. Eisenhower's initial communique in a solemn and sonorous voice. When he finished there was a special fanfare of music, including Russian marches and "Yankee Doodle."

French men and women embraced and wept in the streets of Algiers at the news of Allied landings in France.

Jap Destroyers Sunk in Pacific

U.S. Liberators sank a Japanese destroyer in the Halmahera sea, 300 miles northwest of New Guinea, and probably destroyed another off Manokwari, in the Geelvink Bay area of Dutch New Guinea, on Saturday night, Gen. Douglas MacArthur's communique revealed yesterday.

Meanwhile an American column pushed within two miles of enemy-occupied Mokmer airdrome on Biak Island in Geelvink Bay by outflanking Japanese positions on a ridge north of the field.

Heavy bombers from the Admiralty Islands dumped 79 tons of bombs on Dublon and Eten Islands in Truk atoll and shot down seven of 20 enemy interceptors for the loss of one Allied plane. More than 60 tons were dropped on supply dumps and bivouacs in the Wewak-Hansa areas of British New Guinea.

On the Burma front, Lord Louis Mountbatten's communique reported that Lt. Gen. Joseph W. Stilwell's forces captured a Japanese position at the northern edge of Myitkyina and destroyed enemy defenses to the south and southwest.

Letters to Home Front Kept the Invaders Busy

Movement into marshalling areas had brought about a natural lull in mail from home, but the flow of outgoing mail kept censors and mail clerks chained to their jobs as invasion troops penned letters until boarding the boats.

When they weren't writing letters or playing softball, U.S. troops sprawled in tents jammed with battle equipment, reading or just resting "in the sack."

Armada Moves Within Firing Range of French Coast

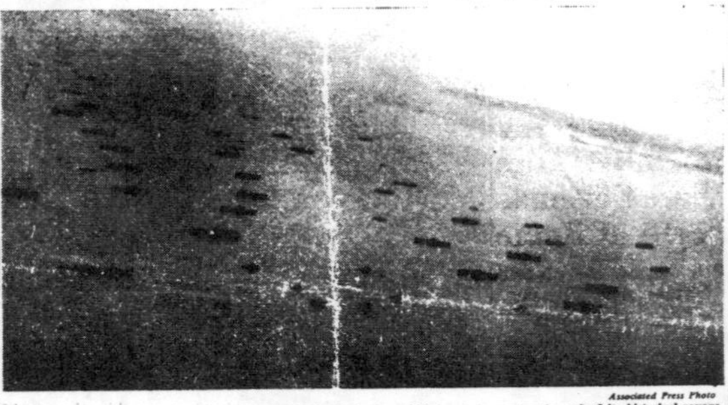

Associated Press Photo

D-Day's invasion coast is barely visible as this aerial picture shows an Allied armada nearing the end of its historical voyage across the Channel early Tuesday morning.

Allied Armies Driving Wedge Into France

(*Continued from page 1*)

landed at the mouth of the Seine." Instantly the electrifying news was relayed round the world.

The Allied announcement came at 9.01 AM, when correspondents summoned to the elaborate invasion press room in London's Ministry of Information were given Communique No. 1:

"Under the command of Gen. Eisenhower, Allied naval forces, supported by strong air forces, began landing Allied armies this morning on the northern coast of France."

A few minutes later American and British broadcasting stations sounded the alert for all of Europe, and in the voice of Gen. Eisenhower himself the eager patriots of the other nations were advised to be cautious until the hour for liberation struck in their own lands. He was followed by the exiled rulers and ministers from those countries.

To France the supreme commander directed an even more emphatic appeal: "Follow the instructions of your leaders. A premature uprising of all Frenchmen may prevent you from being of maximum help to your country in the critical hour. Be patient. Prepare."

The two Normandy ports of Le Havre and Cherbourg were the obvious locale for Gen. Eisenhower to spot the first landings. Both are big ports, Le Havre the largest in France, and ports are vital for an amphibious operation on the scale of this offensive. The ports are close together, so that the attacking forces need not be widely split. And each port is on a promontory of the sea rather than a long lateral stretch of coast like the section opposite Dover; this gives the attacking forces a comparatively narrow front to hold while assembling for the advance inland and makes it possible for warships to give supporting fire from both flanks.

Britain and America, tensely waiting for word of what was transpiring on the other side of the Channel, by mid-afternoon had received heartening word from several sources.

Prime Minister Churchill told a cheering House of Commons soon after noon that the Allied assault was "proceeding according to plan—and what a plan!"

Military circles at SHAEF heard soon afterward that the Allied forces had secured a beachhead and had dug in, although they gave no indication how deep the penetrations from the sea were.

From the German Official News Agency itself came word that Allied tank forces had penetrated several miles to the south between Caen and Isigny. The latter town, though small, is strategically important because it stands on the main trunk road out of the Cherbourg Peninsula and guards a large bay into which run the Rivers Vire and Aure.

Churchill, addressing Commons in tones of confidence, said he could not give any particular details, as reports were coming in in rapid succession, but he added that "the commanders who are engaged report that everything is proceeding according to plan."

"This vast invasion plan," he said, "is undoubtedly the most complicated and difficult that has ever occurred. It involves tides, wind, waves and visibility, both from the air and sea standpoints, and the combined employment of land, air and sea forces in the highest degree of intimacy.

"There are steady hopes that the actual tactical surprise has been attained, and we hope to furnish the enemy with a succession of surprises during the course of the fighting.

"The battle which has now begun will grow constantly in scale and intensity for many weeks to come, and I shall not attempt to speculate on its course. But this I will say, that complete unity prevails."

The extent of surprise which the Allied troops achieved was not immediately announced by supreme headquarters. Obviously it had been impossible to hide the great convoys massed for the attack with only five hours of darkness in the Channel. However, the Germans had been kept on edge for months by the presence of such masses of shipping and, it can now be revealed, by a series of feints, predicted by Winston Churchill months ago, to deceive the enemy.

Several times great fleets of Allied vessels had sailed out of British harbors, carrying invasion forces complete even to war correspondents, and had approached within shelling range of the German defenses on Europe's coast only to turn back. German reconnaissance planes had checked closely on the maneuvers, which were carried out at widely separated points.

Two Invaders Cited

Two GIs took a few minutes off in their marshalling area to receive Silver Stars for gallantry in action during the Sicilian campaign. They are T/Sgt. Edward A. Plona, of Newburgh, N.Y., and Sgt. Robert A. Price, of Far Rockaway, N.Y.

Troops Carry $4 Into France

Each GI in the invasion army was issued 200 French francs (about $4) as his partial pay for May. Those who previously had turned in English money received full value in francs. In their spare time the soldiers gambled "so we can get the hang of the franc."

1st Eyewitness Of 2nd Front

(*Continued from page 1*)

Col. Wilson R. Wood's Ninth Air Force group, piloted by 1/Lt. Richard E. Robinson, of Pittsfield, Ill., I saw the first Americans go ashore. Just as they went into the low surf, our ship and with it thousands of other bombers and fighters carried out the job toward which Eighth and Ninth Air Force airmen have been aiming since the first Fortress opened its bomb bays above Rouen on Aug. 17, 1942. We poured onto every known German strongpoint in the Cherbourg peninsula area in front of the assault craft the heaviest concentrated bombing any spot in the world ever got.

Fountains of smoke and flame and Nazi-poured concrete leaped up along the ridges behind the beaches.

The airmen had been told that on them would rest the task of making the foot soldier's job less bloody. They accepted that task and in its execution bombed from half the altitude they knew could give them a fighting chance of getting home so that their explosives would not miss. To do that job they had gone through a nightmare of flak before they came to the targets.

For long months, the bombers and the fighters have woven a pattern of craters across the ramparts of the Atlantic Wall. The pattern was cut for invasion. On Monday, I flew in the co-pilot's spot of a Marauder piloted by Maj. Paul Stach, of Rosenberg, Tex., to watch the last attack of the many which had come to be called "the pre-invasion blitz."

The bomber men went back to base. They ate and went to bed. At one o'clock in the morning they were called. Sleepy, worn with the strain of two hauls a day almost every day for two months, they walked through the wet night to the briefing. In a plain, undramatic Texas voice, Wilson Wood told them:

"Thirty-three seconds after your bombs hit the target, hundreds of thousands of American boys just as you are going ashore in France. This is the invasion." He talked some more and ended: "Let's kick the hell out of everything Nazi that's left."

Then they cheered, and went out to work.

The clouds broke over the Channel, and suddenly there were more ships than you could see, with the white wakes of them streaming back to the English coast and the dark green of the Channel flat before them to the coast of Europe.

The flak began to come up, but for once the bomber men weren't watching it, because through the murk above the waters off the coast there burst the angry red of warship broadsides, and inland came the answering crimson a few moments later as the shells hit home.

At half the height they've used for bombing the Marauders swept in.

The heavy flak burst around the formations, and tracer from machine guns streaked up past the wings; that's how low they flew.

We went away from the flak and began the long journey home and talked too much over the interphone, because this had been the day.

Awesome Sight as Fleet Bombards

By Desmond Tighe
Representing Combined Press

ABOARD A BRITISH DESTROYER OFF BERNIERE-SUR-MER, June 6—Guns are belching flame from more than 600 Allied warships. Thousands of bombers are roaring overhead, fighters are weaving in and out of the clouds as the invasion of Western Europe begins.

Rolling clouds of dense black and grey smoke cover the beaches southeast of Le Havre as the full fury of the Allied invasion force is unleashed on the German defenses. It is the most incredible sight I have ever seen.

We are standing some 8,000 yards off the beaches of Berniere-sur-Mer, and from the bridge of this little destroyer I can see vast numbers of naval craft of all types.

The air is filled with the continuous thunder of broadsides and the crash of bombs. Great spurts of flame come up from the beaches in long snake-like ripples as shells ranging from 16 inches to four inches find their mark. In the last ten minutes alone more than 2,000 tons of high explosive shells have gone down on the beach.

It is now exactly 7.25 AM and through my glasses I can see the first wave of assault troops touching down on the water's edge and fanning up the beach.

Battleships and cruisers are steaming up and down drenching the beaches ahead of the troops with withering broadsides. The guns flash and great coils of yellow cordite smoke curl into the air. Great assault vessels are standing out to sea in their hundreds and invasion craft are being lowered like beetles from the davits and head toward the shore in long lines. They are crammed with troops, tanks, guns and armored fighting vehicles of all types.

Conditions are not ideal. A fairly high sea is running and the sky is overcast and dark clouds scurry across the sky. Bombers are passing over us in their thousands; we cannot see them, as they are well above cloud level, but the air reverberates with the thunder of Fortress engines. We can see the bombs crashing down on the German gun positions and defences just inland of the first assault troops.

London Calm But Tense at D-Day News

No Celebrations, and GIs Take It Like the Rest, Quietly Go to Work

By Arthur W. White
Stars and Stripes Staff Writer

The small number of American troops left in London yesterday saw few outward changes in the life of the Allies' invasion capital. There were no hooters or noisy celebrations, but on practically every street corner long queues, mostly women, stood awaiting the latest editions.

American and Allied soldiers in non-combat jobs quietly read their papers and went to work, their sentiments the same as those of the MP on guard duty at a headquarters building who said fervently, "Christ, I wish I was over there with them."

GI Joes—and London's—reaction was, "We've waited a long time for this, now let's make it good."

There was a new tenseness among the people in the buses and busy thoroughfares, but everyone seemed to be waiting for the next fellow to show how excited he was. Yanks in London who expected to see the population get het up remembered that most of them had fathers or brothers fighting with the invasion troops.

A girl bus conductress said the only difference she had noticed was that passengers were more polite than ever before.

One policeman, on his beat in Piccadilly, compared yesterday with Sept. 3, 1939—the day Britain declared war. "We waited and worried a long time then before we knew for certain whether we had to fight," he said. "We've waited a long time for the invasion. Now it's here I think everybody will be calmer than ever before. It's the waiting and worrying that gets you down."

American MPs patrolled with orders to send soldiers on pass and furlough from camps more than 25 miles out back to their stations.

Most London Red Cross clubs were half-empty, and everywhere the conversation of American and British workers was of the soldiers, now fighting, who have swarmed through the buildings during the last year and more.

Nazis Fear Blow From East Next

German nervousness over an imminent Soviet offensive on the eastern front rose to new proportions yesterday with the Allied landings in France.

"In view of the new military situation," said Col. Ernst von Hammer, German News Agency commentator, "the German high command is paying particular attention to the lower Dniester sector where a strong Soviet offensive army has taken action stations and where Soviet artillery and mortar fire is gaining in intensity. . . .

"Now that the Allied invasion in the west has been launched, it is likely that the Soviet divisions which have been massed here over a matter of weeks will now go over to the offensive in order to force a decision."

The Soviet communique, reporting Red Army troops continued to repulse German infantry and tank attacks for the eighth day north of Jassy, said the enemy lost 41 tanks and 33 planes in 24 hours.

French Say Underground Already Aiding Troops

ALGIERS, June 6 (UP)—Members of the French underground are already in action helping Allied airborne troops, Andre Philip, French Minister of State, said today.

Andre le Troquer, Minister for the Liberated Territories, said the underground would not make its full weight felt, however, until the mass of the German army in France was engaged.

The War Today

France—American, British, Canadian forces, supported by 4,000 ships and 11,000 planes, land on northern coast of France to open battle for liberation of Europe. Advances announced by supreme headquarters and admitted by Germans.

Italy—Fifth and Eighth Armies pursue Germans north of Rome, but find enemy retreating so swiftly they are unable to make contact . . . Roosevelt warns nation against over-optimism after Rome's capture, says "victory still lies some distance ahead."

Pacific—Liberators sink Japanese destroyer 300 miles northwest of New Guinea, prabably sink another in Geelvink bay . . . Americans push within two miles of Mokmer airdrome on Biak Island.

Russia—Nazis look for Allied landings in France to signal resumption of Red offensive on eastern front . . . Russians repulse tank and infantry attacks north of Jassy for eighth day.

Printed in England by The Times Publishing Company, Limited, Printing House Square, London, E.C.4, and Published by the United States Armed Forces—7-6-44.

June 7, 1944. Falaise, France.
Target: Crossroads.

The town of Falaise was the intersection of two principal roads leading from Paris to the beachhead. By blocking the roads we would be able to slow up Nazi reinforcement of the beachheads. Since there was complete undercast we saw nothing of the fighting troops nor the land mass. We dropped ten 500 lb. GP bombs on PFF from 20,000 feet.

June 8, 1944. Eutemps, France.
Target: Railroad Marshaling Yard, 30 Miles South of Paris.

This was a main supply point for the Nazis at the beachhead. Briefed at 01:30 hours, takeoff was at 04:30 hours and we climbed to 19,000 feet before crossing the coastline. We found that the route and targets were completely covered by low clouds and we had no Mickey. The mission was aborted. We did not drop bombs on our way back to England because the policy was to refrain from bombing cities in France in an indiscriminate manner.

We returned to the base at 10:30 hours with our entire bomb load. This was very risky business. If there was a rough landing, a bomb could break loose and cause a colossal explosion of our plane. My entire crew breathed a sigh of relief when I "greased in" the landing.

There was a gap in missions after the Eutemps trip June 8th, when my squadron operations office posted a notice that I was to go to a rest and recuperation facility for 4 days. I joined several other flying officers on the truck ride to a British Lord's manor near Gloucester in Western England. I guess I was worn out and didn't know it. It was a luxury to have a real bed in a grand bedroom, retire early and sleep through the night. This included the gracious courtesy of British servants who provided orange juice, tea, crumpets, real eggs and bacon, and all the other niceties. It was a grand place to stay for a few days, away from the pressure and stress of the flight line and all it represented.

There were a about 20 of us from various groups who were offered all types of recreation including horseback riding, croquet, tennis, golf, fishing and other diversions. It was tough to think about what lay ahead as the time passed too quickly. My luck so far on the mission path had been too good to be true. Would it continue to hold up during my missions in the next segment of duty with the 8th Air Corps? Only God knew the answer to that.

JUNE 12, 1944. DOUAI, FRANCE (OR VITRY-EN-ARTOIS).
TARGET: LUFTWAFFE AIRBASE.

The target was a Nazi airfield near the Belgian border. Our popular flight surgeon decided to go along since it promised to be an easy mission. We took off at 04:30 hours and crossed into Belgium north of Antwerp, cut down east of Antwerp and then over Brussels. We suffered the most accurate flak over Brussels that I had seen since first flying missions. It seemed like we were going down a bowling alley with flak balls coming at us from every side. They appeared to be aiming at each of our planes, and that is accurate and fearful aiming.

Our squadron surgeon discovered that a short mission is not necessarily an easy mission, and this one was very rough indeed. We located the target and dropped on it at 08:30 hours. Our box lead was hit by flak and dropped out over Brussels. I flew number three lead squadron. We bombed at 20,000 feet and carried 38 100 lb. bombs. Close inspection of our plane revealed after landing many holes and a five-inch piece of a flak shell resting on the oil line of number three engine. A close call. The flight surgeon survived. I have that piece of flak to this day. It is encased in plastic, and I used it as a paperweight on my desk throughout my professional career.

JUNE 14, 1944. PARIS, FRANCE.
TARGET: LE BOURGET AIRDROME.

We took off at 04:20 hours and crossed the coast over the invasion beachhead. The target was reached by 08:15 hours. The Nazis used Le Bourget as a military base. It is famous as the landing place of Charles Lindbergh in the Spirit of St. Louis, at the conclusion of the first transatlantic flight. Now the Americans were back, but with another mission in mind. After a number of 360 degree turns we finally dropped amidst accurate flak from our left at Paris. The flak was very close but didn't hit us. There were Nazi fighters in the area but they didn't hit us either. Then back to the coast and out over dense flak at Dieppe. It was accurate, too.

We got back on the ground at 11:00 hours. Many of our ships sustained battle damage. We carried 18 250 lb. GP bombs, bombed from 23,000 feet, logged seven hours and lost three planes with 30 American airmen aboard.

June 15, 1944. Angouleme, France.
Target: Major Roadway Junction, Just North Of The City.

Take-off was at 04:30 hours. I flew number five low squadron. We crossed the invasion coast and had very little flak over France. We hit the target and departed the coast over the Bay of Biscay. Then up north across the Brest Peninsula and back to England. Our photos and reports showed that we really slammed the target, helping to keep Nazi reinforcements bottled up, away from the beachheads. We carried ten 500 lb. GP bombs and dropped them from an altitude of 21,000 feet. We lost four planes on the mission and 40 airmen.

June 17, 1944. St. Pol, France.
Target: Nazi Airfield Six Miles East Of The City.

I flew number one of the low squadron. We assembled at 09:30 hours at 18,000 feet, we arrived over the target at 11:30 hours, and encountered no flak. Southeast of the target, on our way home, we ran into severe flak. One burst seemed to explode right in front of our nose. I was sure that I had lost every one of the crew. We used to say if you could hear the explosion, it was really close, and, did I hear that burst! I called on the intercom for the count in the front of the plane and we hadn't lost a person. There was one good sized hole in the right wing barely missing number four fuel tank, and another on the top cylinder of number three engine, along with numerous smaller holes. We bombed on radar with 8/10th undercast at 21,000 feet. We carried twenty 250 lb. GP bombs.

June 18, 1944. Hamburg, Nazi Germany.
Target: Shipyard Refineries.

We took off at 04:30 hours and flew the route over the North Sea and Denmark to approach the target from the north. This gave us the prevailing direction of the wind. In this fashion the smoke from the bombing would be carried to the south and our chances of visually sighting the target would be greater. There was scattered cloud cover over the target so we bombed by PFF although the target was faintly visible.

There were an astounding number of our planes from all directions converging over the target. Five thousand feet below, B-24's were bombing and laying out dense contrails. Thankfully, the flak was not accurate but this was the first time that I saw another kind of flak, propaganda flak put up by the Nazis. It was a fireworks type of display and certainly got our attention. We were relieved when we discovered that it apparently had no dangerous qualities.

We sustained one small flak hit in the chin turret. We bombed from 25,000 feet, dropping 38 250 lb. GP's. As number one high squadron, we returned to England by way of the North Sea. We reached our home base at noon.

June 21, 1944. Berlin, Nazi Germany.
Target: City Center.

We were briefed at 01:00 hours with take off at 04:30 hours. This was the first in-depth penetration since D-Day. Additional targets for other 8th Air corps Groups were engine factories in the suburbs. The Ruhland synthetic oil refinery to the southeast of Berlin was attacked by planes from Italy. They proceeded on to Russia for an overnight stay and eventually returned to Italy. Our route in took us to the northeast over the North Sea and then over the Kiel Canal and the Baltic Sea. We flew east in a feint toward Stettin and then turned south to Berlin.

The undercast was heavy over the North and Baltic Seas but cleared some as we approached Berlin. The flak over the target was of the very dangerous "tracking" variety and we had great concern about getting through it unscathed. Maybe we were imagining things but it appeared that they were singling our planes to follow with their guns. Some ships were pretty badly damaged but we escaped with a hit on the skin of the bomb bay doors.

We bombed from 26,000 feet, carried eight 500 lb. GP's and two 500 lb. incendiaries. I flew deputy lead in the low box and logged ten hours. Lt. Krum, on his 29th mission, was badly injured and he had to fly to Sweden when one of his engines was hit. Lt. Wilson, flying his first mission as a plane commander, was hit, caught fire and blew up seven minutes after leaving Berlin. We lost two planes and 20 crewmen.

Though it was heralded in the press, this great experiment and show of cooperation between Allied forces was not a resounding success. We tried having our planes fly from Italy to bomb Nazi Germany, and then land in Russia. They were to be refueled for another mission on their way back to Italy. The Russians were uncooperative and not equipped for Yank planes. One of the pilots told me that it was a first class SNAFU.

JUNE 22, 1944. ROUEN, FRANCE.
TARGET: SOUTH BANK OF SEINE RIVER.

With an unusual shift in our routine, we were briefed at 15:00 hours with take off at 15:50 hours. We assembled at 15,000 feet and climbed to 25,000 when we left the English coast and flew over the troops fighting below. The rapid gain of altitude was necessary because the initial point for the bomb run was so close to our base. The flak was light but accurate, the tracking variety. I flew number one lead in the low squadron in a 12 ship formation, dropped eighteen 150 GP bombs from 23,000 feet. We logged four hours and 40 minutes and picked up a few more flak holes.

JUNE 24, 1944. NORTH OF WATTEN WOODS IN FRANCE.
TARGET: POWER STATION.

This was a familiar type of target for our group. We were briefed at 13:30 hours and took off at 17:00 hours, climbing to 15,000 feet for assembly. We were routed down a flak-free alley behind the French coast between Calais and Dunkirk. It was very unusual in that we did not fly in a group formation but just took off and followed the leader. We opened the bomb bay doors over the English Channel, dropped bombs on the target, picked up some flak and returned to base. It was a real milk run, the kind we wished would happen every time.

JUNE 25, 1944. MONT DE MARSAN, FRANCE.
TARGET: BURIED OIL DUMP.

This target was actually at the small village of Montbartiers on the banks of the Midi Canal, the connecting waterway between the Bay of Biscay and Mediterranean Sea. It was about 35 miles north of Toulouse, which was the major naval seaport for France on the Mediterranean.

We were briefed at 01:30 hours for this very long mission. The target would be near the Spanish border and the Pyrenees Mountains. We took off at 04:15 hours. I flew number one lead of the high squadron, lead box of a 12 ship box. We assembled at 16,500 feet, crossed the coast at the invasion beachhead and were hit by heavy, accurate flak.

I lost both wingmen from hits to their planes and they returned to base at Glatton. I then took number four position low squadron where I picked up replacement wingmen who completed the bombing mission with me. We flew quite close to the Pyrenees Mountains on the way to the target and thus had an opportunity to do a little sightseeing. Fortunately there was neither flak nor Nazi fighters. We hit the target, then went out to the coast and came back over the Bay of Biscay at 500 to 1,000 feet altitude.

The weatherman had warned us that we would be running into something on the way home and he was right. Near the south shore of England we entered foul weather. The "G" box (radio homing device) and the radio compass were not working properly. We didn't know where we were. In fact, it was black outside with a fury of rain.

Fortunately my experienced navigator and radioman were aboard and pulled us through in great fashion. Short of fuel, we landed at an American B-26 base in Kimballton. There was no fog that rainy night. Had there been, we would have been sent to a special airfield that handled fogbound situations with the ditches full of burning fuel for visibility. No one wanted that. I gassed up the plane and flew the 12 miles home. We had bombed from 22,000 feet, logged 11 hours and ten minutes, carried ten 500 lb. GP bombs and found no flak holes.

We were kept very busy flying 20 missions in 49 days since my first run on May 7th to Berlin. Following the mission to Mont de Marsan at the end of June, Lt. Joe Shaffer, my co-pilot, and I took leave for a five day trip up to Edinburgh, Scotland. The Great North Road went right across the end of our principal runway and extended to Edinburgh. We took the train from Peterborough, which was nearby. Edinburgh seemed an ideal place to take a brief vacation since that city was not bothered by those pesky Nazis who were annoying the population with bombs down in London. It was quite different from London which was under a siege mentality with major buildings sandbagged, crowds of soldiers, and bomb shelter directions on every surface.

Arriving in Edinburgh, we knew nothing about the city. As we stepped off the train, a short Scotsman who noticed our bewilderment approached us. In a strong Scottish burr, he asked if he could be of help. This was a very welcome offer to a couple of Yanks in the city for the first time. I have never forgotten this very pleasant man. In fact, I have emulated his example ever since when made aware of people who are from foreign lands, "new" to Iowa and the Americas.

The Scot directed us to lodgings and gave us a few ideas for sightseeing. We settled in and then walked to the famous Princes Street with its giant clock made of flowers, Holyrood Castle, and the huge cannon known as Mons Megs. As we wandered around the city we shopped for table linens to send home to our spouses and did a little antique hunting for other gifts.

We ran across a photography shop just off of the main street. Ideal Studios was at number 10A Greenside Place. The photographer specialized in taking pictures of people in genuine Scottish clothing. This included kilt, bearskin hat, claymore (sword) and everything that makes for a "proper" Scot. He directed us to don the outfits, placed us in front of a backdrop of Holyrood castle, and

Captain Norman Erbe, Edinburgh, Scotland - June, 1944

sighted his large box camera which was about 15 inches square.

"Now stand still." he said. He removed the lens cap with one hand and squeezed the bulb with the other, replacing the lens cover and ordering, "Come back tomorrow."

I just knew that photograph would never come out with such a primitive method. But it did, and it was one of the best pictures I have ever had taken. If I someday get back to Edinburgh, I must check to see if that shop is still there.

Our rest and recuperation time was done. It was time to get back to merry England and the 457th Bomb Group. Both of us felt a sense of apprehension about our future with the 8th Air Corps, and about our life expectancy.

Harry Will did not go with us to Edinburgh, nor did any others of the crew, because they did not fly all of the same missions that we did. This was due to illness and filling in with other crews when needed.

SEVEN: OUR BOMBARDIER TAKEN PRISONER BY THE NAZIS

As it turned out, our bombardier, Harry Will was to be the bad luck guy for the rest of the war. While Joe and I were in Scotland, Harry was scheduled to fly a mission to Leipzig. Below I relate his story in his own words. Where memory failed he made use of some of the descriptions of camp life that appeared in the book *Stalag Luft III* by Arthur A. Durano.

To set the stage for the 29 June 1944 mission to Leipzig, Germany, I have to start with the mission we flew to Laon-Cauvron airfield, since that was the beginning of our problems. On 28 June 1944, we went to the briefing for the mission as usual and the G-2 told us the ceiling of 500 feet for take off would be burned off by the time we returned. It didn't happen.

When we did return to England, the ceiling was still low and we all crunched into a P-51 fighter base. It was a close encounter of the worst kind and we almost collided with another B-17. We remained at the base for several hours and then decided to hedge-hop to our own field one at a time, which worked out satisfactorily. However, we were fed our dinner at 21:00 hours and went to bed dead tired.

The CQ came to our hut between 23:00 and 24:00 hours and awakened the crew who were scheduled to fly, but said nothing to the members of our crew. I was happy because I did not have to fly again that day. Shortly after I went back to sleep the CQ returned. He said that one of the pilots on another crew was sick and we were to fill for parts of that crew.

We had a mixed enlisted crew, some from our crew and others from another. Three of the enlisted men had never flown a mission. This would be their first. We were late, just barely making the navigators briefing and arriving at the airplane just at engine time. The pilot, Lt. Albert Gumuslauskas, started the engines and taxied out onto the perimeter taxi strip. The taxi strip was under construction with a ditch between us and the end of the runway. Our only access was to cross the runway to the other side before the planes began their take off.

Before we could cross, the first planes started to roll and we had to wait until all those ahead of us had taken off. I felt that things were not going to go well on this mission. Al shut down the engines as did the others and I went to sleep, something I rarely did in the airplane. I woke up when the engines started again and we began to move.

It was now daylight. I looked at my watch and saw it was close to the time that we should have joined the formation and on our way to Leipzig. Al got around the strip as fast as he could taxi a B-17, turned onto the runway and took off.

There was no time to fly the three legs we normally flew to assemble. Rather, we headed straight for the coast departure point at Cromer. As we broke through the clouds we got there just in time to be the last plane in the low squadron, 'tail end Charlie.'

We had never flown in that position before but since we were filling in for a new crew, I guess we got their spot. We crossed the North Sea and over the Zeider Zee, then passed by Dummer Lake to feint a course toward Berlin, and then angled down to Leipzig to bomb the engine factory. The clouds were 10/10ths (solid) all the way and bombing was by PFF through the clouds. I was busy with crew checks, fixes, and entering information in the navigation log as we came up to the I.P.

We opened the bomb bay doors and I moved up beside the chin turret gunner to be ready to salvo the bombs when the smoke canister dropped from the Lead ship. I noticed that a large hole in the clouds had opened up over the target area and it should be possible to bomb the target visually. The Lead crew was not prepared for visual bombing, (which to this day I have no reason why) and the next thing I knew we were turning off the bomb run to the east of Leipzig. We were making a 360 around the target to give the Lead crew time to get set for visual bombing and for the boxes to take their positions in trail. This proved fatal for our ship.

One of the crew called on the intercom, 'Navigator, where are we going?'

I replied, 'I think we are making a 360 degree turn around Leipzig so we can bomb visually.' Before he released his mike button, I heard some cursing from the crew member.

As we came around for the second run we had heavy and accurate flak, as well as fighters attacking the formation. Twin-engine German bombers were dropping some type of air-to-air flares into our formation. They could have been for Ack Ack gunners to find our altitude. When we arrived at the I.P., I moved up beside the nose gunner again to drop bombs. I had no sooner left my navigator's position when I heard a sound like someone breaking a plate glass window and felt a jolt to the whole airplane.

The gunner and I turned around to see a large hole in the nose over my desk where a 20 mm shell had come through the side of the airplane. At that moment we didn't realize the shell had lodged in the instrument panel and exploded, wounding both the pilot and the co-pilot. The co-pilot received a chest full of shrapnel and the pilot was hit in the neck. The nose of the airplane was a mess with papers and maps flying and smashed equipment strewn everywhere.

Almost immediately the engines began to rev up and we started down in a steep dive. I heard the pilot say over the intercom, 'Prepare to...' The intercom went dead. We dropped the bombs and the engineer came down the hatch and said that we were to bail out. I turned to the gunner, pulled the emergency release on his flak suit and it dropped to the floor. I then handed him his escape kit and turned toward the hatch to pull the red emergency cord which fired the hinge pins. The door wouldn't release so I gave it a kick with my foot and it flew away.

The plane was in a spin and no one had to tell us it was time. The nose gunner dove out the opening and I grabbed my chest parachute, snapped it to my harness, and dropped out. I had also grabbed my GI (Government Issue) shoes which I held onto tightly. I tumbled until I got tired of it, to below 15,000 feet where I supposed the oxygen supply would be better and pulled the rip cord.

That point was the level of the cloud cover and where I was

when the chute opened. It was a good thing that the intercom, oxygen, and heated suit connections had all broken away, for I had not disconnected any of them before I jumped. I was on my back by chance, not by design. My hands were cold and hurting, and although I had intended to keep the D ring as a souvenir, I dropped it to put my fingers in my mouth. The other hand held my escape shoes. It was frigid at that altitude even though it was summer below.

It was a bright sunny day and when I looked down I could see for miles. The countryside was beautiful below and I heard all-clear sirens. The ground was not coming up very fast and I wondered why I wasn't descending faster. Maybe it was because I weighed only 145 pounds under the 24 foot diameter chute.

As I drew near the ground I saw guns shooting at me and holes were forming in my chute. I began oscillating myself on the chute lines to the point where it almost collapsed. I saw two men operating a combine. When I hit the ground they motioned for me to run away from them. They couldn't see all the men that I had seen coming in all directions. I found out after I was captured that the men were Poles brought in as slave laborers.

I hit the ground harder than I thought I would, but was thankful to be down and apparently uninjured. The nose gunner was not so fortunate, for he hit his hand on something, probably the bomb bay door, when he bailed out.

The men who took charge of me were from an Ack Ack battery nearby. They treated me well, even allowing me to lie down for awhile. I guess I was white as a sheet.

Two of them had me pack my chute into my backpack and took me to an airfield a few miles away. They stopped for beer once but didn't offer me any.

When we arrived at the airfield, a Major tried to interrogate me without success. He got angry and had them take me to the guardhouse where they locked me up. I was given some bread with honey and some tea for the evening meal. I was so bushed that I laid down on a board bed and went to sleep. They couldn't understand that and I heard them occasionally checking on me to see if I was still there.

The next day two men came and took me from jail and we met two other guards with my tail-gunner. The guards then took us to a railroad station where we boarded a train to Frankfurt. The guards emptied a compartment and took it over for the four of us. In Frankfurt they put us on a streetcar with a bunch of people and we rode up to the interrogation camp, Dulag Luft.

I said to the tail-gunner, 'They will be asking you a bunch of questions. Don't tell them anything.' We were parted and that was the last I saw of him.

I was put into a room with no windows or ventilation for four days. I was only allowed out for the bathroom or interrogation. Sometimes the interrogations were twice a day but they only got name, rank and serial number from me.

To pass the time I would sing or whistle songs I could remember. One of these was 'I don't get around much anymore,' which I did without thinking. The men in other cells got a big laugh out of it.

The guards rotated every four hours. I drank a lot of water and kept asking for the use of the bathroom. They put up with this routine for awhile, then they brought a pot. When I was moved from that room I had ten pots under the bed.

After the fourth day, an officer arrived and raised hell about the lack of ventilation in my cell. I was moved to another cell and in the process saw Al, my pilot. The new quarters had a frosted window which was opened once a day to air the place out.

I thought I was being clever as I drew a clock on the floor. I asked the guard for the time and marked it where the sun hit. Over a period of days and lots of guards I had my sun dial. Ten days later they cleaned out all the men in the rooms and put us together in another compound to await shipment. When I told Al about my clock, all the men laughed. They had been listening to a church bell that struck on the hour and half hour.

The German psychology was that by putting us all together, our tongues would wag. We all kept saying, 'Shh, this place is bugged,' but it's hard not to say hello to friends after you have been in solitary.

We were moved from Dulag Luft to the nearby town of Wetzlar. As we entered this camp we were ushered into a large room. There were long tables set up. Interrogators sat stiffly with forms organized on the surface in front of them. They informed us that we were now POWs and needed to fill out the forms. A glance showed that there were questions which we wouldn't answer at Dulag Luft and weren't about to now. The ploy did not work and we held fast to name, rank and serial number.

We were then taken to a building and issued regular GI uniforms. This one set from the Red Cross was to last us the duration.

We remained at Wetzlar for a week, living in tents. We ate in a mess hall and the food was reasonable. It was there that I ran into our engineer who told me he had been shot through the neck with a small caliber bullet as he was being questioned on the ground by German police. The others had tried to stop the man, but too late. He was taken to the hospital where he woke up next to the co-pilot. He had experienced partial paralysis of the right hand, but was recovering.

The tenth day we were loaded on a regular passenger train bound for Stalag Luft III. On this trip I sat next to a navigator who had been held in a Parisian jail and suffered diphtheria while there. We arrived at Stalag Luft III which was the Allied Flying Officers camp at Salgan on the Oder. They photographed each of us and then assigned barracks. My Barracks Chief was a Lt. Colonel and Al and I were put with six other men to form a combined group or what have you. This was to grow to 16 before we left.

There were twelve combines in our barrack—six in each half. The combines of eight men shared Red Cross parcels that were issued each week. Sometimes we received an eighth of a parcel per man and on good weeks might receive a half per man. In addition, the Germans furnished hot water for tea and barley soup or cabbage soup. We never ceased being hungry, especially Al, my pilot.

There was a cook stove at each end of the barrack and every combine was assigned a limited time when they could cook if there was anything to cook. Each combine scheduled the guys in charge of cooking and cleaning up each day.

The day began with one person going to the cookhouse for the hot water for tea or coffee. With this we had two pieces of black bread (which contained sawdust), that was toasted and covered with a type of jelly.

After breakfast, we fell out for appel (roll call or countdown), and calisthenics.

Stalag Luft III was located about 90 miles southeast of Berlin and about one-half mile south of the town, Sagan, population +/- 25,000. This was in the province of Silesia. It was near the old Polish border and on the Bóber River, a tributary of the Oder. The area was well forested, but the trees added little to the natural beauty as they were primarily thin and scraggly pine.

The camp was well away from all combat zones and even further away from any friendly or neutral territory.

The perimeter fence consisted of two separate and parallel barriers about seven feet apart, each about nine feet high with an overhang at the top pointing inward. It consisted of barbed-wire strands six inches apart horizontally and six inches vertically. Between these two fences lay barbed wire tangles that were two to four feet deep. Inside the camp and 30 feet from the perimeter fence was a warning wire, stretched some two feet off the ground that marked no-man's land.

Outside and along the fence stood guard towers at all the corners and others spaced about one hundred yards apart. The barracks were constructed off the ground so inspections for tunneling was easy.

The camp contained four distinct areas. The West side had a large area called the Kommandantur which was for the Germans. In the northeast corner sat the Vorlager which contained facilities for the prisoners such as the 'cooler' (jail), sick quarters (where I spent two months with diphtheria), bathhouse, coal shed and storage buildings, as well as several barracks for Russian prisoners who were used as camp labor.

Once a day we would line up and be escorted to the showers. In the shower, the water was turned on for a brief period for us to soap down. The water went on again for a very brief time to rinse off, sometimes not enough. The Germans thought this a great joke and laughed while doing it. The alternative was a cold shower back in the camp washroom which I did most of the time. That was the same place we washed our clothes while we ran around in our wool underwear.

The designation Stalag was a contraction of the word Stamnlager and can be interpreted to mean a prison for the common stock, army or servicemen below officer rank. The camp should have been called Oflag which meant Officer's Camp. The Germans named all the Luftwaffe camps Stalags.

Our days were usually taken up with walking around the camp perimeter, washing, playing cards, or just talking together. There were classes for those who wanted to take math or any college degree courses that we had teachers for. We also had a limited library where we could check out books for study or reading. Most were old with fine print but it was better than nothing.

When I was released from the sick quarters, I had an accumulation of two months supply of Red Cross parcels to take back to my combine. Needless to say, the guys were delighted when I dumped these into our common stores. I gave the cigarettes to my pilot to share with the others if he liked.

It was December, and we were getting the bad news of the Battle of the Bulge. The German guards got very cocky and told us we would rebuild Berlin before we went home. We did receive Red Cross Christmas boxes that cheered us up and made for a pleasant day, all things considered.

As January came upon us, the war had taken another turn and the German armies were losing on both fronts. Our Senior officers issued instructions to prepare to move out if the Germans told us to. Near the end of the month, we could hear the battle going on in Warsaw, Poland. The night of January 27th, we were told that the camp was to be evacuated in front of the Russian advance. In spite of the best efforts of selecting food, etc., to be taken, we had to leave behind some 25,000 to 50,000 Red Cross parcels.

We were told that an agreement had been reached with the Germans that we would not be chained if we agreed not to escape. Although some did run off there was no advantage to it, and we did not know what the people would do if they caught us.

Our center compound started out about twelve o'clock in a foot of snow and all our possessions (food, etc.) were on our backs. I had a very bad cold and was sure that I was going to die, but managed to keep up with our group. General Arthur W. Vanaman lead the way and set the pace. He would only allow us to walk 24 km. per day. The first night we stayed in barns on several farms along the way. The one we had was brick with open spaces between the bricks and a lot of straw.

I felt so bad I just laid down on the floor with some straw and went to sleep. The next morning I woke up feeling great — I couldn't believe that I was over the worst part of the cold.

Another night we stayed in an old church with small tight pews that we slept in sitting up. We reached Muskau, where we found quarters in a brick factory and a heating plant. The factory had running water and those who could, washed themselves and cooked some food. A good many were suffering from exposure and exhaustion.

All the compounds followed the same routes and arrived at Spremberg, where after a few days we boarded box car (40 and 8's) trains headed south. Normally, they only put forty men or eight horses which is why they were called forty and eights.

We were loaded 60 per car. It was so crowded that we were unable to move. Men lined the walls with their feet aiming inward. I had the misfortune of getting my feet turned sideways for some time until they hurt. Some people on the floor moved for me. What a relief to be able to move my toes and get some feeling back into them.

The only time we could relieve ourselves was when the train had stopped and the guards allowed us outside. No matter *where we were, in a village, town or not, we did our thing beside the tracks.*

Several occasions we were in railroad yards when there were air raids. We were locked in the cars while the guards sought protection. We were not hit, but we sure sweated it out.

Arriving in Mooseburg to our new camp, we realized that it was not going to be a pleasant experience. When I saw the shed type barns that we were to stay in, I couldn't see how they could house all the men involved in our groups. I was right. When we bedded down, there was no room to walk. Conditions were impossible with open trenches for latrines and no good drinking water. We did our best to survive by making blower-type can stoves to boil water and cook food on.

A week or two later they moved us to better barracks. Once again we had a stove to cook on and three stacked bunks to sleep on. Sanitation was not much better and one day when the Abbott (Latrine) was overflowing, we refused to stand roll call unless they brought a truck to pump it out. The Germans became very angry and brought in the dogs. It was very scary but we won the day.

Not long after, the Germans brought in large circus-like tents and we were moved again. Now we were back on the ground again. We would be in these tents until we were released.

On April 29th, Patton's army liberated us and I had the biggest lump in my throat as they raised Ol' Glory over the village of Mooseburg. The gates were opened and we eventually moved out on May 5th. In the meantime the POWs went wild, liberating cars and motorcycles from the local village. Even a cow was brought back to the camp and a big bar-b-que was held. There was a contest to see who could eat a whole Red Cross parcel. Of course, there were sick POWs from this adventure.

The next day we were taken by truck to an airfield at Engalstaud. We waited and waited until nightfall for planes to pick us up. They finally trucked us back into town and placed us in a Calvary training school the Germans had left. There was all sorts of brand new riding equipment which some of the

POW's chose to take. They would have taken saddles also if there had been any way to get them home.

We heard that all liberated cars and motorcycles had to be given up to the Army to be returned to their rightful owners. That evening a G.I.'s radio said that the war in Europe was over, it was V.E. (Victory in Europe) Day. The following morning we were transported again to the airfield to wait for the transports. There were all sorts of German aircraft spread around the field, even a couple of jets. Several POW pilots got a hold of the lighter planes and took them up for a spin.

A Stuka dive-bomber tried to land. Every gun available was firing at the Stuka. It circled once and landed without being hit. Three Germans climbed out and surrendered, stating they were fleeing the Eastern front. They preferred to be captured by the Americans rather than the Russians.

One army major saw some DC-3s in the distance so he fired some flares to attract their attention. It worked and soon a number of transports were landing and taking on POWs. As we were being flown to Reim, France, the pilot let each POW come up front to view the cockpit.

Landing at Reim Airport, we were trucked to a place to be de-loused, losing the clothes we had worn for too long, to be issued regular GI clothing. There was no organized place to sleep that night so I found a grassy spot and went off to sleep right away.

The next day was more organized and we moved into tents. We stayed in the tents a few days until we were shipped out to Camp Lucky Strike at Le Havre. The camp had been a port of embarkation for troops coming from the states so they reversed the process to prepare us to return by boat to the U.S. We received shiny new uniforms and they tried to fatten us up before they let us go. We were given physicals to determine if any of us needed hospitalization.

In a week or so we were put on board the Marine Robin for our trip home. My quarters were in the bow section and very noisy, so I spent most of my time on deck. Entering New York harbor was a once in a lifetime thrill. I'll never forget seeing *the Statue of Liberty.*

There was a strike by the dock workers. It was impossible to get a tug to bring us in. The captain docked the ship without any help by getting close to the dock and using cables and ropes to pull us along the side. We disembarked and boarded a train for Camp Shank. There we were given instructions to talk to no one about our experiences in captivity. After more physicals and processing, I was sent to Ft. Dix, New Jersey, and then home for 60 day leave.

Harry had been imprisoned for a period of about ten months. It was on our return from Edinburgh that we learned that Harry Will and his crew had been lost on the mission to Leipzig on June 29th. (Harry was to be the only person on my crew to have become a casualty of the war by wounds or capture.) He survived the ordeal and returned to the States, resumed his previous occupation in Pittsburgh, and later retired with his wife to Dunedin, Florida. Harry Will and my Crew Chief, Dick Cochrane, from Sauk Center, Wisconsin, called on us in Boone, Iowa, after the war. Neither had changed a bit. However, Harry passed away in January, 1996, as a result of colon cancer.

EIGHT: BOMBER PILOT MISSION DIARY
PART II: July 6 - December 1, 1944

JULY 6, 1944. ST. AMER, FRANCE.
TARGET: NAZI SUPPLY DEPOT.

Our leave of absence came to a close and it was time for us to contemplate returing to the "shooting" war. We took the London train back to Peterborough and our base to resume flights

Our second U.S. bombing session for the day was to concentrate on the supplies intended for the Nazi ground troops. It was what we termed a "no-ball" mission since it was a short one for which we got credit on our mission totals. We were briefed at 13:30 hours for a 16:30 hours engine start time. I flew number two of the Lead squadron in a 12 ship box.

I flew into France at a point north of Le Havre and came out between Calais and Dunkirk. We bombed by boxes without a wing formation. We dropped eighteen 250 lb. general purpose bombs from 26,000 feet and logged four and a half hours. This was the kind of mission we liked to fly, very little flak at the target. An inspection found no flak holes in the plane.

JULY 7, 1944. LEIPZIG, NAZI GERMANY.
TARGET: ENGINE FACTORY EAST OF THE CITY.

We took off at 05:30 hours, assembled at 09:00 hours, and ran into weather over England. We climbed to 25,000 feet and flew over the Zuider Zee, Holland, Dummer Lake, and came into the target from the northeast. On this mission I was flying a spare plane. As it happened, a plane had to abort, and I went with no bombardier. This was not critical. We usually dropped our bombs by toggling a switch at the same time that we saw the lead plane drop his bombs.

We had no flak until we reached the target, but then they made up for it, giving us a huge barrage. We followed the usual practice of dumping large bales of chaff into the air to throw off their aim.

At the same time my hut-mates flying in another aircraft were experiencing a great deal of trouble. Lt. Jack Owens, pilot, and Lt.

Francis Minturn, the navigator on Owens' crew, were flying an old B-17F on this mission. At a point north of Magdeberg, Nazi Germany, where the formation turned southeast to the target, he jettisoned his bombs and broke formation.

He had been having difficulty transferring his fuel from the outer wing tanks. These were also called Tokyo Tanks. It was said that the extra fuel they carried could get you to Tokyo. Owens, the co-pilot Chuck Berta and engineer discussed their options. If they went all the way to the target they would not have enough fuel to return to England. If they jettisoned their bomb load and returned now, they might have enough fuel to make it to Sweden or England.

Owens decided to jettison the bombs and everything else that they could do without, and headed for England alone. Conserving every drop of fuel, he managed to fly lower and lower over Nazi territory and at last reach the comparatively friendly North Sea. That day, however, there was a high sea running and his plane broke in half as it hit the waves. There are normally two dinghies stored in the compartments above the bomb bays. On this plane there was only one dinghy in the compartment.

Lt. Minturn saved some of the crew, but he and S/Sgt Earl Markwalder were lost at sea. T/Sgt. Philip Mural and T/Sgt. Theodore Orlando also lost their lives in the ditching process. The remainder of the crew was picked up by an Air/Sea Rescue ship out of England and brought back to the base at Glatton.

We carried thirty-eight 100 lb. incendiaries, dropped from 25,000 feet, logged nine hours in flight, and lost 37 planes and 370 American airmen on this mission.

JULY 8, 1944. AMIENS, FRANCE.
TARGET: V-1 BUZZ-BOMB LAUNCHING SITES.

We were briefed at 01:00 hours for a take-off at 04:00 hours. I flew lead for a 12 ship box at 25,000 feet.. Everything went wrong, it was really SNAFU. We couldn't bomb the primary targets because of 10/10 cloud cover, so we hit an airfield after "sneaking" around all the flak areas in Northern France. It is hard to imagine a large formation of B-17's "sneaking" around in the air over any civilized land, but we did. We carried eighteen 250 lb. GP's and dropped them from 23,000 feet.

July 11, 1944. Munich, Nazi Germany.
Target: City Center.

Briefed at 03:00 hours with take-off at 07:20 hours. I flew a Mickey plane as Deputy Wing Lead. Our group made up the lead and low boxes. Twenty-five heavy bomber wings went to this target. We were second in a long line of planes to Southeastern Nazi Germany. We first assembled over the undercast which was solid all the way to the target. I took over the Wing Lead over Belgium. At the target my PFF went out. I made a quick 360 degree turn and bombed abreast of another wing.

At the briefing we had been cautioned not to drop west-northwest of Munich. There was an American Prisoner of War camp there. Dachau, one of the most infamous concentration camps, was also located in that area. In 1983, I visited Dachau with its awful reminders of ovens and gassing facilities. My ground visit was a horrible experience.

There was a carpet barrage of flak over the target but we escaped without injury to our plane or ourselves. Although there was complete undercast of clouds, it was easy to identify the target by the shape and concentration of flak being thrown up at us. We went back to Glatton by the same route but were the last planes in the long line, of more than 1000 planes, with ten crew men in each plane. This was not a comfortable place to be since Nazi fighters liked to pick on the last planes in the formation. But we had excellent fighter cover from our "little friends" all the way in and all the way out and saw no Nazis. We did a little sightseeing on the way back, spotting Lake Como on the Italy/Switzerland border through a break in the clouds.

We bombed Munich from 27,000 feet, dropping eighteen 250 lb. general purpose bombs through the undercast. We logged ten hours on the mission.

This and other Munich missions to follow were the longest missions we flew. We had to carry a maximum fuel load as well as a large bomb load. Our Munich missions were at a greater than usual altitude, where the plane controls got very mushy and did not respond normally. Having less control while trying to avoid flak and drop bombs is not a happy situation but we managed. The formation on this Munich trip lost 26 planes which meant 260 American airmen were lost.

JULY 13, 1944. MUNICH, NAZI GERMANY.
TARGET: CITY CENTER.

Munich again. They went the day before without me so I could get some rest. I got up at 01:00 hours for a briefing at 02:15 hours, and engines at 04:55 hours. I flew group lead in the high box. We "shuffled the deck" over England as we assembled. This is exactly like shuffling a deck of cards. With several groups criss-crossing each other at the same altitude while trying to get into formation. "Shuffling the deck" was not a normal event, but it happened in some cases when a plane or a squadron was delayed in take-off and, in their zeal to join the formation over the radio buncher, would fly right through the formation. This was a highly dangerous procedure. A pilot flies his plane in formation and suddenly another plane flies across his front. Very dangerous.

We took the same route to Munich as before while climbing to 20,000 feet. I followed the lead box in on their left. They turned 90 degrees left west of Munich and dropped bombs on the center of town. They had turned left through heavy flak and we turned right and came out on the south of town. Again, we had total undercast and could identify the city of Munich only by the pattern of flak.

This time the clouds opened up over Switzerland and we saw a beautiful sight of the Alps Mountains covered with snow. On this trip we had bombed from 26,000 feet carrying four 500 lb. general purpose and four 500 lb. incendiary bombs. We logged nine hours, lost 16 planes and 160 American crewmen, arriving back to base at 14:00 hours.

JULY 16, 1944. MUNICH, NAZI GERMANY.
TARGET: CITY CENTER.

Back to Munich once more with a total undercast of clouds. Our takeoff was at 05:00 hours. I flew Deputy Wing Lead in a PFF ship. Over the initial point on the bomb run and the target, the undercast was joined by condensation trails which further decreased visibility. I tried to go around it but finally went through the clouds at 27,000 feet. We dropped our five 500 lb. incendiaries and four 500 lb GP bombs through dense clouds. The flak was very accurate. So accurate in fact, we could see and feel the detonations. That was too close. We took a few hits but nothing disabling. We returned by the same route. No planes lost.

July 18, 1944. Baltic Sea, Peenemunde, Nazi Germany.
Target: Rocket Research Station Power Plant.

The Nazis, under the leadership of Werner Von Braun, were conducting research on V1 and V2 rockets, and on the atomic bomb at this location. After the war, Von Braun did research on rockets for the U.S. at a laboratory in Alabama.

We were briefed at 02:00 hours with takeoff at 05:00 hours. We assembled at 09:50 hours. I led the high box of the wing as we flew over the North Sea to Denmark and then over the Baltic Sea hitting the IP for the target at 26,500 feet.

We had some trouble getting the bombing interval established but finally made it. They tell me that we got a "shack," which meant that our bombing was very accurate. As bombardiers go through their training a shack target is set up on the bombing

Return from Peenemunde Mission, July 18, 1944

Left to Right: Beere, Frank, Taylor, Cochrane, Norman, Egri; Front: ..., Erbe, Carson, Auten, ...

range for them to aim at. When they hit the shack itself there is rejoicing.

There was light flak over the target so we made a sharp turn after bombs away, which kept us out of it. We logged nine hours and carried ten 500 lb. bombs. No planes lost.

July 21, 1944. Schweinfurt, Nazi Germany.
Target: Ball Bearing Factory.

This was a very famous target for American flyers. It had been the first major target for the 8th Air Corps and the deepest penetration to

Completion of Mission to Schweinfurt - July 21, 1944 - Back Row: L to R - Maj Perevich, Capt. Erbe, ..., Lt. Auten, ..., ... Front Row - L to R ..., Sgt. Cochrane, Sgt. Frank, Sgt. Taylor, Sgt. Norman.

that time, August 16, 1943. There were very heavy losses. It was also the first shuttle mission of the war. A portion of the planes had headed for our bases in Africa after losing twenty-four B-17s, and thirty-six B-17s lost by flak and fighters by the England-based planes. Sixty planes meant 600 crewmen lost on one mission.

The 100th Bomb Group stationed in England became known as the Bloody 100th hard-luck group because of the many bombers lost on this mission. And now, on the 21st of July, 1944, it was our turn to see if this was as dangerous a target, as its reputation.

I flew number one in the high, 12-ship box. We took off at 06:00 hours, assembled at 14,000 feet and flew over Holland straight to the target at 25,000 feet, after having to climb to get over the many contrails in the air.

We bombed visually since we could see the target. Our AFCE, also known as automatic pilot, was not working satisfactorily so the deputy took over at the IP and dropped on his signal in the target area. The flak consisted of enormous bursts all over the target area and we remarked later that it seemed as if they were aiming their guns at each individual plane.

Schweinfurt had a reputation among the 8th Air Force as one of the most well defended and thus most dangerous targets. Fortunately there were no hits on my ship due to the fact that I made a steep left turn after bombs away. We dropped our bombs from 25,000 feet with five 1000 lb. GP's, logged eight hours and landed at 14:00 hours. No planes lost.

JULY 24, 1944. ST. LO, FRANCE.
TARGET: GROUND SUPPORT.

This target was a line drawn on a map and outlined on the ground by smoke and physical features identifiable from the air. This was the first of two days of the infamous and historic St. Lo mission, where SHAEF command decided that heavy bombers and all other appropriate and available air resources would be called upon to provide direct air support to the ground troops.

Our briefing included in detail the nature and importance of accuracy in our conduct of the mission. We took off at 09:30 hours, assembled at 11,000 feet and flew to Selsybill, England, which was the IP for our target. The Group put up four boxes. I led the Low Box. The formation dropped their bombs from 15,000 feet, each plane unloading two hundred-forty 20 lb. fragmentation bombs in six clusters through 8/10ths undercast. They fell 3,000 feet OVER the road which marked our line for bombing. We saw very little flak and no Nazi fighters, and logged five hours combat time. *[This account above was my own diary entry for July 24th and 25th, 1944.]*

Those in the low box did not bomb and carried our loads back to the base at Glatton. I was happy that it turned out that way. If we had dropped all of our bombs we might have caused additional U.S. casualties, as is described below.

A gripping description of these two days was written by General Omar Bradley as quoted from his book, *A General's Life*, page 279, Simon & Schuster, 1983.

Heavy, continuous rains forced us to postpone COBRA (The St. Lo operation) day after day. There was little we could do except fret in our tents and go over the plan again and again, making minor adjustments. We waited and waited and waited. I have seldom been so frustrated and edgy. I could not sleep. Finally the weather forecasters promised a break on July 24th. The hour for the 2,246 aircraft that would lay the bomb carpet was to be 13:00 hours. To a man the First Army was primed and ready.

To our dismay, a late morning heavy cloud cover moved over the target area. Air Marshall Leigh Mallory sent out a message cancelling the attack, but it was too late to stop all the planes. Some 400 bombers reached France and let go. Owing to a mixup in the orders, bad weather and human error, many bombs fell behind our lines, killing 29 and wounding 131.

One reason for the error was that the planes flew a course perpendicular to our lines rather than parallel to it as I had been assured they would. I have seldom been so angry. It was duplicity, a shocking breach of good faith. I launched an immediate investigation to find out why the airmen bombed on a perpendicular course rather than on a parallel one as promised.

To my astonishment, the Air Force Brass simply lied, claiming that they had never agreed to bomb parallel to the road.

We reset the jump-off for the following day, July 25th. That day the weather cleared. Ike hurried over to watch. The planes came on schedule. 1,500 heavy bombers, 380 medium bombers and 550 fighter bombers. In total these 2,430 aircraft, flying perpendicular to the target, dropped some 4,000 tons of bombs and napalm.

To our horror reports of "shorts" immediately flooded into my CP. The final toll was shocking and ghastly: 111 dead, 490 wounded. Ike flew off to his headquarters in England completely dejected and furious with the Air Corps for killing and maiming so many of our own men. He determined never again to use heavy bombers in support of Ground Forces.

The Official 457 Bomb Group Account of the mission on the first St. Lo day stated:

The four boxes reformed abreast for the run to their assigned areas at 17,000 foot altitude. These covered a rectangle 4-3/4 miles wide by 1-3/4 miles deep. Below, the cloud cover was almost complete. The coast was crossed with the target area sixteen miles away and still the clouds persisted. As no landmarks were visible, course could not be checked and corrected. Finally the formations came out into the clear about a mile north of the road, thirty seconds time for bombs away.

All boxes were about a half a mile to the right of the aiming points but could not turn left because of crowding and breast formation. As American troops were 1500 yards away from the road the four Bombardiers in the lead ships waited until they were sure their bombs would not fall short. Then they hit the toggle levers. All bombs were away except those in the low box.

The lead ship's bombs hung up and the Bombardier, hearing the radio operator call "bombs away" did not attempt another release. The other three boxes reformed and made a 360 over the channel waiting for the high box to go back over the target area. On the second run the clouds had moved over the German positions and no release was made. At this moment WILD BLUE YONDER came over the air from the 1st Division. The entire operation was canceled.

The second day of this mission, July 25th, was the worst day in history for dropping on our own troops. I am thankful that I did not fly on that day. Only 487 of the 1,586 bombers had dropped bombs because orders canceling the mission were radioed while the mission was underway. All planes proceeded to base and the 457th group began landing at 15:00 hours.

The Generals Aide later wrote, General Hobbs said afterwards it was horrible. The ground belched, shook and spewed dirt to the sky. Scores of our troops were hit, their bodies flung from slit trenches. Doughboys were dazed and frightened. General Huebner, who is an old front-line campaigner, said it was the most terrifying thing he had ever seen. A bomb landed squarely on General McNair in a slit trench and threw his body 60 feet and mangled it beyond recognition except for the three stars on his collar and his West Point Ring.

An account from the Nazi viewpoint at St. Lo is described in *Eyewitness to History,* edited by John Carey, on pages 603-604:
American Break-Out in Normandy, 24-25 July 1944:
General Bayerlein

After establishing the Normandy bridgehead, and taking Saint-Lo on 18 July, the Americans broke through the German defences at Avranches on 31 July. This account is by the general commanding the Panzer division that opposed them.

By about 23 July, U.S. troops had gained suitable jump-off positions for their offensive and had taken Saint-Lo. Panzer

Lehr Division held a 6000-yard sector west of the town and, by allocating only weak reserves, had formed a defense zone of 4000 yards in depth. The fifty or sixty tanks and self-propelled anti-tank guns still remaining to the division were deployed in static positions as armored anti-tank guns and the Panzer Grenadiers were well dug in on their field positions.

On 24 July, 400 American bombers attacked our sector, but without doing much damage. My AA battalion even managed to shoot down ten of their aircraft. The expected ground attack did not come.

But on the next day, there followed one of the heaviest blows delivered by the Allied Air Forces in a tactical role during the whole of the war. I learnt (sic) later from American sources that on 25 July a force consisting of 1600 Flying Fortresses and other bombers had bombed the Panzer Lehr's sector from nine in the morning until around midday. Units holding the front were almost completely wiped out, despite, in many cases, the best possible equipment of tanks, anti-tank guns and self-propelled guns. Back and forth the bomb carpets were laid, artillery positions were wiped out, tanks overturned and buried, infantry positions flattened and all roads and tracks destroyed. By midday the entire area resembled a moon landscape, with the bomb craters touching rim to rim, and there was no longer any hope of getting out any of our weapons. All signal communications had been cut and no command was possible. The shock effect on the troops was indescribable. Several of the men went mad and rushed dementedly round in the open until they were cut down by splinters. Simultaneous with the storm from the air, innumerable guns of the U.S. artillery poured drum-fire into our field positions.

In *Straight From The Front* by Ernie Pyle, the war correspondent had this to say about B-17s while on the ground at Normandy.

...And then a new sound gradually droned into our ears. The sound was deep and all encompassing with no tones in it— just a gigantic far away surge of doom. It was the heavies. They came from directly behind us and first they were the merest

B-17G Bomber

---

dots in the sky. You could see clots of them against the far heavens, too tiny to count them individually. They came on with terrible slowness. They came in flights of 12 - three flights to a group. And in the groups stretched out against the sky they came in "families" of about 70 planes each.

Maybe these gigantic waves were two miles apart, maybe they were ten miles, I don't know, but I do know they came in constant procession and I thought it would never end. What the Germans must have thought is beyond comprehension. Their march across the sky was slow and steady. I've never known a storm or machine or any resolve of man that had about it the aura of such ghastly relentlessness. You have the feeling that even had God appeared beseechingly before them in the sky with palms upwards to persuade them back they would not have had the power in them to turn from their irresistible course.

...The first huge flight passed directly over our farmyard and others followed. We spread our feet and leaned far back trying to look straight up until our steel helmets fell off. We'd cup our fingers around our eyes like field glasses for a clearer view, and then the bombs came.

They began ahead of us as a crackle of popcorn and almost instantly swelled into a monstrous fury of noise that seemed surely to destroy all the world ahead of us.

From then on for an hour and a half that had in it the agonies of centuries the bombs came down. A wall of smoke and dust erected by them grew high in the sky. It filtered along the ground back through our own orchards, it sifted around us and into our noses. The bright day grew slowly dark from it.

By now everything was an indescribable cauldron of sounds. Individual noises did not exist. The thundering of motors in the sky and the roar of the bombs ahead filled all the space for noise on the earth. Our own artillery was crashing all around us, yet we could hardly hear it.

The Germans began to shoot heavy, high, ack-ack. Great black puffs of it by the score speckled the sky until it was hard to distinguish the smoke puffs from the planes.

And then someone shouted that one of the planes was smoking. Yes, we could all see it. A long faint line of black smoke stretched for a mile behind one of them and as we watched there was a giant sweep of flame over the plane from nose to tail. It disappeared in flame and it slanted slowly down and banked around the sky in great wide curves, this way and that way, as rhythmically and gracefully as in a slow-motion waltz. Then suddenly it seemed to change its mind and it swept upward, steeper and steeper, and ever slower until finally it seemed poised motionless on its own black pillar of smoke. And then just as slowly it turned over and dived for the earth - a folder spearhead on the straight black shaft of its own creation - and it disappeared behind the tree tops.

Before it was done there were more cries of 'There's another one smoking, and there's a third one now!'

Chutes came out of some of the planes, out of some came no chutes at all. One, of white silk, caught on the tail of the plane. The men with binoculars could see him fighting to get loose until flames swept over him and then a tiny black dot fell through space all alone.

And all that time the great flat ceiling of the sky was roofed by all the others that didn't go down, plowing their way forward as if there was no turmoil in the world. Nothing deviated them by the slightest. They stalked on slowly and with the dreadful pall of sound as though they were seeing only something at a great distance and nothing existed between...

As we watched there crept into our consciousness the

realization the windrows of exploding bombs were easing back toward us flight by flight, instead of gradually forward as the plans called for.

Then we were horrified by the suspicion that these machines high in the sky and completely detached from us were aiming their bombs at the smoke line on the ground. - and the gentle breeze was blowing the smokeline back over us. An indescribable attack of panic comes over you at such times. We stood tensed in muscle and frozen in intellect, watching each flight approach and pass over us, feeling trapped and completely helpless.

And then all of an instant the universe became filled with a gigantic rattling as the huge dry seeds in a mammoth dry gourd. I doubt that any of us have ever heard that sound before, but instinct told us what it was. It was bombs by the hundred hurtling down through the air above us. Many times I've heard bombs whistle or swish or rustle but never before had I heard bombs rattle. I still don't know the explanation of it, but it was an awful sound.

We dived. Some got in a dugout, others made foxholes and ditches and some got behind the garden wall, although which side was "behind" was anybody's guess. I was late for a dugout - the nearest place was a wagon shed which formed one end of the stone house. The rattle was right down upon us.

I remember hitting the ground flat, all spread out like the cartoons of people flattened by steamrollers, and then the squirming like an eel to get under one of the heavy wagons in the shed. An officer who I didn't know was wriggling beside me. We stopped at the same time, simultaneously feeling it was hopeless to move farther - bombs were already crashing around us. We lay with our heads slightly up like two snakes staring at each other.

I know it was in both our minds and in our eyes—asking each other what to do. Neither of us knew. We said nothing. We just lay sprawled, gaping at each other in a futile appeal, our faces about a foot apart until it was over.

There is no description of the sound and fury of those bombs *except to say it was chaos and waiting for darkness. The feeling of the blast was sensational. The air struck you in hundreds of continuing flutters, your ears drummed and rang, you could feel quick little waves of concussion on your chest and in your ears.*

At last the sound died down and we looked at each other in disbelief. Gradually we left the foxholes and sprawling places and came out to see what the sky had in store for us. As far as we could see other waves were approaching from behind. When a wave would pass a little to the side of us we were garrulously grateful for most of them flew directly overhead. Time and again the rattle came down over us. Everything about us was shaken, but our group came through unhurt.

I can't record what any of us actually felt or thought during those horrible climaxes. I believe a person's feelings at such times are kaleidoscopic and uncatalogueable. You just wait— that's all. You do remember an inhuman tenseness of muscle and nerves. An hour or so later I began to get sore all over, and by mid-afternoon my back and shoulders ached as though I had been beaten with a club. It was simply the result of muscles tensing themselves too tight for too long against anticipated shock.

July 29, 1944. Merseburg, Nazi Germany.
Target: Synthetic Oil Plants Southwest Of Berlin.

We were awakened and ate breakfast at 01:00 hours with a briefing at 02:30 and takeoff at 05:00. I flew Deputy Wing Lead in a PFF ship. The group put up three 12 ship boxes. Clouds forced us to go up to 15,000 feet for our assembly and we then crossed the English coast at 08:00. This was a large scale effort with over 1,200 bombers and 700 fighters involved. There was no flak on the way in but massive smoke from previous hits the day before obscured the target. We turned a sharp right after bombs away and heading over the channel ran into low clouds. We split up and returned to base individually. We bombed from 25,000 feet and logged eight and a half hours carrying 20 250 lb. GP bombs.

July 31, 1944. Munich, Nazi Germany.
Target: City Center.

It was my 32nd and last mission, a red letter day. We were briefed at 04:00 with takeoff at 06:00. The wing assembled at 24,000 ft. I flew deputy wing lead. One thousand three hundred bombers were dispatched to targets in the Munich area. The 457th group with seven other combat wings were assigned the Allach BMW Aero Engine Works as their visual target, the City its PFF target. After forming on the Glatton Buncher, (the radio signal on which we aimed with our radio compasses) the Division assembly-line flew to the coast, which took considerable effort to maintain proper position. Across the North Sea and southeast over Belgium, constant deviations were made to avoid the prop wash of 94th Bomb Wing ahead. Near the Rhine the altitude was increased to 26,000 ft. because of clouds.

The official historical record account of my 32nd and last mission reads,

Before the formation reached its IP of Donauworth, P-51 scouts radioed that a visual run could be made on the primary target. The boxes broke into trail formations for the bomb run. The wing had been crowded out at the IP so it came in on a slightly different heading than planned. All along the run, a thick undercast obscured the ground so PFF remained in control of the lead box with the high and low boxes flying closely in trail. Bombs hit the southern part of the city. The other two boxes released on smoke markers from the Lead Box at 13:10 from 26,000 feet. Fire from 170 mm. anti-aircraft guns was particularly effective on the low box while less so on the other two. Lt. Kauffman's plane was hit, the right wing and tail cut away. Three chutes opened.

Rally was accomplished off-course southeast of the city. Returning, considerable time was gained because of strong tailwinds. The Wing separated into boxes over the North Sea and arrived individually to base. Sixteen heavies failed to return out of 1,181.

My personal diary account is, in part:

The trip to Munich was without incident. 10/10ths cloud undercast until we reached the target when it became 8/10ths undercast. We bombed PFF on the center of Munich. Flak tracked the lead ship for a while but not seriously. The boys behind us saw a lot of flak. There was one direct hit on the right wing of a ship in the low box. He went into a spin and down. No parachutes were seen by the crew. The return was uneventful.

Lt. Jaraszlow, the same pilot who had burned up his engines idling in the February cold at Goose Bay, Labrador, many months before, was flying in the tail of my ship to report the status and location of planes in the formation. He found on arrival in England that he psychologically could not take the stress of seeing the flak ahead of him, knowing he would have to fly through it. Because of this he spent his "mission time" in the tail and reported to the Commander the condition of the formation. Strangely, looking rearward at the flak bursts that missed our plane did not bother him at all.

Some pilots on completing their missions buzzed the field and/or the tower. Not me! Of the missions I had flown, 2,380 American airmen were lost. I was not about to risk cartwheeling into my own field after surviving all that the Nazis could throw at me.

When I went overseas the formal tour of duty for pilots and crews was 25 missions. After a while the Brass changed the rules and determined a normal tour should be 30 missions. Then they changed the rules again and stated that 35 missions was to be the requirement. Fortunately, they gave credit for the missions already flown so that my quota was to be a total of 32 actual missions. In retrospect, my diary entries of missions get more matter of fact as the totals and targets accumulated. The danger of flights over enemy territory had escalated with the number of missions and increased distances.

Twenty-three hundred and eighty Americans were lost on the missions which I flew. I had dropped 158,160 pounds of bombs on Nazi Germany and occupied France. The fact that not one of the members of my crew was ever injured or wounded during this experience does not indicate that I had a "safer" time of it than others.

110

Each mission could have been our last day of life on this earth. All of us were totally cognizant of this fact as we took off for Berlin, Munich, Sorau, Hamburg, Brussels, and other targets.

Some pilots and crewmen volunteered for a second tour of duty. That was permitted, and that person was awarded a 30 day leave in the States before reporting back for duty. It was never an option for me. I felt that my string of luck had run its course, and others could handle the balance of the bombing runs. During my tour I had picked up a promotion to the rank of Captain, and accumulated medals and decorations including the Distinguished Flying Cross and the Air Medal with three oak leaf clusters.

During its 1,008 days in action against the enemy, the Eighth Air Force burned a billion gallons of gasoline, fired 99 million rounds of machine-gun ammunition, and 1.464 billion pounds of bombs. It lost 5,982 bombers, 3,000 fighter planes and 146 other aircraft, and more than 46,000 of its men were killed, wounded or captured by the enemy. These facts are from *One Last Look* by Philip Kaplan and Rex Alan Smith.

After the completion of my tour in combat, my new assignment was to report for duty to Alconbury the air base where I first delivered my plane on the trip from the U.S. to England just four months earlier. About ten miles from Glatton, Alconbury had a threefold mission. It trained PFF navigators in practice flights over England, sent out PFF navigators at night to map possible enemy targets such as marshaling yards and enemy cities, and performed modification work on B-17s as necessary for the PFF function.

Those pilots assigned to PFF mapping responsibilities took Mickey navigators and a minimum crew when flying alone over the continent at night to carry out their functions. Since I had finished my tour of combat my role was to fly PFF navigators in training missions around England, which usually ran about five hours per day. This was pleasant duty. It was daytime flying with regular daylight hours. We bunked in barracks with about 15 other pilots, spending our time playing cards, reading, or working out on exercise equipment, and usually took weekends off to go to London or some other inviting place to see a stage show or movie.

Trips to London were nearly routine while stationed at Alconbury.

The Lieutenant of burned-out-engine fame in Labrador, and tail-gunner pilot in flak, Milton Jaraszlow, was stationed with me at Alconbury. He was Jewish, from New York City, and achieved additional fame among his associates when he was the recipient of a large package of Kosher food for Rosh Hashanah. He shared all of it.

One weekend he and I decided to go to London and I suggested hitchhiking. He had no idea what I was talking about, but climbed aboard when a lorry full of British soldiers stopped to pick us up on the road. The lorry later pulled over and without a word, all the Limeys (British) got out and walked away. We waited for a long time in the vehicle, fearful they might leave without us. They eventually returned and climbed in. It was tea time and they had stopped at a pub for tea. Jaraszlow was so impressed by the free ride to London, he later made a habit of hitchhiking.

In wartime, London was a serious and uninviting spot. The public buildings were surrounded by sandbags six to ten feet high. Public fountains were boarded over and looked very dreary. The statue of Eros had been removed and stored for the duration. Picadilly Circus was a favorite meeting place for Yanks, and others.

Blackout was enforced to the greatest degree possible. Civil Wardens roamed about insuring that no glimmer of light shone through windows and doors. Vehicles displayed only a pale blue light on front and rear. It was very difficult for strangers to get around at night in the huge metropolitan city. Add to that the dense fog and smoke from the bombing and the coal burning fires, it was hard to even walk anywhere after dark.

The blackout was a burden to travelers but inside buildings it was a different story. With blackout-drapes and curtains secure, life went on almost as usual. Movies and various entertainment centers did a brisk business and were great if you could find them in the night.

The London taxis were wonderful. The drivers knew the city like the back of their hands, and did not gouge or take advantage of Yanks. Of course we would overhear the remarks about us: Over-sexed, over-paid, and over here.

This was buzz-bomb time in London. The Nazis had developed rockets in their research at Peenemunde on the Baltic coast. I had bombed that station on July 18th after crossing the North Sea and

Denmark. The official report stated that we "got a shack" when there. They had been involved in this research for years so our bombing of the installation had little effect on weapons already developed. We also had buzz-bomb launching sites for targets on the French and Dutch coasts. They were concrete sites aimed particularly at London. We hit them, but we weren't successful in knocking them out.

V-1s and V-2s were collectively referred to as Buzz Bombs. The V-1 was the first model. Its fuselage was about ten to 15 feet long and filled with high explosive. It had stubby wings and tail, and launched off iron rails pointed toward the prospective target. Flying at relatively slow speeds, about 100 to 125 miles per hour, it made a putt-putt sound as it went through the air. When the sound stopped, it was out of fuel and dropped to explode on the target.

The V-2 was larger, carried more explosives and was much faster than the V-1. British and American fighter pilots were sometimes successful in hitting them in mid-air. Their payload of high explosives was very destructive whether dropped by our fighters or landing due to lack of fuel. People on the ground could hear them as they came in. When the noise would stop everyone ran for cover. There was really no defense against them. Slit trenches, sand bags and bomb shelters were useless since there was no time to seek protection. It was a very scary weapon.

The V-1 and V-2 flying bombs in 1944 cost London more than 30,000 casualties. The evenings the Londoners had expected to spend in pubs or theaters, were often spent in bomb shelters.

Ira Eakin vividly recalls the V-2 rocket that struck a crowded nightclub just after he and a crewmate had left it to return to their room in the nearby Rainbow Corner Red Cross Club.

We'd just gone to bed when the damn thing hit, and our floor buckled and bounced. I threw on my pants and shoes, and Abe was so excited he put both legs down one leg of his pants, and there he was, he couldn't get them off or on. I said, "Let's get the to hell out of here before the whole building caves in!" He said, "*##*, I'm a coming, but first I gotta get my legs out of my damn pants." (from One Last Look *by Philip Kaplan and Rex Alan Smith)*

I usually stayed at the Regents Palace Hotel while in London. This was just off of Picadilly Circus and pretty much in the center of things. The rates were special for servicemen at that time. One night when going to bed I heard the familiar putt-putt of the buzz-bomb coming in, then the ominous quiet and sudden tremendous explosion as it hit about a block away. Sleeping was difficult that night.

One of my barracks mates was a pilot from Texas, Lt. John Hancher. John had not finished the required number of missions so he had to make those solo PFF flights over the continent at night. He was a lawyer and we called him Judge. John's wife was an army nurse serving in a U.S. military hospital in Le Mans, France, and he wanted to see her. It was 6 October 1944. Paris had been liberated less than a month and there was still fighting going on in the suburbs, with the front lines not far away.

We discovered we could hitch a ride the next day on an evacuation plane (C-47 or DC 3) which was to go to Paris. This would suit us just fine for several reasons. I had always wanted to see Paris and had dropped some bombs on one of their airfields. There was a load of freight on the plane as well as an evacuation nurse who would be bringing wounded soldiers back to England on the return trip.

We took off at 09:05 hours and landed at Villa Coubleau airport just outside of Paris at 11:00 hours. As we flew in we could see the beautiful Gardens of Versailles. But the airport was something else again. Many huge hangars were gutted or bombed out, and piles of wrecked Nazi planes and equipment were everywhere. We saw General Eisenhower's plane land but he wasn't aboard. Among the debris our Air Corps Technicians salvaged and crated Nazi aircraft engines to wait shipment to the States. We tried to catch a ride on a plane to Le Mans or Chartres but had no luck. We decided to hitchhike instead and hopped a ride on a truck into Paris.

We exchanged our money for French Invasion Francs, 16 pounds for 3200 francs or $64. The French Francs had been brought in by our army and had distinctive markings on them, the only "good" money to be used.

The streets were littered with rubble and citizens were darting from building to building. Our ride from the airport took us to the center of the town where we were able to see the bombed out bridges over the River Seine. We heard frequent sniper fire and felt that we should have packed our .45 caliber pistols on this trip. We always carried them on our missions, but now when we were face to face with the enemy, we were empty-handed. Our infantry was hard at work in Paris, cleaning out snipers who didn't believe that the war was finished there. We missed seeing the Eiffel Tower because of the haze and smoke.

Finally we were able to hop another truck on the Red Ball Highway to Chartres. The Red Ball Highway was a very impressive transportation invention, designed to expedite the movement of supplies and fuel from the coast to the supply depots close to the troops. Most of the roads in France between principal cities had been in existence for hundreds of years and were wide enough for only one lane of traffic for the most part. The U.S. Army converted one lane parallel roads into east-west divided highways. They were thus high speed thoroughfares for the transportation of goods and people.

Alongside the roads were double lines of 5 inch pipe which pumped fuel to the front lines. Military Police were in charge of the traffic so there were few delays. The efficiency and dispatch with which the Red Ball Highway ran was amazing. Fuel and maintenance depots were every two miles. The forests and scenery all along the route was beautiful, even around Paris. The road conditions were very good except through villages, where they reverted to a single cobblestone lane.

While riding in a jeep from Chartres to Le Mans, we were the target of angry name-calling by some of our own tank soldiers. We were wearing our leather flight jackets and they immediately identified us as pilots who had bombed American troops at St. Lo.

There was evidence of war the entire way; foxholes every 20 feet and an occasional overturned truck or burned-out Nazi half-track. Few towns showed the ravages of the war although they said that Caen, St. Lo and Cherbourg were in shambles. The electric railway was running again in the Le Mans area but only for freight. We met a French interpreter who described a Flying Fortress bombing attack on Le Mans as a terrifying nightmare.

We found the hospital in Le Mans and most importantly, John's wife. The hospital was built just prior to the occupation and modern in every respect. I stayed in a room at the hospital in the corner of which was a three foot square platform of tile, raised about three inches, with a hole in its center and several water knobs at the side. This was a water closet or stool, my first view of this type of bathroom equipment. I carefully examined it to see how it worked and decided to ignore it for the balance of my stay.

The officer's club was a former air raid shelter below ground with an entrance from the garden. The roof and walls were poured concrete five feet thick. The bar was stocked with wines left by the Nazis and the club was furnished with Nazi furniture, rugs, radios and glassware. It was very nice.

We attended the Saturday night party at the club while we were there. It was great fun and we enjoyed liberated wines, champagne and interesting conversation. The nurses lived in tents on the hospital grounds and doctors lived on the fourth floor of the hospital. There were Nazi soldiers among the patients who had been shot while trying to escape. In securing blood for transfusions, some of the Yank combat soldiers refused to give blood if it was to be used by a Nazi.

Le Mans was on the front line when the Yanks took over the hospital and it was obvious that the Nazis had made a very hasty departure. A high point of my visit was a real treat, white bread. After several days of this vacation I hitched a ride back to Alconbury to resume my duties as a pilot for navigators in training.

Much later, in the 1980's, John Hancher had some business with a client who had a connection in Boone, Iowa. On the phone, Hancher quizzed Lloyd Courter of my former law firm whether he knew a fellow from Iowa by the name of Norm Erbe. It's a small world.

NINE: SAILING TO SAFETY

My assignment at the Alconbury Air Base became boring and, it seemed to me that my experience could be put to better use in the Armed Forces than flying students around England. My days were brightened with the receipt of E-Mail letters from Jackie with an occasional package of goodies, which consisted of popcorn, cookies, and other edible delights. While I was in England Jackie had, of course, gone back to Boone to stay with her parents while I was overseas. She soon decided that her time must be filled with something productive, so she went to work at a local bank and helped to conduct the local War Bond Drive. Her letters were frequent and very welcome, telling me the news about her and the family. The overseas mail in those days consisted of what was known as E-mail. This was a special form on which the letter was written. Then it was censored. The final step was for the post office to photograph the letter and send the film overseas. Then it was processed into a five by five inch piece of paper at the destination and mailed to the soldier. My mail home required that I censored my own outgoing mail and sign my name in the upper right corner of the envelope instead of a stamp and send it off.

Jackie had many school girlfriends in Boone with whom she frequently related comparing stories and experiences of their spouses who were at war. Mary Jo lost her husband Paul Thorngren, a P38 pilot, over Italy. He had been a groomsman at our wedding—Millie Ward's husband Bob Ward was a P.O.W.—so the girls enjoyed an occasional session with the local psychic who as I understood it was a whiz at telling fortunes and interpreting Ouija board readings.

I was becoming quite impatient to get back to the States and finally received orders to report to Grenock, Scotland, for transportation back home. A luxury liner named the NIEUW AMSTERDAM had been converted to a troop ship. The conversion process apparently consisted of clearing out the original cabin furniture and replacing it with 20 bunks to a cabin, four high.

The food on board was excellent, with two sittings a day. They obviously had not replaced the chefs.

A naval gun was installed on the fantail of the ship.

In 1944, 90 years after Sophie Festner sailed from Europe to New York, I, her grandson, sailed again for America. While she found it treacherous to sail at the mercy of wind and storm, I found it treacherous looking out for Nazi submarines. We returned to North America as a single ship, and not part of a slow convoy. Our protection from submarines was the lonely marine gun-crew manning the deck gun.

All was quiet on the crossing except for a presumed enemy submarine nearby as we neared our destination, Halifax Nova Scotia. Perhaps it was the gun crew just using some ammunition and getting target practice with their weapon. Ever since that trip I have had a soft spot in my heart for the Holland American Line, but have unfortunately not had a chance to travel on one of their ships.

Our port was Halifax, and we made it in good shape. We then traveled north on board a "troop train". This really puzzled us, since the U.S. was south. It turned out that Halifax was on a peninsula, and one must go north in order to go south and back to God's country. The train took us to Boston then to New York, and finally to St. Louis, where I disembarked and threw my arms around my wife, Jackie.

At Jefferson Barracks in St. Louis, I checked-in to advise the army where I wanted to be reassigned. I selected Atlantic City, New Jersey, for my post since my brother, Fred, was stationed there. He was awaiting reassignment and I thought we could get reacquainted with him and his wife, Ednamae.

Jackie and I headed for Iowa on a night train, and were back in Boone for a thirty-day vacation, which was filled with speeches to civilians at the Service Clubs and the Veterans organizations, sharing with them the experiences I had had in the war in Europe.

Word arrived to report to Atlantic City, and off we went for a new adventure. The first order of business was to report in and find living quarters. All we could find was a three room apartment with no windows and minimal helpful furnishings so we proceeded to check out sheets, blankets and other things to make the place livable. The supply sergeant was most helpful in this regard. Later we had dinner with Fred and Ednamae at a local hotel.

Little did we know it was to be the only time we would be together in Atlantic City. Fred got his orders to Germany the next day and had to leave for his next assignment. He was destined for a unit of the U.S. Strategic Bomb Survey. Members of this unit were required to have some proficiency in the German language as their task was to assess the impact of our bombers from the standpoint of targets we had bombed.

I was a little surprised that he could qualify for work using the German language, since, to my knowledge, the only German he had was as a youth listening to German spoken by our parents. Granted, I too, was able to understand what they were talking about when they didn't want us to know.

Fred asked me if I wanted him to bring home a souvenir from his German assignment. This was a welcome suggestion, since I had been as close as five miles in the air but never on the ground in Germany. I suggested a small German pistol would be most welcome. He brought back a small German Luger pistol which I took apart several times and put it back together, though I never did fire it. It was a 7.65 MM which is now on loan to the Boone County Cultural Center and Museum.

No sooner had Fred received his orders than I received orders to report to Fort Sam Houston, Texas, to attend a one month school in Separation Counseling administered by The Adjutant General of the Army. There was a glitch. The school session started two days prior to the receipt of my orders.

So we had several problems. I had checked out a number of items from the supply sergeant to improve the conditions in our windowless apartment. I would have to clear the Post before leaving. The second problem was to make arrangements to get Jackie back home to Boone, and the last was to get myself to Fort Sam Houston immediately.

Post officials had never heard of a spouse "clearing the post," yet that's the way we did it. I'm sure she used a great deal of tact and persuasion to convince that supply sergeant and other post signatories to accept the fact that I was on my way to Texas and she was turning in all of the property for which I had signed. She also arranged for her own transportation back home. She did an outstanding job.

Meanwhile, I was hitchhiking rides on planes in the general direction of Texas. First, I changed planes in Washington, then at Memphis and, finally, to my destination in San Antonio, where I reported in late for my class.

It was good to get back to my old post where it all began. I ran into a fellow Iowan, Major Emmet Tinley. The name Tinley from Council Bluffs was familiar to me and it turned out that he was related to a man long connected with the National Guard in Iowa, General Matthew Tinley.

The course work was interesting and would prove to be helpful. We were given our preference as to location for our next post and I requested Ft. Sheridan, Illinois. With that approved I cleared the post and took off for Boone to pick up Jackie, and then off for Ft. Sheridan to look for housing. Fortunately we found a furnished two bedroom house not far from Highland Park and Ft. Sheridan, close to the North Shore railroad line which ran from Milwaukee to Chicago, and close to Ravinia Park, which held weekly musical concerts. There was a knotty-pine bar in the finished basement as well as a grandfather clock against the wall of the dining room. We were happy to have the house.

I was to be the Air Corps Liaison Officer at the Separation Classification Center at Fort Sheridan. I counseled Air Corps soldiers about their records and benefits for their spouses and families as former servicemen, evaluated how their military jobs might match civilian jobs on the outside and described additional benefits for their spouses and families.

One day I had quite a surprise when the next person on my list for counseling was a Colonel by the name of Jacob Arvey of Chicago. He was the political boss of the Democratic Party in Chicago and Cook County, Illinois, and had been so for years. He had gotten a great deal of publicity when he served in that role before the war and the publicity continued even while he was in the service. What could I add to what he already knew?

While we were at Ft. Sheridan, my brother Herbert, known as Cap, was assigned to the Great Lakes Naval Training Station at Evanston, Illinois, as a dentist. He had been transferred from service in Hawaii.

Cap was a nickname which had been given to him by our father. The name came from the comic strip entitled The Katzenjammer Kids, which was popular in our childhood days. Herbert was given the name Captain and I was named Colonel. His nickname stuck with him, while my nickname was used only by our father. Interestingly, during the post-war period, Cap served in the Naval Reserve and attained the rank of Captain. I served in the National Guard and attained the rank of Colonel.

Cap was married to Laurie Karch in St. Louis during July of 1945. I served as his Best Man at the wedding as he had done for me when Jackie and I were married in 1942. Following the wedding, they obtained an apartment in Evanston.

About this time our sister, Olga, who had been an invalid with a serious heart ailment, decided that she could obtain better care for her condition in a sanitarium in Colorado. She moved west, and I decided that Cap and I should fly out to Colorado to see her. I was still on flying status which required that I fly at least four hours each month in order to qualify for the 50% increase in pay for hazardous duty. Visiting Olga would be a good way to get the hours in.

Since I was stationed at Ft. Sheridan, I had to scramble to find a nearby Air Corps installation which had planes available for me to fly. I finally settled on Orchard Place, which was located near Des Plaines, Illinois. At that time it was the site of a Douglas aircraft plant. Now it's known as O'Hare Airport. The baggage abbreviation for O'Hare is ORD, taking its name from the Orchard name of the war years.

There were three planes available: a C-47 (DC -3), a C-45 which I had flown in Advanced training, and an AT-6 which was an advanced single-engine trainer. Although I had never flown in or piloted an AT-6, I felt that it would be the best plane of choice for our flight out to Denver to see our sister Olga.

The mechanic gave me a cockpit check showing me where the various controls were located. I then installed Cap in the front as navigator and I jumped in the back seat as pilot.

Following takeoff I was busy keeping the plane at the right attitude and didn't put the wheels up until I had some air under me. When I had about 4,000 feet of altitude I finally put my head into the cockpit and found the switch for pulling up the wheels. My navigator did a fine job with a lot of help from the railroad. He found the railroad tracks known as the 'iron beam' which we followed all the way to Denver. It was a beautiful summer day and the visibility was excellent. After a couple of stops for fuel we arrived in Denver and called on our sister. We went to see her again the next morning and then left to return to Orchard Place Airport in Chicago. I'm glad we made that trip. Olga died in August 1945.

In our spare time, Jackie and I tended our Victory Garden, which we had planted shortly after arriving in Highland Park. And then came the end of the war in Europe on May 8, 1945. Cap, the girls and I thought we should celebrate along with the crowd down in the Loop in Chicago. We took the North Shore train downtown and found the greatest celebration that had ever been seen. Thousands and thousands of people filled the streets. All of us were very happy to finish that war in Europe. It was quite a party.

It should not have been unexpected that some hard-nosed General thought it was inappropriate for servicemen to be engaged in a wild celebration. When the time came to celebrate the victory in the Pacific, we were forbidden to go to the Loop.

Jackie and I had our first exposure to television while at Fort Sheridan. Television screens were located in some of the war-effort plants in the Chicago metropolitan area. They were frequently used to help promote and sell War or Victory Bonds. Part of the program was to find soldiers who had just returned from combat to help sell the bonds. We were asked to go to the television studios of WBBM in Chicago, where they filmed our interview for the War Bond effort. It was an interesting experience to be involved in this new technology which would not come into its own for another ten years or so.

Now that the war was over in Europe, interest in the "point" system became of greater importance to the military. This was a system by which a relative priority for discharge from the Armed Forces could be established for those who had served in the armed forces. A certain number of points was given for length of service, rank, marital status, dependents, decorations, time spent overseas, emergency nature of health of the soldier or his dependents, economic emergency of the soldiers family and other factors. All of these were determined at his place of duty. If it added up to the announced level for discharge, he was sent to the Separation Center to be discharged.

I checked to see if everything was in order for the soldier. When I was through, he knew about his benefits and I would be able to wish him the best of luck. Congress had passed the GI Bill of Rights, which provided financial support for higher cost education as well as loans for purchasing a home. I was one of those checking on my cumulative number of points and eagerly looking forward to release from active duty to return to law school at Iowa City.

LAW SCHOOL- UNIVERSITY OF IOWA

The day finally arrived for my separation from the service, and Jackie and I started our search for housing in Iowa City, effective with accumulated leave pay to December 3, 1945. Law school was already two weeks into the term. We found an apartment immediately across from University High, owned by Mrs. Fiske, the widow of an architect. She made it abundantly clear that she would have no children or dogs staying in her apartment units. At that time we qualified on both counts, no babies and no dogs. We found out in the summer of 1946 that Jackie was pregnant and due in February 1947. We had looked forward to having a child since 1943, and at last the time had come. I told Mrs. Fiske the good news and she simply said we had better look for another place to live. Now this seemed very unfair, and it was probably unlawful and in violation of housing regulations, but we didn't fight it. It was much easier to move.

About this time, Jackie's former roommate Mary Ann Goldzier from her sorority days at the Kappa Alpha Theta house in Iowa City was returning to the State University of Iowa. She and her husband, Delbert Ringena, were also looking for quarters, and we decided to join forces. Del had served in the Air Corps also. They had a baby named after Jackie. We located an unfurnished house just off of Burlington Street which would be adequate for all five of us. It was a two-story frame house with a study, dining room, living room and kitchen on the first floor, and two bedrooms and a bath on second.

We shared the rent of $40 per month, and also shared the utility and food costs. The GI Bill provided Del and my funds for tuition, an allowance for books, and a monthly stipend in cash for rent or whatever we cared to use it. A very important source of assistance were the Ringena parents and the Doran parents, with contributions of meat, eggs, and vegtables. There was no refrigerator or stove. Del, Ringena's father, was a medical doctor who lived in Brooklyn, Iowa, and he gave us a used refrigerator in which he had kept his medicines. Left on our wish list were beds, a stove, and some sitting furniture for the main floor. We hit the Salvation Army and used-furniture stores for the bare necessities. We were able to find a four-burner kerosene stove; which Jackie had experience with, when we lived at Buckroe Beach, Virginia. We also found a table and chairs and a few pots and pans for cooking. We secured beds and mattresses as well as study desks and chairs.

Jackie and Mary Ann took turns in the kitchen and, of course, Jackie won the prize for the best cooking. They decided that the kerosene cookstove looked too grungy and that it should be painted. The completed paint-job was very nice but when heated for the first time, the black paint burned off into tiny particles that floated around the room like small insects. Nevertheless the stove did look a bit better.

Jackie had just a few hours left to graduate from the University. She had majored in political science and went to confer with the head of that department to inquire about what she needed to graduate and get her degree. He assured her that she could take almost anything she found interesting since all of her requirements for political science were fulfilled. She then took a number of art courses, courses on home-making, sewing, and other courses which related to the family. She was slated to receive her Bachelor of Arts degree at the February 1947 commencement exercises when she would be nearly nine months pregnant.

She managed to make that event with fellow graduates on each side of her remarking that she shouldn't have the baby just yet. She countered, "Never has a graduation gown covered so much." Although a pregnant woman is a much more common sight on college campuses these days, it was not so in the 40s. Our daughter DeElda Lou was born on February 18, 1947.

Jackie wanted to breast feed our new baby. All went well until a week following the birth, when Jackie had an attack of appendicitis; an operation required a hospital stay of a week to ten days. Shortly after surgery (Jackie's mother came to help) we found that the baby would not tolerate anything but mother's milk. One of my more critical duties consisted of visiting the patient in the hospital and taking mother's milk from a breast pump back to the house where Baby Dee was fed by her grandmother. This worked great, except that on one of these trips I spilled the milk in the car. I felt guilty and embarrassed. Jackie's mother put me back in the car with instructions for Jackie to drink lots of tea. It worked.

With all of this commotion at home, I was trying to get through law school. It seemed like almost all the students in Law School at this time were veterans of the military. When I took my first law classes in 1940-41, I had joined Gamma Eta Gamma, one of three law fraternities. They promised help getting through exams and the entire course of study. I figured that I needed all the help I could get. One of our long time professors, O.K. Patton, told us we should look to the right and left of us. One of us was not going to be there next year. He was about right.

While in Law School, I was elected president of our fraternity chapter. I was concerned about the lack of contact with practicing lawyers and members of the faculty, so I established monthly fraternity luncheons at which a practicing lawyer would be the guest speaker, relating some of his experiences and providing advice as to how it really was out there in the real world. This was a novel concept, for we students had had no contact with the actual practice of law prior to graduation.

We also invited our law school professors to join us and address subjects which were of special interest to them and to us. One of our favorites was Professor Percy Bordwell, a national authority on the law of Property. His dog, a collie, came to class with him. Professor Bordwell gained renown among the students by giving the reading "Casey at the Bat" at social functions.

School was tough but I managed to get through it and earn my degree. Then I took the "Bar Exam." The Bar Exam was given to law students who wanted authority to practice in the State of Iowa. Twice a year it was made available in Des Moines or Iowa City. The written exam took two days, and the oral portion a half day.

On completion a list would be posted that afternoon of those persons who passed the exam. If your exam number was not on the list, you didn't pass and had to take it again. As can be imagined, this was a very tense time for students who had spent seven years studying Liberal Arts and the Law.

I passed on the first try, in 1947. You never knew what grades you received on the Bar Exam, nor in your courses. You just went to school and hoped to be among those who understood what the professor was saying and that he liked your answers. My next step was to practice law in Boone. Jackie's father, Lant Doran, was one of the top practitioners of Law in Boone County and Central Iowa. He graciously invited me to be a member of his firm, which consisted of himself as senior member and his two nephews, A.V. Doran and Al's brother, Ted Doran: Doran, Doran, Doran was the firm's name.

THE PRACTICE OF LAW

The practice of law involved me in the usual problems looking for solutions for the client. Counseling clients for those seeking a divorce, infrequent duties representing persons charged with criminal violations, and the administration of estates for those who are heirs in the last will and testament. Any of these were quite interesting. We received a call one morning asking me to come down to a farm in the southern part of the county and to bring my typewriter since the gentleman wanted to prepare a will. Since I had taken typing in high school and had a portable typewriter, I was selected for the job. When I arrived at the farm all I could see was what appeared to be a deserted farm house and buildings completely surrounded by overgrown bushes and trees with no sign of life. Disregarding the signs of abandonment of the premises, I knocked on the back door and hearing a faint "come in," I walked in to the kitchen. The kitchen table was littered with used dishes, dried bread and mouse droppings and I discovered that the voice had come from the dining room. There sat a figure in a rocking chair next to an oil heater which was emitting heat, although it was a hot July day. A shotgun was leaning on a steel safe which was next to the chair. A few feet away was an steel army cot with a blanket. Several windows gave a view out through the bushes, trees, and brambles to the gravel road and entrance to the farmyard.

The gentleman in the chair was my client who was dressed in farm clothes. We will call him "Jim." Jim wanted me to draw up his will. He knew exactly what he wanted done with his property when he had passed away. This developed in our conversation. In addition to several modest cash bequests to two nephews who, he said called on him only to ask for money, he wanted his farm of 120 acres to go to several neighbor friends, who looked after him and brought him food. I cleaned off the kitchen table, mouse droppings and all and proceeded to type up his last will and testament. After having it properly witnessed, I

126

departed to go back to Boone and place the will in our vault, wondering what treasures were in that steel safe next to his chair.

I was told that the shotgun was used when strangers had the audacity to enter his driveway. They did not come back. Jim died some months later and the executor and I did an inventory of his possessions. Upon opening his strong box we discovered the usual items—deeds, contracts and other papers as well as $200 in gold U.S. coins. I handed them over to the executor and remarked that they were valuable, probably more than the face value. He took them to the bank in the nearby town and deposited them at their face value. I nearly flipped my lid but there was nothing to be done. We then proceeded to have the largest antique farm sale for some time, since he was apparently a "saver."

Shortly after this experience, the District Court Judge appointed me to the position of Referee in Probate for Boone County. This position was an officer of the court with duties consisting of reviewing the Probate proceedings of all estates which were to be presented to the Judge for his approval prior to the closing of the estate. The Referee was charged with the responsibility of checking to see that the laws for administration of the Estate had been complied with. That the heir had received the assets to which they were entitled and that the persons entitled to receive the proceeds of the Estate, had properly received these assets, and was given a receipt for their share in the estate, that all taxes had been paid, that all court cost paid, and that the Estate was ready to be closed. The referee then certified all of this to the Judge and he would sign the closing order of the Estate. The Referee did not receive any compensation for his part time duties, except for a vary modest fee for each case.

The legal profession has at times been criticized for undue length of time it takes to "get things done." This is especially true in the settlement of Estates for decedents. The laws of each state impose certain time restrictions on the settlement of estates to make sure all expenses are paid, before the distribution of the assets and the closing of the Estate. Many times the actual closing extends far beyond the time limit.

This is the situation which I encountered when I was named Referee of the Court by the Judge. I examined all of the Estates and Trust proceedings on the books and ledgers of the Clerk of Court and found a large number of them still open and unresolved, some of them as long for as 30 years from the death of the decedent. In some cases the attorney who was handling the Estate had passed away and the heirs of the original Estate were still waiting for their distribution. I spent a great deal of time "catching up" with the backlog of work in this area.

My starting compensation from the partnership was $75 per month. Jackie, myself and the bank had purchased a house in Boone for $7,700. It had an oil burner in the furnace and sometimes the fuel bill equaled or exceeded my monthly salary. My practice was the usual type of work to be expected in a small Iowa town. It consisted of personal injury, probate, insurance, workers compensation, domestic relations, contracts and minor criminal cases. Boone had a population of 11,828. I backed up the partners in their work doing research, and they invited me to sit in on some of their case conferences.

One of the interesting cases which sometimes arrive at the desk of a small town law firm was a letter from the Yugoslavian Consul General in Chicago. He related a fascinating account of a missing person from Yugoslavia, and asked for help in finding and identifying this person. The missing man was John Ivan Zauhar, who had come to the United States about 1920 and found work with other Yugoslavs in the lumber camps and mills near Bend, Oregon. His wife and son remained in Yugoslovia. After a four year absence from home, he saved enough money to return to Yugoslavia, and fathered a second son, in 1925. He then returned to Bend, Oregon.

He again saved enough to return home in 1928, where he fathered a third son, and made his last return trip to the logging camp in Oregon. In 1938, Zauhar was hit in the head with an ax and rushed to the lumber company hospital for treatment. The blow caused blood to collect in his skull. A trephine operation was performed on the right upper rear area of the skull to relieve pressure from the collection of fluid on his brain. The operation left a hole in his skull about the size of a nickel. Zauhar recovered and returned to work in the forests at Bend.

By 1947, the logging operation and its hospital had closed. Zauhar had saved enough money to return to Yugoslavia and began his cross country journey by train to terminate in Uniontown, Pennsylvania, where he planned to visit with relatives before boarding a ship for his home. But Zauhar never arrived in Uniontown, according to the Consul

General. The train sped across Nebraska. Zauhar became faint and walked up to the men's lounge. While sitting in the lounge he had become violent, picked up a chair and threw it at the window, shattering the glass. The railroad conductor wired ahead that there was a violent person aboard the train who should be taken off at Boone, Iowa. On arrival the train was met by Boone police officers who took Zauhar with them to the police station, where they emptied his pockets and put him in a jail cell overnight.

The next morning they gave Zauhar several dollars from his billfold to go out for breakfast and when he returned they would return his property and he could be on his way. Zauhar took the money and went to a nearby cafe. He never returned to the police station. What the consul didn't know, however was that after Zauhar's disappearance, some months later a body was found alongside the railroad tracks west of Boone. It was decomposed with unrecognizable features and some evidence of animal disturbance. There was no identification at all on or near the body. When the effects of John Zauhar were examined, it was found that he had a money belt, which had been turned over to the bank. It contained more that $2900. Thus, the identity of the owner of the money belt as well as his other personal effects became of greater than casual interest. The police notified Zauhar's family but no one had followed up until the Consul General's letter to our firm in 1953.

The period of time between the disappearance of John Zauhar and the discovery of the unidentified body was several months and no real connection was made between the two.

The body was taken to the local funeral home and a coroner's inquest was convened to determine, if possible, the identity and cause of death. The coroner, Garland Hancock, was a local funeral director. The Coroner's Jury consisted of three men: E. H. White, a magazine distributor, G. H. Wallentine, a minister, and Marvin Sturtz, the Boone County Superintendent of Schools.

A principal witness at the hearing was a noted and experienced pathologist from Des Moines, who had the body and skull X-rayed at the hospital. Other physical evidence were the 8 teeth found near the body, as well as the teeth in the skull of the decedent. The pathologist testified that the nickel-sized hole in the upper left rear side of the skull was caused by a .45 caliber bullet. He also stated that the victim had been shot and died as a result of the shooting thus leaving the Boone police with an unsolved murder.

The Coroner's jury concluded that the body was that of an unknown man who met his death as the result of a bullet wound in his skull. The body was buried in a grave in Ridgeport Cemetery in Boone County, its location unmarked.

Now, six years later, the consul general's letter gave me the ammunition I needed to re-open the inquest, and it told us about Zauhar's trephine operation. But Zauhar's operation was on the right side of the skull, while the unknown body had a gunshot wound according to the pathologist, in the left side of the skull and no trephine operation on the right.

My first step in response to the mystery was to visit with the Sheriff about the incident and the Coroner's inquest proceedings. The sherrif went to the closet in his office and took out a quart fruit jar in which were a number of human teeth. The Sheriff, Steve Beaulieu, opened the jar and spread them out on the desk top and we both examined them. I called on my dentist brother, Dr. H.C. Erbe, and Dr. Frank Sunstrom, another local dentist, to examine the teeth, and to review the teeth that we could see in the X-ray film of the skull.

I then discussed with the Sheriff the procedure which was followed at the inquest. It was his opinion that the person who had taken the X-ray picture of the skull had reversed the film when marking it, thus causing the right side of the head to be confused with the left side of the head. If true, this was extremely important to the identification of the deceased, Zauhar.

Another critical bit of evidence contributing to the identification of the deceased were the dental records. I wrote to the president of the Bend County Dental Society and explained our problem of identification, requesting that he contact members of the dental society to see if any of them had worked on John Zauhar while he was an employee of the lumber operation.

We were lucky. He found a dentist Dr. Peterson who had done dental work for John Zauhar. I sent Dr. Peterson the description by the Boone dentists of the work which had been done to the teeth of the deceased and asked him to verify that it was indeed the skull of John Zauhar.

Still trying to fit together pieces of the puzzle, my letter to a law firm in Portland, Oregon, revealed that the lumberman's hospital in Bend was no longer in business and that the whereabouts of the hospital records were not known. They also stated that the neurosurgeon who had done the trephine operation was deceased.

I then contacted a Des Moines pathologist to determine whether the X-ray film was consistent with the theory that it was a bullet hole which caused the death of that person. He stated that it was not a fresh bullet wound in the skull but rather the result of a healed trephine operation which had been performed some years ago.

With this I felt there was sufficient evidence to consult with the Coroner about the possibility of reconvening the inquest following an exhumation of the body parts necessary to establish the identity of Zauhar. He agreed that the identification of the body was likely if exhumed and the inquest were reconvened to consider this new evidence.

Under the laws of the State of Iowa, exhumation of a body is permitted only upon obtaining a permit from the State Board of Health with good cause shown. The cemetery sexton warned me that the body would not be exhumed until I had the necessary permit in hand. At my request, the coroner fixed a date for reconvening the inquest, and asked the original jurors to serve at this hearing. I invited prospective witnesses to appear and testify on the facts of the matter.

On the day fixed for the inquest, the Coroner, members of the jury, the sheriff, the county attorney, the pathologist, the sexton and I, all assembled at the Mineral Ridge Cemetery at 9 AM to exhume the body. The sexton forgot to ask for the Public Health exhumation order and proceeded to try to recall which unmarked grave was the correct resting place of the deceased.

He finally found the one he was looking for and began to dig. Upon reaching the wooden box he jumped down and opened the top of the box. He handed up the skull and lower jaw. The pathologist asked him to bring up several vertebra as well as the hyoid bone from the throat. The sexton then opened the lower portion of the box and checked to see if any bones were broken and found them all to be intact. He replaced the cover and filled the grave.

The group adjourned to the Welin Funeral Parlor for a reconvening of the inquest. The pathologist sawed around the circumference of the skull to determine whether the inside of the cavity contained a .45 caliber bullet, as alleged. Finding none, the pathologist then washed out the skull and testified that the hole was caused by a trephine operation and not by a pistol shot. This was based on the regenerative bone tissue which had grown around the hole, as differentiated from a shattering of the bone if it had been a recent pistol shot. He then testified that the hole was in the upper-right rear of the skull instead of the upper-left rear, and was the result of a trephine operation. He also testified that there appeared to be no damage to the vertebra nor the hyoid bone. Damage to these body parts many times indicates death by strangulation.

The local dentist, Dr. Frank Sunstrom, testified that the dental work performed on the teeth was the same dental work described by Dr. Peterson of Bend, Oregon, on John Ivan Zauhar. I then testified that a letter from the Social Security System stated that there had been no payments into the system since Zauhar had departed Bend, Oregon, nor had there been any claims against his social security number since that time.

The Internal Revenue Service had written that there were no filings of income tax returns or applications for refunds from him since that time. His relatives in Uniontown, Pennsylvania, wrote stating that the steamship ticket which they held for him had not been used nor was the railroad ticket from Boone to Uniontown used.

The Chief of Police recounted the circumstances of John Zauhar's arrival in Boone and his departure from the police station on the morning following his arrival, and the fact that he did not return. The police department had asked that his luggage be returned to them for safekeeping and that a trunk, footlocker and suitcase be returned to Boone. They were kept on the back of the stage in the auditorium of the City Hall.

An officer of the Citizens National Bank then testified that the money belt and pocket change had been turned over to them for safekeeping and they had held the same in their vault until the present time. It consisted of $2998.89. It was then testified that there had been no communication by John Zauhar with any relative nor any other related person since he was taken off the train and sent from the police station for breakfast in August of 1947.

The coroner's jury then met to consider the new evidence and reconvened to announce that; "We, the jury, do find that the body which was disinterred this morning, July 29, 1953, is the body of John Ivan or John Anton Zauhar, and that John Ivan or John Anton Zauhar did not meet his death by reason of a bullet through his head, and that the cause of death so far as we are able to determine, is unknown."

They suggested that his mental disability, resulting in his removal from the train, may have caused him to follow railroad tracks, and that he may have been struck by a train which, with exposure, may have caused his death. With this official finding of the identity of the deceased, it was then possible to open a guardianship for his assets and my appointment by the court to protect his assets and my authority to hold them for his Estate. I was appointed as guardian of his assets by the judge.

I then went to City Hall and opened the foot locker, the suitcase, and the steamer trunk. I found among the contents a black silk dress, a five pound package of sugar, several pair of lumberman's hobnail boots, long underwear, gloves and other personal clothing which might be expected in the luggage of a person leaving the Northwest of the United States.

These were entered on an inventory sheet which I sent to the widow in Yugoslavia. Contact was made with the Citizens National Bank and the funds held by them were used to establish a guardianship checking account. There was then filed with the Internal Revenue Service an application for refund of the overpayment of income taxes as well as an income tax return for the decedent, and a letter to the railroad for refund of the unused railroad ticket from Boone to Uniontown, Pennsylvania.

As guardian of his estate I collected all of the assets of the estate including the contents of the luggage, proceeds of two insurance policies, as well as application for Social Security benefits for the spouse in Yugoslavia and forwarded all of this to the Yugoslavia Counsel in Chicago who receipted for it on behalf of the surviving spouse and family. I then opened an estate for the deceased John Zauhar. I do not know how much of the cash she received but I did ship the luggage and contents directly to her and she would have received the Social Security benefits in Yugoslavia from the time of his death in the United States.

I discovered several group life insurance policies and collected the principal amount for his heirs on behalf of the deceased. A claim was made in the estate proceedings to reimburse the insurance companies for their cost in trying to establish the identity of Zauhar. This was denied. It had been planned to cremate the body instead of reburying the remains but in order to do this it was necessary to obtain the consent of the surviving spouse. Communication with the spouse had to be accomplished through the Yugoslavian consul general in Chicago, Illinois. This process took an unusual amount of time with translations and distance, as well as certifying in their Chicago office the contents of the document with a number of official seals and stamps. Consent for the cremation arrived one week following the date of recovening of the Coroners jury and reinterment of the deceased. His body still rests in Ridgeport Cemetery in Boone County, Iowa.

TEN: MY LIFE IN POLITICS TAKES OFF

My father-in-law, Lant Doran, was also a former State Senator and a leader in the state Republican party. Lant took me along to political affairs of the Republican party and encouraged me to get involved in politics as a way of getting to know people so that I could build my law practice. The best way to do this was to volunteer for the job of Treasurer for the local Republican organization. The holder of that job was required to get out and raise money, and to meet and get acquainted with the local candidates. This was not a desirable job and anyone who volunteered for it would not be popular since he would be asking for money all the time. On the other hand, he would get to know the people in the community and that was my goal. I felt that it would help considerably in establishing my law practice, and it did.

As it happened, I had advanced from the job of Treasurer to the County Republican Chairman in the spring of 1952. At the time Ike was thinking about running for President. When the National Republican Convention was about to start in Chicago, I sent him a telegram in Denver inviting him to stop in Boone for an old fashioned chicken dinner on his way to Chicago. He accepted the invitation and then the pressure began. I had to plan the event, including the location, food, who would cook it, how many would eat it, and who would be on the guest list, all within a 36 hour period.

Every self-styled VIP in the state claimed to have special connections with Ike and was surely entitled to have dinner tickets at the shelter house in McHose Park in Boone. I had space for 300 people and made 2,700 enemies, yet my father-in-law, Lant Doran, who was a Taft supporter, did receive a ticket. I met the soon-to-be President's train, rode in the parade, ate with Ike and introduced him for his principal farm speech on his way to Chicago. It was a very exciting time.

One of my classmates in Law School was a friend from Nevada, Iowa, Dayton Countryman. He was elected to the position of Attorney General of Iowa in 1954 and he asked me to serve as his Special Assistant at the Iowa State Highway Commission in Ames. I felt that I could help him out by specializing in the Iowa law of roads and the Iowa law of drainage. I could become an expert in these fields and get good experience in trying condemnation appeal cases before juries throughout the state. I accepted his invitation.

While in Ames I served as Special Assistant Attorney General and as General Counsel to the Highway Commission, trying condemnation cases in the courts of Iowa. This was 1954, the period of preparation for the construction of the Interstate Highway System. Planning, designing, and acquiring right of way for new highways made the Highway Commission a very busy place to work. In the legal department, we were particularly busy with the problems involved in buying property from landowners when they didn't want to sell.

One case at the western edge of Clinton County was an interesting example. The property owner was a single man of about 60. He had farmed his 300 acre farm since he was a youth. His sister kept house for him and helped with the farm chores. They lived in a nice, large frame house and had a number of sizable farm buildings and sheds to the south of the house.

Our right-of-way agents had been negotiating with him for about a year for the right to place the new highway between his house and the out-buildings. He wouldn't even talk price for the land needed. After numerous contacts by our Right of Way agents they admitted defeat in a negotiated acquisition. When this happened, the State, through its exercise the law of eminent domain, proceeded to condemn the property. Notice was given to the property owner and three condemnation commissioners, usually rural realtors who are knowledgeable about farm land values, examined the land and reached a consensus as to its value and the dollar value of the loss to the remaining land.

Their verdict and a check for the appraised value figure was then filed with the Clerk of Court. The Sheriff served notice of the appraised value of the property on the farm owner, advising him that he could appeal their finding to the District Court but must do so within 30 days if he wanted to preserve his appellate rights.

The procedure was followed correctly, but the property owner did not appeal and thus his appeal rights were lost. The farmer refused to let the highway surveyors and engineers onto his property. He carried a shotgun and threatened to use it on them if they approached his land. The Commission specialists were convinced that he would use his gun as promised and were at a loss as to how to solve the problem.

They came to me for the answer. I decided to set a date for the

136

confrontation. I asked the sheriffs of the two adjoining counties to meet me at the farm at a designated time. I explained the situation to the Highway Patrol and asked them to join us, too. On that date with this show of force I engaged the owner in conversation and pointed out that he had given up his right to appeal, and he was required by law to permit the specialists to come onto the land, since it was now the property of the State of Iowa. The man finally agreed and we obtained the necessary land for the highway. I never understood why he had not used his right-of-appeal.

My two years as Special Assistant Attorney General was at a time when there were many challenges and new, exciting legal issues developing in highway and drainage law. Since the Federal Highway Administration was during this time involved in construction of the Interstate Highway System, I was particularly busy trying jury cases in the courts of Iowa. These were principally cases on appeal from the valuations fixed by our Right of way Appraisers. The Chief Engineer asked me to prepare a simplified booklet of highway, roads, and street laws which could be used by Highway Engineers and County Engineers who were not trained in the law but were required in their work to carry out some of the provisions of the Iowa Law. I wrote such a volume for their use. It was designated as a research prospect of the Highway Commission. I subsequently prepared another book on the Drainage Laws of the State of Iowa. They were titled the Iowa Highway Road and Street Laws 1956, and The Iowa Drainage Laws 1956. There was a total of about 650 pages in each volume.

As we neared the end of Attorney General Countryman's two year term he told me that he was seriously thinking of running for the U.S. Senate seat held by Bourke Hickenlooper, Iowa's senior senator. He gave it a lot of thought and decided to go for it. As soon as he announced that decision, I decided that I would run for Attorney General of Iowa.

Jackie and our three daughters, DeElda Lou born in February 1947, Jennifer Lee in October 1948, and Kevin Lynn in February 1953, helped a great deal in this, my first step into statewide politics. It meant folding and inserting announcement letters into envelopes for mailing to the Republican officials and a list of Iowa voters. Most of this work was done on the kitchen and dining room tables.

Meanwhile, I was also engaged in traveling around the state trying jury cases for the highway commission, speaking to various service clubs and Republican groups. There were family pictures to be taken and campaign materials designed. I was successful in the primary election campaign, and won the general election held the fall of 1956. I also won re-election in 1958.

The Attorney General is a constitutional office elected to a two-year term, which has since been changed by constitutional amendment to a term of four years. The Attorney General is the chief legal officer of the State and heads the State Department of Justice. The powers and duties of the office include representing the departments and agencies of the state government, giving legal advice on questions of law, and representing the state in court. The office issues written opinions on questions of law submitted by elected and state appointed officials, and represents the state in all tort claim actions. All criminal appeals from the ninety-nine counties to the Supreme Court are handled by the office of the Attorney General. On request from a County Attorney, the Attorney General's office assists in prosecuting difficult local criminal cases.

The duties of the office of Attorney General of Iowa have increased remarkably through the years. It took only one attorney on my staff to handle all criminal appeals to the Iowa Supreme Court in the late 1950's. My total staff at that time was 12 Assistant Attorney Generals. By 1996 this had grown to 12 attorneys who presently share just the criminal appeal load from the court. The number of assistant attorneys has mushroomed to 110 lawyers because of additional responsibilities given to the Attorney General's office by the legislature. The office now has a current annual budget of nine million dollars.

The office of Attorney General was located in the East Wing of the Statehouse. My first days in office I had the job of filling a staff roster, which totaled nine lawyers. One of the most outstanding assistants was Oscar Straus, who had retired from active practice in Des Moines when he was in his late 60's. When I met him he was in his late 70's and working in the Attorney General's office. His recollection of facts and opinions was phenomenal and he was able to cite the book and page number of elusive opinions which had been written by the office in years past. Other exceptional staff members were C.J. Lyman, Don Swanson, Frank Bianco, Kent Emery, John Eddy, Leonard Abel, Hugh

Faulkner, Edward Hayes, Richard Brinkman, Mike Forrest, Bob Helmick and Lloyd Courter. A major responsibility for the Attorney General's office was to carry forward to the Iowa Supreme Court all appeals in criminal cases from the District Court, as well as appeals from the Iowa Supreme Court to the U.S. Supreme Court. I argued one case before the U.S. Supreme Court, which was affirmed midway through my term.

CLEANING UP CASE BACK LOG

I discovered upon my arrival at the Office of Attorney General that there were hundreds of court cases resting in the files which had never been disposed of. These included state law violations in various areas of interest. The original suits were initially handled by the office and then simply allowed to be stored in the file folders. Fines and possible imprisonment could have been imposed. These 1,580 undecided law suits brought by the State went back some thirty years. We reviewed these and made determinations as to their fate. Either we would prosecute them or invoke the Statute of Limitations to get them dismissed. The defendants in these cases were entitled to have them removed from the record.

STATE LEGAL COUNSEL

We also engaged on a daily basis in the process of researching and writing legal opinions in response to questions posed by state officials, legislators, and county attorneys regarding Iowa law, involving the operation of their offices and the legality or illegality of actions they proposed to take. Normally these matters were not of sufficient importance to seek court rulings, but there was simply a need for guidelines with which to operate. The more important opinions were placed in book form every two years, indexed and keyed to the appropriate code section of the law to be considered as precedent. As can be imagined, over the years the questions repeated themselves and unless one had a prodigious memory, he had to "re-invent the wheel."

I decided to organize these opinions. I hired a woman with legal training to index all the legal opinions of the office, by subject and title, identifying the question and answer, then place this information on index cards in a Rolodex file. It was a cumbersome method, but the best method available in the pre-computer era. It increased the efficiency of the staff many fold and reduced wasted time and effort.

ANTI CORRUPTION LAW ENFORCEMENT

Another big project of our office was to fight corruption in state contracting. One of the largest categories of state contracting involved road and highway construction—one of my areas of particular expertise and experience.

The State Highway Commission held lettings on highway contracts each month for road projects in the State of Iowa. These lettings of contracts were for the construction of bridges and culverts as well as surfacing or paving roadways.

Counties were required to obtain approval of the State Highway Commission before proceeding with a state funded project, and their contracts were also part of the state contract lettings. The Commission held the purse strings and was charged with total responsibility for appropriate and lawful handling of funds. These funds included the monies from the federal government as well as fuel tax revenues ear marked by the State constitution for roadways.

In 1957, an investigation by the Highway Commission disclosed that various road contractors were involved in "bid rigging" which involved exchanges of information between contractors engaged in the bidding process. This was illegal under State and Federal law. Our office brought several prosecutions and a number of the contractors were found guilty, assessed fines, and given prison terms.

TAX REFORM

Another of our projects concerned tax law. The State of Iowa had an income tax which was not cross-checked with the Federal Income Tax. As a result there was widespread failure to pay state income tax. We corrected this problem by changes in the regulations and improvement of state enforcement provisions.

FISCAL ACCOUNTABILITY

Cash flow to the counties from the State Treasurer was handled by each County Treasurer and County Board of Supervisors. These funds were often substantial, depending upon the size and activities of the counties. Some counties hired a fiscal agent to determine investments and lawful distribution of these funds to the various recipients. This practice was contrary to the law and we put a stop to it.

BABY SELLING

There had been a business of bringing babies into the state and selling them to couples who desperately wanted children. The practice was unregulated, with no oversight by agencies to ensure that the babies were lawfully available for adoption and that the families were suitable to receive them, and the problem was growing each year. It had become a serious problem in the counties which had larger population centers. My office investigated and, through publicity and threat of legal action, we were able to halt the practice.

ELDERLY CARE

The need for nursing homes for the sick and elderly was increasing each year and resulted in the proliferation of unlicensed facilities. Licensing identified them and gave the social service agency the responsibility to inspect for proper operations in the interest of the residents. We advertised this problem and obtained compliance, though I suspect a number went out of business.

ANTI-PORNOGRAPHY

Distribution and sale of pornographic magazines had reached a pitch where lewd and indecent materials were available to everyone. It was a profitable venture and pervasive throughout the state.

I brought in the Director of Public Safety and asked him to prepare a plan to collect certain offensive magazines and use them as evidence in subsequent court cases in different jurisdictions in the state. I wrote a letter to county attorneys stating that, in my opinion, 42 magazines were obscene, and asked them to bring criminal charges against the publishers if the magazines appeared on newsstands in their jurisdictions. I also called magazine wholesalers to a meeting, told them I would enforce the State obscenity laws, and asked them to remove the cited magazines from the newsstands.

Four Star Publications of New York and 17 other publishers filed an injunction suit, contending my actions applied to the initial pickup of the magazines as well as to future issues of the magazines. A similar injunction petition was filed by Knight Publishing and Sir Kay Publishing Co., both of California. The two actions in Federal Court were combined for trial. The plaintiff claimed censorship.

Federal Judge Van Pelt of Omaha said he was making no decision as to the constitutionality of the Iowa law or whether any of the magazines involved were actually obscene within the meaning of the state statute. He said, "This court believes that eventually in the different localities of Iowa, juries should determine in criminal cases whether any of the plaintiff's magazines are or are not obscene." The judge indicated that the common conscience of various areas of the state may be the ruling factor in determining the question of obscenity. He said the common conscience might be different in urban areas as compared to rural areas, in river towns as compared to the interior, and in highly industrialized centers as compared to educational centers. The judge dismissed the suit and smut magazines disappeared from the newsstands of Iowa.

Hanging Out the "Shingle"

My job as Attorney General included the responsibility for administering the Bar Examination to law school graduates who wanted to practice in Iowa. I have previously described the complete lack of dignity with which candidates who successfully passed the exam at that time were notified of their success. I felt that there should be greater emphasis placed on the successful completion of the formal education and training of prospective lawyers.

I therefore arranged to have a luncheon served to the successful new lawyer applicants, invited the four or five lawyers who were on the Board of Bar Examiners who read the essay papers of the students, and asked the Chief Justice of the Supreme Court of Iowa to deliver a brief address. I also had Certificates of Admission prepared prior to the luncheon and these were delivered to the students along with a congratulatory handshake by the Chief Justice.

One always spoke of "hanging out their shingle" when they entered practice. We purchased some cedar shingles and inked their names along with the words "Attorney at Law" on them for presentation to the new lawyers. It was a welcome change which provided a great deal of dignity to the admissions procedure for the Bar. Forty years later I still meet lawyers who tell me that they have the shingle on their office wall.

When I was elected and took office as Attorney General, I had asked the Boone County Brush and Palette Club to help me out with furnishing my office. I wanted artwork by local artists. They were selected and hung, to be changed about every six weeks. This worked out well as they received exposure and recognition for their talents and I had an attractive office. I had followed this same procedure as Governor. Those paintings were done by the State Art Clubs.

Years later, serving in the Transportation Department in Chicago, I inquired about their paintings. Finding they had no list or record of their collection, I persuaded the Chicago U.S. government GSA people there to prepare an inventory. I was able to obtain from the U.S. General Services Administration the loan of some of their art works for my office.

ON THE EVE OF A DICTATOR'S DOWNFALL: BASTISTA IN CUBA

As the state's Attorney General, I was invited to the Second InterAmerican Congress of Public Law Administrators, in Havana, Cuba. I agreed to speak on the rights of the individual under the laws of our jurisdiction. I had not heard of the organization, but soon discovered that it consisted of Attorneys General and Public Law Administrators in each country of the Western Hemisphere. Meetings were held every three years, the first being held in Sao Paulo, Brazil.

Their second letter advised that all expenses would be paid by the host nation. This was to be the first venture out of the country by Jackie and me. We didn't know what to expect in Cuba in 1954. President Batista was having a difficult time maintaining control as Fidel Castro was leading a "citizens' revolution" in the hills and mountains of Cuba. When we landed at Havana Airport we were met by a uniformed soldier who stated that he was to be our guide, driver and guard during the course of our stay. He whisked us through customs and drove us to our hotel, which was new and situated on the banks of the sea. He told us he would return for us at 4 PM to take us to the of Palace of Justice for the formal dedication of the edifice.

Jackie and I unpacked and settled in, relaxing and enjoying the view of the sea from our tenth floor balcony. As 4 PM, approached, we leisurely dressed, believing that the dedication ceremony was just another event on our agenda. We went down to street level and found our very nervous driver waiting for us. When we arrived at the Palace we found that everyone was waiting for us so they could begin the cermonies.

As we joined the crowd, the band began to play, and things began with a flourish; music, speeches, ribbon cutting,—the whole nine yards. We all then were escorted inside to the Supreme Court chamber, which seated about fifteen judges around a large horseshoe shaped bench. More speeches were given, then we met the Attorney General of Havana and his spouse, as well as the Attorney General of Cuba, who asked if we would like to go for a brief tour around Havana. We agreed with pleasure. Our car for the tour was a limousine, with a driver and another person in the front seat. Jackie leaned forward and noted that the right seat passenger had a submachine gun accross his lap.

First the Attorney General took us to the home of his daughter so that we could see a "typical" Havana home, then we went to see the Havana Country Club, with a very beautiful new clubhouse of white marble. We arrived at the Country Club and got out of the car. Walking up to the building, the Attorney General of Cuba, bemoaned the fact that the United States media was so very critical of Batista. Couldn't I do something to convince them that Batista was good for Cuba? I tried to assure him that it was very difficult if not impossible to manage the media in the States.

We had reached the clubhouse, all the time being followed by the driver and his friend with the submachine gun, who walked in the bushes at the side of the sidewalk. As we strolled into the lounge, we paused at a table for introductions to the ladies sitting there playing bridge, members of the Bacardi family of Bacardi rum fame. After visiting several other Havana sites we finally returned to our hotel.

The next day we were again suprised by a ceremony. Our driver took us to the Palace of Justice and then to a special room that was apparently a gallery of VIP portraits, some of which were covered with large cloths. Upon our arrival one of the officials approached Jackie and told her that she would have the honor of unveiling one of the pictures. She was truly embarrassed, since we had no idea that she would be honored with this privilege. Had she known she would have worn more appropriate clothing. As it was, she wore a "hot weather casual" dress and carried it off in an outstanding manner.

After the unveiling, we were all toasted with champagne cocktails. We then got down to work with the various papers prepared by those in attendance. I was the only person from the American delegation to prepare a paper, although there were about 25 Attorneys General at the meeting. I was elected Chairman of the U.S. Delegation. This was quite an honor—but it also had its problems.

A mid-week diversion was scheduled for the conference participants. Our group was taken in Greyhound buses for a one and a half hour ride to a school for children of government employees. We were escorted by many motorcycle police, each of whom had his sirens screaming full force as we went through the country villages. The parade was fast and noisy, scattering children, chickens and pigs, and caused astonished looks on the faces of natives that watched as the "official" buses and motorcycles flew by.

Upon arrival at the school we were taken through the barracks, noting each child standing at attention at their foot-locker and bed, in very strict military fashion. The children, dressed in khaki, were ages six to seventeen, boys and girls. After barracks inspection we were taken to a reviewing stand to see them pass in review. Oddly, they had formed the companies with the oldest at the head and the youngest students at the rear of the columns. As can be imagined, the youngest and shortest had to make long strides to keep up with the pace in front. It was almost heartbreaking to see those little tykes trying to keep up and still march properly.

Our hosts were very proud of the school, which was for the children of poor government workers who couldn't afford schooling. For most of us in attendance the military atmosphere was too much.

At lunch, Jackie mentioned to me that she had become nauseated on the bus trip. I mentioned it to our Cuban host, who responded that a relative of his had been shot in the hills and they had to go back to Havana in a limo. Would she like to go back with them? She said "no thanks."

While some of our delegation were on the tour of the school, part of our delegation went hunting, including Bill Saxbe, then Attorney

General of Ohio and later to be appointed U.S. Attorney General. They bagged over 200 ducks. There was no legal limit so they were quite pleased with themselves. I wondered what was to be done with all of those ducks.

Our meetings were interspersed with free time to tour the beautiful city of Havana. It was a wonderful, interesting, experience, except for the slight problem which concluded the conference. That afternoon was taken up with various resolutions of gratitude to the hosts, pledges for law changes and procedures in the future, and an anticipated invitation for the next conference from one of the attendee nations.

Hearing no invitation from the countries attending, they came to me, as Chairman of the American delegation, and asked if I would invite them to have the next conference in Washington, D.C., three years hence. This was my initiation to the mysteries of foreign policy. If this followed precedence, the host government was obligated to provide rooms and meals for all delegates. Of course I knew I was not the one to speak to; others in our government did this sort of thing. I excused myself and told them I would have to confer with the U.S. Embassy in Havana on the subject. I called the Embassy, explained my dilemma, and waited for the answer, which was just what I expected. There was no representation at all from the U.S. Justice Department or any agency of the U.S. Government at the meetings, so a response would be more complex. I expect that the lack of attendance by the U.S. was a purposeful omission from the conference, in addition to the fact that Batista was about to leave the country and Castro was soon to take over.

I went back to the conference hall and was immediately called on. I reported that we would attempt to get a formal invitation, and if successful in our attempts, give them a very sincere and happy welcome which they would long remember. There was generous applause.

That night we went to the Trocadero, the finest night club and dining place in Havana. The food was very good, the drinks great, and the floor show terrific. It was a lovely and memorable day for all of us. The final evening in Havana featured a reception at the President's Palace with Fulgencio Batista receiving and visiting with all the attendees. It was a beautiful building modeled after our national Capitol building, located in a plaza and surrounded by other government structures.

146

The roofs of the buildings surrounding the capital plaza were lined with armed soldiers guarding the capitol building. Soldiers were also stationed within the palace itself. Huge bouquets of beautiful roses decorated the tables which held the evening refreshments. Later, our Cuban hosts took us to their apartment across the street and showed us a hidden drawer in their bedroom chest which held a pistol, passports and other papers needed for a sudden departure. When Castro took over the family did not leave, but I believe our host was imprisoned.

On my return to Iowa, I wrote to Senator Hickenlooper and the Departments of Justice and State, explaining my dilemma concerning the invitation expected three years hence, and asked them for help. Of course I knew the answer: no money. About two years later, I had a phone call from the Council of State Governments saying three persons were in their office who described their organization and were inquiring about a possible invitation from the U.S. to entertain the Third Congress of Public Law Administrators. I felt embarrassed about not being able to reciprocate the invitation, but was helpless to take action.

KRUSCHEV IN IOWA

Nikita Kruschev came to the United States for a visit with Senator Henry Cabot Lodge as his tour leader. The Russian leader arrived in Iowa and stayed at the Ft. Des Moines Hotel from September 22 to 24th, in 1959. He dined at the Fort Des Moines Hotel in Des Moines and I was one of the guests at that function. I was a little early for the dinner and watched as his security detail went about the room and checked under each of the tables for uninvited guests. It was an interesting evening. We had a rather slow conversation at the table because of the difficulty of conversing with members of the Premier's party who did not speak English. Kruschev's remarks were as would be expected.

Eleven: President Eisenhower

I had several opportunities to visit with President Eisenhower. Mamie Eisenhower was born in Boone, Iowa, though her family moved to Denver when she was a small child. Mamie's Uncle Joel Carlson was an officer in a local bank and he and his wife Carolyn, who was the school nurse, lived in Boone for many years. Before and after the war, Ike and Mamie both visited Boone several times a year.

I have already written of the time I hosted IKE for a Pre Election in Boone. While I was Attorney General I had an appointment to see him in the Oval Office. He had just returned from a trip to South America. The trip was one on which a U.S. military band had accompanied him to Brazil to play at several functions. The plane crashed and a number of the band members were killed. He, of course, was very busy and I hardly knew what to talk about other than Uncle Joel. He was most gracious.

Later during the Nixon Administration I attended a Republican conference and picnic at IKE and Mamie's farm home in Gettysburg, Pennsylvania. It was a lovely spot and he was a very charming host. Later Jackie and I decided to take in a show in New York. We arrived at the last moment, lucky to get seats in the center section. The show that night was "The Unsinkable Molly Brown" by Meredith Willson. At intermission Jackie turned around and said, "There's Ike behind us." I turned around and there they were with Maurice Stans, a cabinet member. Ike recognized me and referred to me as "his boy." They did not leave their seats for intermission and we soon had people asking us to get his autograph. We found that we were unofficially guarding and protecting our President from the autograph seekers.

Visiting with President Eisenhower.

We've been to the Eisenhower Presidential Library in Abilene, Kansas, and believe it is one of the finest, especially since it contains mementos and gifts from his World War II experiences. We have also entertained his grandson, David Eisenhower, for dinner at our home in Boone. He is a fine young man.

Twelve: Landing In The Governor's Chair.

In 1960 I decided to run for Governor of the State of Iowa. The family helped again in folding, inserting and mailing announcement material from their work tables in the kitchen and dining room. There were six Republican candidates to face the Republican voters in the primary election in June.

Jackie was an absolute jewel, directing and waging this campaign as well as she had done in our two Attorney General's campaigns. Although Jackie did not encourage me to run for office, once I decided she spent all of her energies helping to make it a reality, doing a marvelous job. The best campaigner in the family, she worked hard and everyone loved her.

Entering the races for Attorney General and Governor, I pledged to myself that I wouldn't use our money to finance the costs. I felt that if people weren't interested in me enough to contribute, it would be unwise to run. Our last war chest amounted to over $100,000. This was about the time when TV ads were just coming into their own. Our advertising decisions were addressed to the comparative effectiveness of billboards, newspaper ads, direct mail, radio, or that new invention, TV, which was terribly expensive. The campaign was a very hectic time, with a great deal of travel and speaking around the state. David Fisher, a Boone native and student at Grinnell College, was my driver on the summer campaign trail. He performed that role in a very superior manner. I changed my remarks at each stop but the other candidates never varied from theirs. By the end of the trip I could almost give their speeches verbatim.

I was successful in the primary, having reached the required 35% of the votes. By then there were only three Republican candidates for Governor: myself, Bill Nicholas, a turkey farmer from Mason City, and Jack Schroeder, a State Senator from Davenport. The score was Erbe-81,869; Nicholas-68,033; Schroeder 75,599. Then came the General Election in the fall. Our friends in Boone, under the leadership of our next door neighbors, Stan and Maxine Redeker, devised a very effective campaign tool. (Stan would later perform outstanding service

151

as president of the State Board of Regents and was reappointed to the Board by the Democrats.) They asked their business friends in Boone to acquire a mailing list of their Iowa Business Association members. Each of the Boone members then wrote a letter to a member on the list, extolling the virtues of my candidacy for Governor. This was a tremendous help in reaching voters that could not be contacted in any other way.

They added another facet to the campaign by organizing a "Neighbors For Norm" effort. At least two couples accompanied me to my speaking dates to hand out campaign material at stores and speaking sites. Then they would precede me to the next speaking site and do the same thing.

Among those on the team were Jim and Jean Flanagan, Stan and Maxine Redeker, Bob and Francie Fisher, Pete and Juana Sandberg, Bill and Pat Ryerson, Bill and Jo Doran, Paul and Barb Lilly, Bill and Jeanette Westfall, and Wayne and Pauline Cramer. This was probably the most effective and best organized grass roots campaign effort that I have ever witnessed, and a real testament to our friendship.

In the General election in the fall of 1960, I received 645,026 votes and my opponent, Lt. Governor McManus from Keokuk received 592,063. It was thrilling, yet my parents were not impressed. When I practiced law after the war, I had taken a step down in their eyes. Lawyers were shady. And when I entered elective politics, all was lost. Politicians were crooks. Therefore there was no pride of achievement for their youngest child with my election to the post of governor.

I was startled once after my election when visiting with a cousin who lived in a Chicago suburb. He actually voiced the same view, that I must be tainted with the brush of corruption and political chicanery in my service as governor. This bad reputation was the model for all politicians for those citizens who lived in the voting districts of the Chicago metropolis and you were painted with the corrupt politics of that area. I was insulted and depressed that this view would be expressed by a relative, but then I remembered the German Lutheran conservatism under which he was raised and recognized it for what it was.

My father-in-law, Lant Doran however, was a natural political animal. He enjoyed the give and take of political maneuvering, took me along to the various political meetings he attended, and thoroughly reveled in the process. He had served several terms as State Senator in the mid 30's and became widely known as someone who gets things done. He was mentioned as a probable candidate for Governor a number of times but never made the jump. Unfortunately he died of a brain tumor before the election. He told me that it would cost a farm to run and serve as Governor of the state and he was right.

Once the returns were in and I had won with the significant help from my friends in Boone and around the state, Jackie and I went to Mexico City and Acapulco for a week. I didn't want to talk to anyone for a while, since I had been doing only that for over a year. I had developed calluses between the fingers of my right hand from all of the handshaking.

As we boarded the Braniff plane at the Des Moines Airport, we discovered that we were joining a very prestigious party consisting of VIPs from different cities who were on the maiden flight from the Twin Cities to Mexico City. There were special welcoming ceremonies in each city where the Braniff plane stopped and we joined them in their celebration. Our short stay in Mexico City with the group included a call on the President of Mexico in his Palace, as well as a stop at the home of Cantinflas, the famous Mexican actor who played in the movie, "Around the World in Eighty Days".

Then we were off to Acapulco. Upon our arrival we went to our beautiful hotel, looking out on the ocean. As we entered the plaza outside the hotel, we noticed a parade of marchers carrying a black casket on their shoulders, We discovered the parade was a protest against the Governor of the State of Guerero. He had taken the land of residents without paying for it. When they objected, he had them hung by their testicles. No wonder they were protesting. A "TIME" magazine article the following week described the problem and stated that the President of Mexico had removed the man from office. I got some good natured advice about the pitfalls of serving as Governor of a State.

The hotel owner heard that I had been elected to the post of Governor of Iowa. He had relatives in Cedar Rapids so we became fast friends. He invited me to have lunch with some of the Mexican government VIPS, the Tax Collector, and several more notables including the Secretary of Agriculture. Jackie was swimming in the pool, so we had to get word to her that she too was invited While we were eating our host asked me what our hobbies were. I confessed to an abiding interest in photography and Jackie explained her fascination with Indian artifacts. At the conclusion of the luncheon he presented us with colored clay caricature models of each of us in a frame about 6 x 9 inches, Jackie gazing at an archeological stone and me using a camera. They were very good likenesses.

Then he presented her with a beautiful teak box about five inches square and one and a half inches deep, the lid formed to represent the Bay of Acapulco in turquoise and silver. A truly beautiful gift. He then said that one couldn't give a box with nothing in it. He had placed inside a carved alabaster skull made by ancient residents of Mexico. It was about one and a half inches high with two holes in the top for use as an amulet. It has not been out of the Acapulco box since that time.

Thirteen: Erbe Sworn In As Governor Of Iowa

We left soon and returned to the Iowa job for which I was elected. I held budget hearings and drafted my inaugural message. The Budget hearings were in the office of the State Comptroller. It was the first time that a Governor personally conducted these hearings. Since money is the basis for government in national, state, local and personal operations, budget hearings and the resulting bills were vitally important and would, if enacted, determine the direction, scope and programs the organization would take over the next few years.

Getting sworn in at Des Moines

The ceremony when I was to be sworn in as Governor was held in the chamber of the Iowa House of Representatives with our families, friends, lawmakers and guests present. There I was sworn in as Governor by the Chief Justice of the Iowa Supreme Court. A reception was held for all in the Governor's office, and later the family went to a hotel to prepare for the Inaugural Ball at Veterans Memorial Auditorium that evening. The ladies wore beautiful long gowns and many of the men wore tuxedos and black tie. A reception line formed and we had the opportunity to shake hands with most of the visitors as they all walked down the line of state officials who were waiting to greet them.

A grand march later in the evening was a high point. After a long and exciting day Jackie and I retired to the hotel as the band played on through the night. The next morning we had our first look at the Governor's residence. Our daughters, DeElda, Jennifer and Kevin, with their mother's help, selected the bedrooms that they would occupy for the next two years. Our

With the family at the Governor's office

oldest daughter, Dee, was in junior high school at the time and the other two, Jennifer and Kevie, were in middle and elementary schools. For the move to the Governor's Mansion, the Boone Schools had just passed them on because it was so near the end of the term. At the time, the Governor's Mansion was the house at 29th and Grand Ave.—not the mansion used today, which belonged to the Hubbell family during my term of office.

Dee was later to go to Iowa State University at Ames, where she graduated, Jennifer went to Colorado State University at Fort Collins Colorado. She then transferred to Boston University, finishing her college education at DePaul University in Chicago and earning a Masters Degree in Business Administration from Coloumbia College at Chicago. Jennifer by that time was also caring for our first grand child, Justine, while Jennifer worked in Chicago and went to night school. Kevi finished high school in Arlington Heights and then went to Beloit College in Wisconsin, and while there decided to go to the University of Iowa where she received her degree in Women's Studies.

THE KENNEDY INAUGURATION

The inauguration of President Kennedy was to be held on January 20th, 1961, after my inauguration as Governor of Iowa and Jackie and I planned to attend, so preparations had to be made for that event. Jackie's mother, DeElda Doran of Boone, was a life-saver as she came to Des Moines for the care and keeping of the Governor's daughters while we were away in Washington for the Kennedy Inaugural ceremonies.

In Washington, the Governor of each state had a military escort assigned to them for the duration of the event, as well as an auto, which had a license plate especially made for the state he represented. My military aide was an Air Force Captain from Atlantic, Iowa. On the day before the inauguration we were to assemble in the main ballroom of the Shoreham Hotel to greet friends from our state who were in town. The perimeter of the ballroom was arranged with booths for each state. Each booth contained several chairs, the state flag and a sign identifying the Governor. Visitors walked around the ballroom, stopping at the state booth of their preference.

The booths were organized in order of their date of admission to

156

the Union. This practice turned out to be routine at all Governors' conferences and other meetings where states are represented. About 3:30 PM the President-Elect made his way around the room, stopping at each booth and visiting briefly with each Governor. Of course, photographers and newsmen followed every action very closely. When President-Elect Kennedy came to us, we welcomed him and had a very brief conversation. As President Kennedy was introduced to Jackie, he said "we have a lot in common" and Jackie retorted "and don't think it doesn't give me a lot of problems in a good Republican state like Iowa." Where in the world she came up with that remark I'll never know. As he walked away from our booth he suddenly turned around, came back to our booth, patted Jackie on the arm and said, "I'll see you later, Jackie." For a brief while I was afraid she might consider becoming a Democrat.

Good friends of ours, The Attorney General of California, Stanley Mosk and his wife Edna, invited us to join them for some of the Democrat parties in the evenings, both before and after the inauguration. We enjoyed them very much. Several members of their group were movie stars from California and Jackie still remembers thirty five years later how we spent the evening with this or that movie celebrity. Stanley Mosk has since served as Chief Justice of the California Supreme Court.

It snowed the evening before the Inaugural. It was not very heavy by Iowa standards but it did accumulate to about three inches and succeeded in tying up the entire city of Washington. That night we ran into Bob Phillips, formerly of Des Moines, who had moved to Washington with the American Petroleum Institute. His wife was in the hospital having a baby and it was impossible for him to get a taxi or any other means of transportation to get to the hospital. I told him to take my assigned car and get to the bedside of his wife. He did so and welcomed a healthy baby boy.

The next morning we had our car back and it was time to leave for the Inaugural Ceremony. The weather was cloudy and threatening to snow. As we neared the Capitol, traffic was halted all around us in a traffic jam. When we saw Bobby Kennedy and his wife walking in the snow nearby, we got the message, got out of our car and started walking, too.

They gathered the Governors in a special room in the Capitol and

Inaugural parade, 1961 —
greeting President Kennedy

when the time arrived, we were led out to our special seating on the steps of the East Front, behind the podium. The other special guests, Congress and VIPs, gradually arrived and were seated. The uniform for the platform guests was tuxedo, top coat and top hat.

I had never owned nor worn a top hat and mentioned this in a press conference in Des Moines prior to our departure. Several days later, I had a top hat presented to me by the Corn Producers Association. In appreciation for my first top hat, I sent them each a membership card naming them to "Governor Erbe's Top Hat Club" with thanks.

We sat on chairs behind and above the podium and, although chilly, we had a good view of Robert Frost reciting a poem he had written especially for the event. Smoke and fire erupted from the podium during his reading and caused some excitement which was promptly taken care of by the Secret Service and will go down in trivia history as the question, "Which President had a fire at the podium during the course of his Inaugural Ceremony?"

As we sat through the ceremony, my feet were getting colder and colder. I stamped them as quietly as I could and remarked to the Governor of Michigan, John Swainson, my seatmate, that my feet were getting cold. He responded that he didn't have that problem as he had stepped on a land mine during the Korean war and had lost both feet. Governor Swainson was later appointed to the Federal Court in Michigan but he got into a little trouble and was sentenced to the penitentiary for some misdeed. Another of my colleagues that day, Governor Otto Kerner of Illinois, also served time in the penitentiary. We saw to it that President Kennedy was properly sworn into office.

The Inaugural Parade followed the ceremony. Jackie and I rode in an open car and again our position was determined by protocol, the date of Iowa's entrance into the Union.

I had arranged to have the Iowa National Guard Military Academy Company and the Iowa National Guard Band from Fairfield, Iowa, march in the parade. The last Inaugural Parade in which Iowa participated was during President Eisenhower's second term. At that time each of the Governors riding by the reviewing stand doffed their hats in a salute to the President as they passed the reviewing stand.

Governor Loveless, my predecessor, neglected to acknowledge President Eisenhower in this respectful manner, which made every Republican in Iowa very unhappy. I decided to correct this situation in the best way imaginable. As my car passed the reviewing stand, I stood and grandly doffed my hat to President Kennedy. Unfortunately, a TV commercial came on at just that moment with a pitch for bleach, so Iowans watching the parade missed the whole thing. I haven't purchased Purex since then.

An Academy For The Iowa National Guard

I had served with the Iowa National Guard since being back in Law School after the war. I first held the position of flying officer, and after Law School served as Judge Advocate General in the unit. The Guard had good training and excellent esprit de corps. Vacations for the family yielded to my two week National Guard summer training camp as long as I was involved. I thoroughly enjoyed the training and the experience of service in the Guard.

After the state election, my new duties with the Iowa National Guard were to help organize and establish the Iowa National Guard Military Academy at Camp Dodge. This was a two-year weekend and two week summer training course for selected Guardsmen. Upon completion of the program the cadets were commissioned as Second Lieutenants. It was generally modeled after West Point with strict rules and rigid training imposed by tactical officers.

Jackie and our daughters came out to watch a formation several times and at one such session the soldiers had to take off their helmets, put them on the ground in a straight line, and then step away from them. Kevi asked her mother whether the soldiers were really pushed so far into the ground that only their helmets showed. She was reassured that the tactical officers weren't really that mean to the soldiers.

I taught a number of classes at the Academy including Military

*Camp Dodge,
August 1960*

*Teaching at
Iowa Military
Academy,
August 1960*

Ready to take off

Law, Leadership and Military History. Teaching these fine young men, volunteers all, was a very fulfilling and rewarding experience and I enjoyed every minute of it.

My rank in the Guard was Lt. Colonel. On the weekends I reported to the Adjutant General of Iowa as my superior. Yet, during the week when I wore my Governor's hat, I was his boss. I was probably the only Governor in the country where this anomaly was true.

LIFE IN THE GOVERNOR'S MANSION

During 1961, the first winter in the Governor's residence, we had a very heavy snowstorm which took down power lines throughout the Central Iowa area, including those leading into the residence. We were using candles for two days. Traffic on the streets was difficult if not impossible, and no one was available to shovel out the lengthy driveway.

At that time the prison system located their trusties on a farm northwest of Des Moines at what is now the Living History Farm. I called the Assistant Warden at the prison farm and asked him to send a bus load of prisoners with shovels to dig us out. He was happy to do this and the prisoners were glad to get outside and have some exercise. They also appreciated the coffee and cookies that went with the completion of the job. To prevent future service interruptions, the power line into the residence was later replaced by one running underground.

On another weekend several weeks later, we were expecting relatives who were driving in from Minneapolis. Jackie left the front door unlocked. About midnight she heard the front door close and went down the steps in her pajamas to welcome them. She opened the vestibule door to see a complete stranger, a man about 40 years of age standing inside the vestibule. At the same time she got a whiff of whiskey. She looked at him and said, "What in the world are you doing here? If you don't want every cop on the west side of Des Moines crawling all over you, you will turn right around and get out of here!"

To her utter amazement he did just that. She quickly locked the door and went back upstairs to get me.

"There was a man downstairs trying to get in the front door."

I said, "Where is he now?"

"He turned around and walked down the sidewalk"

I said, "Then go back to bed."
"So much for my knight in shining armor."

Jackie did a wonderful job of entertaining the many guests and Iowans who wanted to tour the Governor's residence while in Des Moines. The first priority was the legislators and their wives for breakfast. Jackie, our single cook, and a kitchen helper started out at 4:30 in the morning to prepare the food. They served it to the legislators, all 150 of them. Then the State Officials, the Supreme Court Justices, and the Republican Party Officials, all of whom were served meals. We also entertained friends and supporters from Boone. It was a very busy schedule.

People came to the residence by the busload to visit and discovered that it was not designed to entertain such large groups. They went upstairs and checked-out the bedrooms, closets and chests, expecting to see satin sheets and treasures in the drawers. The house belonged to the State of Iowa and it was their right as voters and taxpayers to view their property.

All the while Jackie was carrying out this very sizable load of cooking, submitting to the invasion of family privacy, and raising our three daughters, I was over at the Statehouse trying to convince the Legislators that they should adopt programs for the betterment of the State of Iowa.

There was no free time in the Governor's Office. But in retrospect I can look back and say that the voters really didn't seem to care whether I was working hard or not. It sometimes felt like they just wanted a person in the Governor's chair to come to their dinner parties. We could have been out every night. The job was difficult on my marriage, I saw little of my family. Jackie did an outstanding job of spending time with our children while I was on the road or in the office.

I had no guards. My driver was a young Air Guardsman, Don King, who carried my meeting notes for speeches, and extracted me from conferences in the office when I was due for my next outside engagement. A very valued assistant in the office was John Lewis. He anticipated every need and handled matters with the greatest tact, skill and understanding.

Other outstanding staff members who made the internal business of the office function included, Jim Maggert, Executive Assistant,

Our introduction
to the Governor's
Mansion for
the first time
January 1961

Shampoos Cares Away

(Tenth of a Tribune Series)

By Lillian McLaughlin

BOONE, IA.—One day in September, 1942, the Kappa Alpha Theta housemother at the State University of Iowa rose at dinner to read this telegram from an six force captain, a former husband at the sorority house:

"Tell your little Theta girl Norm will be home the last week in September."

Jacqueline Doran of Boone, shock on the campus to assist with rush week activities, knew what that meant if none of the others did: The captain had pulled strings for her fiance to get a leave. And on that leave she was to be married.

The "little Theta girl" now is Mrs. Norman Erbe, 37, wife of the attorney general of Iowa.

The daughter of the late Lugi Doran, a former state senator, the granddaughter of an Iowa legislator and the great-granddaughter of a Wisconsin lawmaker, she has fitted easily into the public phase of her husband's career.

Her most partisan constituent, she says with a nod northward to Des Moines and its statehouse: "He's just exactly where he belongs. He's unbelievably happy."

In their comfortable two-story home on Story street here, Jackie Erbe looks back on her 17 year marriage, and even farther to when she and Norm were born. At opposite ends of Boone street.

Her Memories Are Affectionate and Gay

A candid woman with a gift of laughter, her memories are affectionate and gay.

Norm was her "first fellow," but until she went to Iowa State College, transferring her second year to the State University of Iowa, their dates were rare.

"Probably not more than five or six," she recalls. "My father was strict. But Norm would watch me at orchestra practice in high school. I played cello.

"After practice, he'd make a friend of his walk by my house with him every night—about a mile and a half. The friend finally rebelled, and forced him to get acquainted with me at school.

"I was a freshman and Norm was a junior with a letter on his chest. He couldn't have been more beautiful," Jackie Erbe said.

Norm was the son of the Rev. Otto Erbe, a Lutheran minister in Boone for 43 years before his retirement.

"To earn spending money Norm worked part time at a florist shop. Whenever there were parties, I'd have flowers."

As Wife of B-17 Pilot, Moved 23 Times

Norm went off to S. U. I. and on one occasion

Jackie's parents permitted her to go to Iowa City for a dance.

"It was exquisite agony," Mrs. Erbe recalls. "I wonder if my daughters will go through that, too."

Jackie followed Norm to S. U. I., and into pre-law. At the end of her junior year, World War II broke out, and Norm went into the air force. They were married in September, 1942, and Jackie, as the wife of a B-17 pilot, embarked on the most fantastic chapter of her married life.

"I made 23 moves during the war. We cleaned, white-washed, painted apartments from coast to coast.

"I worked at all sorts of jobs. In Washington state once, I worked in a canning factory, which supplied a Seattle orphanage with canned goods.

"One day Norm telephoned and said, 'I'm leaving in an hour. I'll see you in Florida.'

Husband Went Overseas

"I was 21, a small-town girl, who'd always been sheltered at home. I drove from Washington to Boone. A friend of my father's checked the car when I arrived and said, 'There isn't a single bearing in it!'"

At Buckroe Beach, Va., Jackie remembers going out on the beach with about 15 other wives to watch their husbands leave for overseas.

"The planes flew over the beach and dipped their wings. We'd read the numbers on the plane and knew which one was ours. Our girl collapsed, weeping. Her husband never came back. It was almost as if she'd known."

Whenever "things get bad," Jackie Erbe says, she always washes her hair.

On that lonely, fight-

ening day she washed her hair three times.

Returned To College

When he returned she joined him for another succession of moves, finally to Ft. Sheridan, Ill., "where Norm separated everyone else but himself."

"We lived at Ravinia, had a big victory garden. We planted five different kinds of corn, and just when everything was ready to eat, Norm got out of service. We had to leave that enormous garden."

They were married five years before their first daughter was born.

"We were impatient to have children. But now that I have three kids in hand, I'm delighted that we had those few wonderful years alone."

The two returned to S. U. I. Norm to obtain his law degree. Jackie to complete her undergraduate work.

"But I wanted to change my major. I went to Dr. Kirk Porter, head of the political science department. I told him I was married. I was going to have a baby; I wanted to study things that would help me make a home."

"Do you know, that old dear swung it. Oh, my, I had a wonderful year. I took child care, home budgeting, sculpture, plans, costume designing, if only

every girl could have just one year at college like that!"

Seven days before the Erbes' first daughter, De-Elda (DeDe, now 13), was born, her mother got her bachelor of arts degree.

"I had planned to get the degree in absentia. But my parents had looked forward for so long to the day they'd see me in cap and gown. My mother assured me no one could tell I was pregnant in the big loose robe."

"All friend of Norm's sat next to me, and all during the ceremonies he kept hissing, 'Not yet . . . not yet!' Afterwards I had my picture taken, and when I saw that photograph?"

Mrs. Erbe clasped her hand to her forehead and shut her eyes in horror.

In 1947, Erbe was graduated in law and began practice with Jackie's father in Boone. DeDe was followed by two little sisters, Jennifer, now 10, and Kevin, 6.

Active In Politics

As a Boone housewife, Jackie Erbe has entered into many activities. She belongs to the "chairs" of P. E. O., worked in her church (Episcopal) guild. She helped organize Boone County Hospital's Volunteer Hospital Auxiliary.

With her husband she has worked actively in politics, on precinct and county levels, in the Young Republicans, Republican Women's Council.

"At both feel strongly that active participation should be given by everyone at some time. It is hard sometimes to self people on this idea when you are Republican. They're apt to take you're just selling yourself."

In their home life, the Erbes are an outdoor family. They enjoy hosting the Indian relics "any place within driving distance."

This week Mrs. Erbe has mounted some of their most unusual finds on velvet, in framing them for handsome wallpapers. She is an amateur artist, at present is planning a mural in her dining room of oak or maple limbs and leaves.

"The paper you buy has Chinese trees, or others foreign to Iowa," she says. The Doran family owns a beautiful wooded area near Boone, 47 acres of native timber, and the Erbes often go there for picnics or target practice with hand traps.

They hunt for mushrooms ("I had no mushrooms, red haws at Yoder Dede mushrooming when she was a baby?"). They look for May apple blossoms, and leaves at "soon as they're edible."

Travel Family-Style

In their family are a collie dog, two cats, 22 goldfish, countless butterflies and "right now, even a toad."

If Jackie is painting posters for a community project, the little girls are given cardboard from the daddy's shirts as they can make posters, too.

"With the competition of television, you have to find things for youngsters to do, or they'll end up comatose," Mrs. Erbe says.

They travel family-style.

"If you take the kids along you don't have to worry about them, and Norm's so proud of the girls when they're all starched up and their hair curled," she says.

At a national meeting of attorney generals, Jackie went to Chicago with Erbe, and Grandmother Doran brought the children in by train at the end of the convention.

"We had a cocoon at home and had been writing and watching for the moth to emerge. First thing Kevin told me when we met them at the train in Chicago was that a Cecropia — a gorgeous gray and coral thing

—had emerged.

"The day after I'd left!"

Admits Life Has Changed

As the wife of Iowa's attorney general, Jackie Erbe admits her life has "changed appreciably."

Erbe commutes each day to his office in the State Capitol.

"The drive to Des Moines gives Norm time to go over business in his mind. Then, school here is only a block and a half away. And we love Boone. . . ."

She stepped over to the hearth to poke a log fire into flames. ("When I have a fire I want it to crackle so I know it's going.")

"You know we had a chance to get around so much the first years we were married, we got a clear look at the country. We couldn't wait to get back to Boone," she said.

"Even in the wintertime the very Iowa hills are beautiful," she said

An excellent cook, Mrs. Norman Erbe of Boone offers caramel cake in her attractive kitchen, which was designed by her husband, who is striving a second term as Iowa's attorney general.

Capital Sidelights

[Chicago Tribune Press Service]

WASHINGTON, March 12—In the latter days of the reign of Sherman Adams, President Eisenhower had become a political pariah, especially in the midwest. It is interesting to see how far he has come—to the point now where state candidates are following the time honored tradition of coming to Washington to get the Presidential blessing. Of course, the President can't take part in the primaries but he can perform the clasping of hands and say a quotable word or two to the hopefuls.

Mrs. Tankersley

Amidst the current procession the Red Skeltonish visage of the Iowa gubernatorial candidate, Norman Erbe cropped up this week. Erbe is Iowa's attorney general and is in what is rapidly boiling down to a two man race for the Republican nomination for governor. It turns out that Mamie Eisenhower's uncle is a fellow townsman of Erbe's in Boone, Ia., and that he set up Erbe's White House visit. It was refreshing to hear Erbe's dignified but definitely middle west "gee whiz" reaction of meeting the President and being in the White House. For instance, he was very interested in the organizational procedures of the White House. Here is a man who is going to borrow whatever he can ideas that might be useful to him in the executive mansion in Iowa.

Reports It Looks Like Good Republican Year

Of course, with Erbe being a state - wide candidate it was pretty hard to draw him out on national issues. He's for the federal method of reapportionment and something to do with the decennial vote on a constitutional convention and other complicated constitutency of Iowa must be pretty hep if these are the issues on which they choose their candidates.

Erbe brings the glad tidings to Republicans in Washington that it looks like a good year for Republicans in Iowa. He says that the opposition (which he refuses to name-call) will doubtless use Secretary of Agriculture Ezra Taft Benson as a whipping boy again but that it won't wash with the farmers this time. Mostly what encourages Erbe is the interest and attendance at Republican meetings and rallies. This is almost at the pitch it was in 1952. More people than had reservations showing up, not enough chairs to hold the crowds, and other similar happy problems have beset the committee workers.

Ike's Old Popularity Back, Erb Believes

Erbe attributes this to the President. He says President Eisenhower has shown such world leadership this past year that all his old popularity is back and some left over for Republicans in general.

The word around is that Erbe is the winner, first in the primary, which would be the toughest part of the fight. If he is, Iowans can look for economy of government. Erbe talks like a Hoover commission man about consolidation of departments, etc. And furthermore his family owns an Arabian horse.

* * *

From beleaguered Cuba comes a wonderful phrase, from the pen of a wonderful woman whose lands and properties are gone, whose husband will soon have to move her to the United States. She says that in adversity one learns of friendship and the values of one's children and that this is some compensation. And then she says that she now feels courage because she realizes "that the Lord squeezes but he does not choke."

BAZY McCORMICK TANKERSLEY

Mrs. Erbe-- Campaign To Win Friends

a R. Wake

By Judith Grimm

DES MOINES (UPI) — A handsome woman with a broad smile moved down the assembly line shaking hands and speaking personally to workers.

The wife of the governor of Iowa parrotted no Republican slogans nor handed out any campaign literature.

Mrs. Norman A. Erbe, better known as "Jackie", has traveled the width and breadth of the state during this election campaign, and the one two years ago, meeting groups or talking individually with people, including factory workers.

The avid campaigner, a blue-eyed brunette, said that when she visits a factory she does not ask a worker to vote for her husband or quiz him about his party affiliation."

"Seem Human"

"I want to make my family and husband seem as human as those of the worker. I want to make Norm seem as much a person as a coworker on the next machine." Jackie said.

"I want people to know from her children and that the governor's kids have to be helped at school once in awhile and his wife doesn't always fix the perfect dinner." she added.

"We want to be accepted or rejected for whatever we are." She said. "I want to make a voter decide—I don't want him to just take someone's word."

She said she is a "great believer in partisan politics" but realizes there are some voters who do not vote a straight party ticket.

"I feel it's my duty to influence people not voting on a strict party basis," the tall, friendly mother of three girls explained.

"I don't feel right staying home and keeping the home fires burning now that my girls are in school. I don't campaign for Norm just because he is my husband but because I feel he is eminently well qualified," she said.

Comfortable

In spite of her heavy campaign schedule, Mrs. Erbe said she is home every night "except about one pa month."

"Norm feels more comfortable if I'm home. It was getting to the place where someone else was raising the children," she said.

Mrs. Erbe, a gracious hostess, has opened the governor's mansion to any organized women's group in the state to show them "I'm just keeping house like I always have."

She said her children, DeElda, 15; Jennifer, 13; and Kevin, 9, are getting a great deal out of their lives as the governor's children and seem to be experiencing no particular problems.

"I feel the girls are gaining social poise, and their classmates treat them no differently in school than anyone else," Mrs. Erbe added.

"I bet I give out more cookies per minute after 3 p.m. than most mothers give out in a lifetime. Jennifer and three of her friends consumed three quarts of milk and four dozen cookies one night after school," she added.

Election Party

Mrs. Erbe said her oldest daughter "thinks she is old enough to entertain and has fixed up a room in the basement for an election night party."

When Mrs. Erbe is away from home, her personal visits with factory workers aren't her only way of campaigning. She also takes part in such activities as coffees, breakfasts and teas, many of which are sponsored by Republican women's groups.

A tireless campaigner, she greets one and all with a spontaneous warmth.

With genuine friendliness, she carries out her goal of making others feel "at home" with her family.

Christmas Card 1961. L to R: Jackie, Jennifer, Dede, Kevin, Norm.

Governor Erbe's Staff 1961. L to R: Alice Barr, Lt. Don King, Carol Terafren, Jim Maggert, DeLoma Hunt, Governor Erbe, John Lewis, Jackie Day, Lela Bertholf, Bob Hullihan, Russel Ross.

Russell Ross, a professor of Political Science at the State University of Iowa at Iowa City who was a classmate of mine at the University before the war, Jackie Day, my confidential secretary, Carol Terrifren, DeLoma Hunt, Lela Bertholf, Bob Hullihan and Alice Barr. This staff took care of all of the many duties of the office which also included the issuance of Notary Public Certificates for the state. All of them were dedicated and hard working.

The KRNT newsman, Russ Van Dyke, called one night and said that he had just received an anonymous call. A man was angry at the Governor and presently on his way out to the residence to kill me. This got the attention of the local police and Highway Patrol. An agent from the FBI sat in the kitchen and waited for his arrival. We went to bed. The caller never showed.

It was customary for the Governor to appoint his military staff, those in the political realm who had been significant in the campaign to elect him as the top political figure in the State. After taking office, I had prepared miniature Army Colonel insignias and presented these as well as a large certificate indicating the conferring of this honor.

Those people appointed Honorary Colonels were: Colonel Marjorie Edson, Storm Lake; Colonel Shirley Carson, Independence; Colonel James Flanagan, Boone; Colonel Stanley Redeker, Boone; Colonel H. P. Sandberg, Boone; Colonel Robert Fisher, Boone; Colonel John Oberhausen, Dubuque; Colonel Warren Dunkel, Sioux City; Colonel Charles Gee, Shenandoah; Colonel James Younggren, Keokuk; Colonel Robert Gamrath, Fairfield; Colonel Robert Day, Washington; Colonel Harry Slife, Cedar Falls; Colonel Robert Vernon, Cedar Rapids;

Colonel Daniel Whalen, Davenport; Colonel Arthur Jacobson, Waukon; Colonel Don Hogzett, Oakland; Colonel Sam Ozdoba, Orange City; Colonel Charles Hughes, Emmetsburg; Colonel E. A. Hicklin, Wapello; Colonel Richard Lindeberg, Ft Dodge; Colonel Edward Gann, Sigourney; Colonel G. A Hannum , Albia; Colonel Dwight Purcell, Jr, Hampton;. Colonel J. C. Moore, Winterset; Colonel Ivan Goddard, Muscatine.

BRINGING STATE GOVERNMENT INTO THE COMPUTER AGE

One of the first jobs I addressed was that of obtaining a Certified Public Accountant to serve in the position of State Comptroller. I was very fortunate to obtain the services of Marvin Selden, a CPA and a native of Cedar Rapids, who had been in the accounting profession for a number of years. The need was great. For too many years the financial affairs of the state had been managed on the basis of "this is the way we have always done it". When it came to the matter of budget for the state departments and asking of the State Legislature, the amounts used were the ones requested last year. We desperately needed financial information which was accurate, providing the basis for forecasting of the finances of the State.

Marv Selden was a very outstanding State Comptroller. We met often, most times after working-hours in my office with our feet up on the desk, considering innovative, desirable and achievable future plans for the State of Iowa. It was a very exciting and rewarding experience to share plans for the state with such a knowledgeable and efficient person.

IBM cards were used for the recording of information and the handling of these cards was by processing machines. The placing of the holes punched in the cards gave a rough outline of the information stored. The number of cards was in the millions and each state office would order their supply individually. We changed this practice, purchasing in volume and thereby reducing the cost to the taxpayer.

Marv Selden - OMB director for Iowa

Business institutions were just coming into the computer age. Adoption of the program meant dedication of a fairly large room, raising the floor level about 5 or 6 inches for the many electric cables, and finding room for the bulk of the machines themselves in the space allocated. What a relief it was to know, after their installation and use, that the figures we were getting were timely and accurate.

One of the major problems was that the placing of a new computer became a status symbol in the departments. Every administrator felt that he must have a computer if his department were to do its job properly. Marv Selden acted as the watchdog on this subject and did his usual high quality job. I look back at the goal of finally having the State of Iowa operating on a business like basis as one of the most important achievements of my tenure in the Office of Governor.

SELECTION OF JUDGES BY MERIT

Another change which I was able to effectuate while in office was that relating to selecting members of our Judiciary. It had been the custom, indeed the law, for all courts in the State, from Justice of the Peace to Supreme Court, to be "selected" by popular vote. This was a degrading situation to the Judiciary. As an attorney and member of the bar, I felt very strongly that judges should be removed from the thrust of partisan politics. This would eliminate their having to carry on political campaigns, a waste of time and effort of raising funds to secure the vote of the partisan electorate.

The Missouri Plan of selection of judges was unique among states in removing them from politics. Our legislature would not adopt the plan for our own state, yet I instituted it as a policy of my office as Governor. I followed it in making judicial selections for State judges from a list of nominees prepared by the organized bar. Three names of lawyers were submitted to me to fill a vacancy on the Iowa Supreme Court, from which I selected Bill Stuart of Chariton, Iowa, to be my appointment to the Court. He served with honor and distinction on the bench of the Iowa Supreme Court and was later appointed judge of the U.S. District Court. It worked and I am very proud that I gave it the push that it needed for later enactment into law.

ANAMOSA PRISON - MENTAL HEALTH

I visited all State mental and correctional institutions as part of my job. I began by inspecting the Men's Reformatory at Anamosa, shocked to find that they were operating an old fashioned and horrible "snake pit" under their roof. It was a typical Middle-Ages type of care, given to those prisoners who had a mental condition. In effect, it was no care at all. The prisoners were naked, sitting in their own excrement and completely ignored by prison officials.

When I asked who was giving them care, the response was that there was nothing that could be done for them. I asked about professional psychiatrists or psychologists. Their answer was that the budget wouldn't permit it.

Who was responsible for the operation of the reformatory at Anamosa? ...The Board of Control.

Who was responsible for the Mental Health Institute at Mt. Pleasant? ...The Board of Control.

Did Anamosa ever talk to the professional mental health people at Mt Pleasant? ...Well, no.

It was closer from Anamosa to Mt. Pleasant than from Anamosa to Des Moines. I suggested strongly they make an immediate request to the Board of Control for the services of a trained mental health person from Mt. Pleasant. I was disgusted. The old practice would not be allowed to resume and Iowa would never again permit this shameful neglect.

When I returned to Des Moines from the institutional visits, I contacted the Board of Control myself. I wanted to insure that professional mental health services were made available to every correctional institution in the State.

TOURISM AND IOWA MODEL

I made a distinct point in my inaugural address of the value of the tourist dollar and the need to increase spending to attract tourism to the State of Iowa. I pointed out that a simple way to attract travelers on the crossing interstate highways was to erect signs, extending a warm invitation to travelers to pause at certain "designated farms" just off the interstate. Offer them a cup of coffee or lemonade, and a short visit with the farmer, who would be happy to show them how an Iowa farm is operated. The Legislature failed to appreciate the potential of such good public relations. I appointed a Tourism Committee of Citizens with John Brockway as the chair. He did a wonderful job of promoting tourism to the people of Iowa.

Professor William Murray from Iowa State University, took the lead in establishing the Living History Farm on the interstate highway near Des Moines. They presently claim 150,000 visitors to the Farm each season. The Des Moines Visitors Bureau proclaims that of all the states in the visitor and tourist business, Iowa is unique with Living History Farms. The Iowa Sesquicentennial (150 years) bike ride across America did a similar job of inviting people to come to the state when we celebrated our Sesquicentennial in 1996.

While I was in office, the media was spending considerable time and effort to convince people that we were having a brain and people drain to other states. We were headed for mediocrity. Of course the Governor was given the lion's share of the blame for this supposed situation. Feeling the pressure, I initially had billboard sheets prepared for placement on roads heading West which read, *THERE IS NO CALIFORNIA.* But I soon cooled down and decided that the best way to keep people was to make our state a better place.

ATTENDING THE WORLD PREMIER OF "THE MUSIC MAN"

The Music Man movie was completed in 1961 and they were to have the first showing of the movie in Mason City, the storyline's location. Jackie and I were invited to the opening by Meredith Willson, author of the orginal music stage version and a native son of Mason City. Jackie and I looked forward to the hospitality of Mason City and the rubbing of elbows with movie stars and Meredith Willson. We joined the officialdom of Mason City for the fun. Arthur Godfrey was one of the special guests along with Shirley Jones, Robert Preston and Jack Cassiday.

Part of the social occasion was a party presented on the lawn of the MacNider Estate, located a short distance from the city limits of Mason City. General MacNider had been a one of the first commanders of the American Legion after World War I and a top officer of the Second Infantry Division, which bore the patch of the Indianhead insignia. He named his Mason City estate 'Indianhead' in honorable remembrance.

I wore this same patch when I first entered the army in July of 1941, while assigned to the division at Fort Sam Houston, Texas. The movie was a smashing success, and the original music is still being produced on stages around the country.

Cartoon - Summer 1961

GOVERNOR ERBE'S FIRST YEAR

After his first year as Iowa's chief Executive, Gov. Norman Erbe has issued a New Year's statement that "it was tougher than I expected."

There were some disappointments and some hopes. The Legislature enacted less of his program than he thought it should have. Filling of major offices was more difficult than expected. Other elective officials didn't go along with him on central purchasing. Even some appointive department heads were rigid against change.

He hopes for greater advances in 1962 on use of data processing machines and on the campaigns to promote industrial development and tourism in the state.

Almost every Iowa governor has found the office less powerful than it looked. Almost any of them could have made a similar statement about the disappointments he encountered. Few of them would have done so. They would have feared that it might be regarded as a confession of inadequacy or error. Yet most of them ran into the same difficulties.—the powers of the Legislature and the other state elective officials to say "No," the scarcity of able persons willing to take state jobs and the resistance to change.

Governor Erbe's statement is pleasing in its humility and frankness and it may auger well for his second year in the office that he is able to recognize the problems which arose during his first year. Iowans should also recognize the source of these problems. They may be removed by making some of the minor state offices appointive instead of elective and by giving the governor more authority over state departments. Being governor would be a happier experience if the governor had more cooperation and less competition.

(Des Moines Register-Tribune 1961)

GOVERNOR'S CONFERENCE

The annual Governors Conference was held in Honolulu that year of 1961. I planned to make it more interesting by taking a cruise ship over to the islands. It was the ship "Lurline" which was to provide us with 4 days of rest and relaxation.

Our family flew to the west coast in a C-47, also known as the DC-3 or Gooney Bird. The up-drafts were frequent and bumpy, so much so that Jackie became nauseous. By the time we reached New Mexico, she was REALLY air sick. She deplaned there and said she was not going to get back onto the plane; she had had enough. That was a real dilemma.

The pilot felt responsible, stating he would never fly her again, but he did. She was eventually persuaded to get back onto the plane and we flew on to San Francisco where we were to board our ship for a restful cruise to the Hawaiian Islands.

All of us had been looking forward to it and the old adage came into being, "If anything can go wrong, it will." The stevedores at the dock were on strike and no boat was moving. We proceeded to the airport and arrived in Hawaii three days early.

Governor Bill Quinn was most gracious at our early arrival and included us in several events which were in process prior to the start of the Governor's Conference program. One of them was an evening dinner with top military brass at the Governor's home in the mountains of Oahu. It was interesting to meet these personalities about whom I had read for some years. We were honored to be the recipients of a lei which was of green leaves, as distinguished from the flower lei. They were a special honor reserved for only the most honored guests.

Our daughters Dee, Jen, and Kevi learned to surf-ride the waves at Waikiki under the watchful eye of a champion surf rider. We also took a tourist ride around the island of Oahu, driven in a car with a Honolulu policeman Dan Sisson at the wheel. The time arrived for the rest of our staff, and Jackie's mother and her sister to arrive by plane. We went out to the airport and greeted them with a lei and a hug and a kiss.

The official program began with a Hawaiian luau and business meetings. There were visits to the Shark Research Station of the University of Hawaii, the Pearl Harbor sunken ship memorial, and the cemetery at the Punchbowl. We also enjoyed a ride to a nearby island with the Governor's family. Governor Quinn rode in a giant catamaran to where a wealthy oilman, Mr. William Paley, had a home and a wonderful spread of food and drinks waiting.

The conference was held in Royal Hawaiian Hotel with a grand square table. The State Governors were placed by protocol in the order of their admission to the Union. This meant that the Iowa Governor always sat next to the California Governor Edmund "Pat" Brown, which was a nice touch since he was supposedly attracting a great number of the citizens of our state. We adopted a series of resolutions concerning the conduct of our states as well as directions to the Federal Government on how to improve the operation of that entity.

172

Most of the resolutions were ignored by anyone who was in authority after they made their initial splash in the newspapers. This was normal. Also normal was the attention given by the national media to those members of the conference who were running for President in 1964. This was a good forum for politicians to grab headlines as well as a good travel assignment for members of the media.

The situation has not changed in the years since I attended Governors Conferences. The Governor attendee is the recipient of very nice gifts from the host Governor as representative of his state manufacturers. They are very nice occasions. Resolutions are soon forgotten after the one or more candidates for President have obtained their national headlines.

The following year, 1962, the Governor's Conference was held in Hershey, Pennsylvania. Since we were so near to Philadelphia, we took a day to drive to Independence Hall for the dedication of the restored building and hear President Kennedy give a speech. Following the conference I took advantage of our geography by driving our personal car up to the New England states and Boston with the family. When we arrived I very soon discovered that it would be impossible for me to drive to all of the historic places in that historic city since I didn't know how to do it and at the same time keep from getting lost.

I drove to the Statehouse and dropped in on John Volpe, the Governor with whom I had just been meeting at Hershey. I explained my problem and asked him to assign a trooper as a guide for the historic city. He did better than that. He gave me his limousine to take the entire family. But there was a trade-off. I had to give a speech to the legislature which was sitting at the time. I finally agreed, dressed in tourist clothing and with all the enthusiasm of an Iowa tourist. I made a number of remarks about Iowa which were received very graciously by the legislature of Massachusetts. Only then was it time for the tour with our trooper. He did a great job. We hit all the special spots of Boston and vicinity and really enjoyed this lesson in history. I flew back to Des Moines to go to work and the family drove the car home.

We had a major Republican Conference and fund raising gala in Des Moines. It was held at the KRNT theater where show business types from California and politicians delivered a combined show and speeches for the Iowa Republican Party. Pearl Bailey, Edgar Bergen and his dummy, Charlie McCarthy, Jackie Mason, the Andrew Sisters were the headliners, and they all entertained.

Nelson Rockefeller explains it.   *Welcome to Governor Rockefeller.*

Nelson Rockefeller, the Governor of New York, was running for the Republican nomination for President of the United States. I knew him rather well from our work together at Governor's conferences. He came early that day. He was known for his varied collections of Polynesian Art. One collection he claimed was owls. I took him to every antique area we had in Des Moines, looking for owl artwork or anything relating to it. It was a long day.

After the KRNT caper, we went to the Governor's residence with the special guests in tow. Jackie was wearing a mink stole. One of the Andrews sisters was wearing the most gorgeous mink coat that my wife had ever seen. Jackie suggested a trade. This sister said, "Not on your life!"

Pearl Bailey had a daughter named Dee, also. The girl was having a serious eye operation the following day and Pearl was worried. But she was the life of the party, a truly charming person in every way. We continued to maintain contact with her in later years. Meanwhile, Nelson Rockefeller was intent on charming party officials that were present. His aide spent the evening in the kitchen with the cook and servants, even though we invited him to come join us. Edgar Bergen was intent on nothing, standing in the corner of the living room and not saying a word.

THE GOVENOR'S RE-ELECTION.

The re-election campaign was a busy time for us. Bill Nicholas of Mason City, who was a primary candidate in the 1960 election, ran again for the Governor nomination and again was defeated in the primary. I won my fifth straight statewide victory carrying primaries and general elections from 1958, 1960 to 1962. But it was to be my last.

With Vice-President Nixon.

When prohibition was to be repealed by the U.S. Congress in 1933, the States scrambled about to determine a method to control the sale and distribution of this "new" threat to society—demon rum. In 1934, the Iowa Legislature was called into a special session to consider its own options.

The resulting laws read:

1. The State of Iowa was to be the sole vendor of alcoholic spirits. The State Liquor Commission would choose the brands permitted to be sold.
2. The approved liquor brands could be sold in state operated stores only.
3. Purchasers were required to have a liquor permit book in which all purchases were to be entered along with the date of purchase.
4. Liquor offerings were to be displayed on store walls on the "Bulletin Board," along with the price.
5. That alcohol was not to be consumed in a public place, including any public restaurant.

And penalties were provided for all violations.

Private clubs were exempt from being designated "public places." So called private clubs sprang up everywhere, a nominal fee charged for membership. One could buy his bottle at the State liquor stores, take it in a sack to his private club and spike his drink there, or leave his bottle there with his name on it and have it served to him by his waiter.

This was an irritation and bother for the entertainment and food services since the sale of mixed drinks was or could be a substantial part of their income if liquor-by-the-drink was permitted. It was a phony subterfuge of getting around the law by the "club" route and a slightly burdensome bother for one who wanted to carry his bottle in a sack and spike his own drink.

Columnist Donald Kaul writing in the Des Moines Register remembered the way liquor was handled by the state in one of his articles.

This was the drill. You'd walk into a state liquor store and the first thing you did was study the menu on the wall and fill out an order blank. Then you'd take the order blank to the cashier who would take your money AND record your purchases in your own personal liquor book, which you were required to carry around with you like a passport. THEN, you would take the receipt and hand it to a clerk who would go get your liquor and bring it to you. It generally took a half-hour, if there wasn't a crowd.

It was supposed to discourage the purchase of alcohol I think, but it didn't work. After all that, you really needed a drink.

It was a hot and burning issue. The drys in the state felt that liquor should be controlled and any relaxation of the law would result in a reversion to the tavern and speakeasy days.

The issue was proposed in the Republican State Convention and a plank emerged in the platform supporting the existing administration of the liquor laws. Since the only liquor sold in the state was that obtained from the list found on the board or in a sales list distributed by the liquor commission, it was obvious that the discretion of the commission to place a liquor brand on the board had a significant economic impact for the liquor industry supplier.

The addition of a label or brand to the board was influenced by the sales philosophy of the manufacturer. It brought about the concept of "samples" of the product, which were delivered to the commission in case lots at no charge. As a result, rumors arose that there was a sizable inventory of "samples" established and a "sample" room at the commission.

Frank Miller cartoon after election, November 1962.

I asked the Bureau of Criminal Investigation to investigate this and ascertain the donors and recipients of this largesse. Of course, no tracks were left of the transactions. No one knew where the stockpile had come from. The question remained: "What happened to the thousands of bottles of free liquor?" No answer was ever found but the pay-off practice was stopped.

FOURTEEN:
ON THE THE RE-ELECTION CAMPAIGN

During the campaign, liquor-by-the-drink was almost a non-issue until late in the campaign. The other party candidate promoted the repeal of the Iowa Liquor Control Act and we then had an issue that everyone could understand. He was a member of Alcoholic Anonymous and made no secret of it. I personally felt we should repeal the Act and could probably be called a "wet." But since our Republican platform dictated no repeal and the drys had supported me in the last election, I felt that I could not in good conscience turn my back on them nor on the people who the Governorship represented. I stated that if the legislature passed a liquor-by-the-drink law, I would sign it. This was not enough and we had a single issue campaign.

ERBE FAVORS LIQUOR STUDY, (REG.TRIBUNE)

Gov. Norman Erbe said Friday he favors thorough discussion by the 1963 Legislature of the state law prohibiting sale of liquor by the drink.

The governor was asked at a news conference for his opinion on a plank in the Republican state platform calling for a re-examination of the law.

Previously, Erbe said he had seen "no concerted agitation among the people" for legalizing the sale of liquor by the drink. He said Friday his personal views had not changed.

"The platform calls for a reappraisal of the law and I will do everything I can to help," Erbe added.

Erbe said the liquor issue was not discussed at a closed conference here Thursday with legislative candidates and holdover senators.

The meeting was mainly a "get acquainted session," he said. Chairmen of legislative committees studying property tax relief, state aid to schools and taxes submitted progress reports, Erbe added.

The popular vote did not reflect the landslide predictions for Erbe in the polls. Hughes 430,899 - Erbe 338,955. It was a difference of 96,944, or 41 votes per precinct, the closest plurality until 1970 when

Robert Ray was re-elected over his opponent.

I was devastated at the results of the election. My principal pain was that I had failed to measure up to the confidence and hard work which all of my supporters had invested in me. I had failed them. The night after the election, the only friend who called in person was Herb Plambeck. He came to the house and expressed his sorrow at the election result. I will never forget his kindness.

This was a marked contrast with the hundreds of political people whom I thought I had known as "friends" over the last six years in State Politics.

I became very embittered at the political State of Iowa. I had, without a tax increase, lottery, horse races or riverboat gambling:

1. Provided a $20 million increase for buildings at State colleges and universities.
2. Increased State aid to schools by 25%
3. Maintained an anticipated $118 million surplus in the state treasury.
4. Set up procedures to collect unpaid taxes to increase state income, an estimated $4 million per year.
5. Increased emphasis on industrial development, economy and efficiency in state government.
6. Created Iowa's first tourism program.
7. Started a continuing program for removal of curbs from Iowa Highways as a lifesaving measure.
8. Increased funds for urban streets and roads by 62%
9. Increased agricultural land tax credits.
10. Passed the first legislative reapportionment bill in 57 years.

The post election period was one of trauma and disappointment. The most common comment was—"Oh, he won't have any trouble finding a position." I really thought that was true.

Before I left office, a man asked to see me one day. He asked for my help to get a certain brand of whiskey on the board at the Iowa Liquor Commission, and since I was leaving office he would make it "right" for me. I was so outraged at the suggestion I threw him out of my office.

It was impossible for me to return to the practice of law in Boone. And I expected that there was an opportunity just around the corner which would arrive at any day. The family did not want to leave Iowa and I thought that my talents could best be utilized by staying in the state.

After a several month hiatus, I decided to join Investors Diversified Services as an investment adviser. It wasn't long and l found that I was personally unsuited for that role and resigned. Then another search of possibilities. I was over-qualified for about everything and no offer of a position. Eventually Diamond Laboratories, an animal health production company in Des Moines retained me as their in-house Legal Counsel.

All the time my children were going into college. It did cost a farm—my undivided interest in two farms in Boone County that had been inherited from my parents.

For a while I had served as executive Vice-President of the American Chiropractic Association which had its national headquarters in Des Moines. Then after a daily search of the Wall Street Journal, I discovered an ad for Executive Vice-President of a health related organization. I answered the Ad and the response was for me to come to Chicago and interview.

The position was Executive-Vice President of the National Paraplegia Foundation stationed in Chicago. The interviewers consisted of two paraplegics, one a lawyer in active practice in the Loop, and the other a wealthy easterner. The third interviewer was a gentleman by the name of Ted Spiegel of the catalog family of Chicago who had no disability.

The job was to raise money for research and increase public awareness of the problems in the field of spinal chord injuries. The office was in the center of the Loop on Michigan Avenue and the Chicago River. The staff consisted of a badly crippled woman who had polio, and a veteran of World War II who had sustained a spinal cord injury and had spent his life in a wheel chair since that time.

We were concerned with barriers, research being done by neurologists, and raising money. My office was on the 17th floor. I commuted to the Loop every day by train since my office overlooked Michigan Avenue. I had a ringside seat for the riots in the streets of Chicago during the 1968 Democratic National Convention, the sideshow which allowed Mayor Daley to provide such a negative

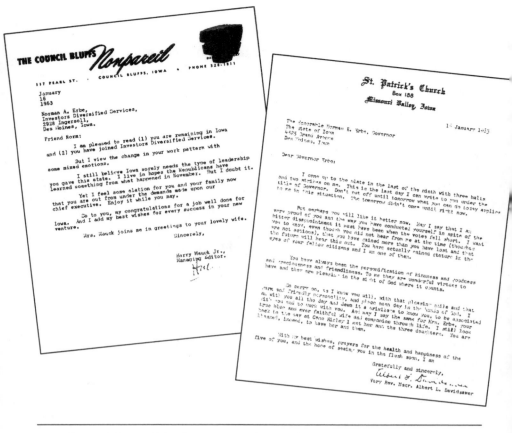

reaction to the political process of America.

The move to Chicago had been traumatic for the family. Kevi was a junior in high school and all of her friends were in Des Moines. She wished to stay in Des Moines to complete her high school education but that wouldn't work at all. There was gloom and doom in the Erbe family. When I got off the commuter train at Arlington Heights in the evenings, my first question would be, "How is Kevi?" The situation became so troublesome that Kevi went to the high school principal and they graduated her a year early so she could move back to Des Moines. We found her an apartment in Des Moines for the summer. Dee was in college at Iowa State and Jennifer at Boston University. Kevi remained the single most traumatic event for us besides losing the election. Later she attended Beloit College and was a University presidential student leader during the riots at the University of Iowa.

I had expected when coming on board that the people who had interviewed me would be the core of my fund raising effort. They were acquainted with the philanthropists in the Chicago and national

With Erbe's Going Iowa Loses A Good Governor

In a few days Iowa Governor Norman Erbe will hand over the mantle of his office and step out of public life.

We think Governor Erbe is a fine gentleman and that he has made this state an excellent governor. Proof of the first has been most evident in his conduct during the "lame duck" days of his term. He has extended every possible courtesy to his elected successor Harold Hughes. Moreover Republican Erbe has passed up a number of opportunities to take political advantages of Democrat Hughes.

The real measure of Erbe's ability as governor has been largely nullified by his party's failure to reelect him to office. He was a forward looking executive who had inaugurated a well thought out plan for bringing a much greater measure of businesslike administration to this state than it has formerly enjoyed.

Such a plan cannot be conceived, inaugurated and carried to fulfilment in one short, two-year term. Many, if not all, of the goals Erbe had in view will be lost with his going. This is most unfortunate and we suspect that many Iowa Republicans, party leaders and voters alike, who failed to support their candidate for governor at the last election will have cause for some sober reflections, many of them unpleasant, in the months ahead.

Unfortunately the disciples of the divided allegiance philosophy which has permeated the Republican party in Iowa for some time and which contributed directly to Erbe's defeat, seem to have learned nothing from this object lesson.

The recent decision by Republican legislative leaders to go their own way and play the upcoming legislative program "by ear" is indicative of this failure. In making their decision these leaders chose to ignore an earlier plea by Republican State Central Committee chairman, George Nagle.

Nagle had suggested that the elected legislators would do well to give some consideration to proposals advanced by the people responsible for their election, namely the central committee, district committee people, county chairmen and their organizations, in hammering out a legislative program.

One of these days all segments of the Republican party in Iowa will wake up to the fact that they no longer have "sheer weight of numbers" going for them in this state. With that realization, it is to be hoped, will come the companion truth that, unless they find a common ground on which to hang together they are going to do a very workmanlike job of hanging themselves and their party separately.

Gov. Erbe was a statesman

By
Dan
Bied

The Des Moines County News
West Burlington, Ia. 10-1-81

Until a few weeks ago I had nearly forgotten about a man named Norman Erbe, a likeable politician who served a 2-year term as Iowa governor in the early 1960s.

But, thanks to a "People" feature by Gene Raffensperger in The Des Moines Register, I learned that Erbe is both alive and well and, nearly as important, back in his hometown—Boone, Iowa—where he's known as "Governor Erbe" or, more to his liking, "Norm."

I met Norman Erbe on a flying trip to Fort Sill and Fort Leonard Wood nearly 20 years ago when, in his role as Iowa's governor, he visited with Army Reservists who had been called to active duty in the wake of the Cuban missile crisis. Some of the inductees felt they'd gotten "the shaft" and Erbe, an Air Force vet with combat decorations, went to see them first-hand to allow them a chance to "sound off."

Along with a dozen or more Iowa reporters and photographers, I accompanied Erbe to Oklahoma and Missouri where, in fact, the GI's "beefs" were few and far between.

Erbe felt he had been misquoted in a Register article which, he maintained, made his attitude toward the reservists more callous than it actually was. This was a main reason for his trip, in sub-zero weather, which resulted in reinforcement of his contention that the reservists had not been called-up without justification.

Erbe proved to be a personable, approachable gent and took time out from a card game on his Air National Guard plane to talk to me about circumstance in which the reservists found themselves. We also talked a bit about the

'liquor by the drink' issue in his re-election campaign, and I told him I would try to clarify his attitude toward the reservists in my articles for The Burlington Hawk Eye.

On arrival at Fort Sill, Erbe received the customary cannon salute. I was standing next to him at the time and recall his slight grin when I remarked, in jest, that "I didn't know they gave newspaper people a 19-gun salute."

That night, in the service club, Erbe got a measure of revenge by introducing me as "military editor" of The Hawk Eye which, actually, was the smallest newspaper represented in Erbe's entourage.

After the trip I sent a copy of my articles to Erbe and was impressed to receive a warm hand-written "thank you" for quoting his comments on the reservist flap as accurately as I could.

Erbe left Iowa for several years and, as mentioned, I had lost track of his whereabouts.

Today, Raffensperger noted, Erbe is out of politics while Harold Hughes, who was elected in 1962 because (in Erbe's opinion) the Governor "refused to endorse liquor by the drink," is pondering a return to the political trenches.

It was interesting, in reading the article about Erbe, to recall that the 1962 election was pretty much a "single issue" sort of campaign in which, looking back on it, Erbe underestimated the issue's impact.

It's also interesting to note that Hughes, the winner, was a reformed alcoholic ... and that Erbe, a social drinker, was actually opposed to Iowa's "crazy liquor laws."

And, by way of additional reflection, it is interesting to ponder the fact that single-issue political campaigns are not a recent, exclusive entity devised by the Moral Majority or other partisans in the political right-wing.

"People probably won't even remember my name now," Norman Erbe was quoted as saying in Gene Raffensperger's feature story.

I remember him, if no one else does, and appreciate the integrity which, though he thinks it cost him re-election, forced Erbe to focus on issues (including fiscal responsibility) he considered more important (if less emotional) to Iowans than "liquor by the drink."

Norman Erbe was the sort of public servant my father had in mind when he used to say "we need more statesmen and fewer politicians" in local, state and national government.

FOR MORE than a decade the United States has not maintained a balance in its economic, political and military commitments.

This is the gist of an essay by foreign affairs analyst James Chace who, a review in The Los Angeles Times points out, fears we are "well on the way to national bankruptcy" by proposing billions for exotic weaponry gadgets

that, in the long run, may do us more harm than good.

"Our need," Chace wrote, "is not for huge, more complex weapons systems. but first to strengthen conventional arms and forces with a simpler weapons.

"Until we get our economic house in order," Chace (managing editor of Foreign Affairs) adds, "we could rearm ourselves to the teeth and still be weak ... if we remain (economically) insolvent, how can we have a foreign policy at all?"

HERE IS food for thought, gleaned from my insider's newsletter, in regard to social security retirement benefits:

"A person who retires at 65 this year and who has paid the maximum tax each year (1937 through 1981) has contributed a total of about $14,800.

"His benefits of $753 a month will return every dime he ever paid in within 20 months. And if he lives to 79, his current life expectancy, he will collect $126,500—not counting cost-of-living boosts."

UNCONFIRMED rumors: the Jimtown Hilton may add a bridle path, heliport and indoor pool with cabanas at Waters Park ... Dick Fry, our retired postmaster, is partial to UPS ... Charlie Rukgaber, the IAAP pipefitter, may be enticed to endorse the health food store at Westland Mall ... several mall clerks were mistaken for statues during the recent display of sculpture works ... and the Woolco store, seeking to upgrade its "5 and dime" image, may add a fur salon, a cocktail lounge and a line of do-it-yourself oil filters for Rolls Royces.

arena. Unfortunately, this was not true. My compassion and interest in the spinal cord injured was at a very high level but the withdrawal of the 'heavy hitters' of fund raising made my work very difficult, if not impossible. This impaired my efforts to the extent that I eventually felt that I should submit my resignation to the officers, stating that they just couldn't afford me in their staff organization.

Campaigning at the Sydney, Iowa, Rodeo in September, 1961. Pictured here with daughters DeElda, Kevin and Jennifer.

FIFTEEN: BACK IN FEDERAL SERVICE: ALASKA, IDAHO, OREGON, AND WASHINGTON

After a number of months, Governor John Volpe, who had been named Secretary of Transportation, asked me to take a look at a new program as Regional Representative of the Secretary of Transportation in the Federal Regional Council structure in Seattle, Washington. I was to represent him and the agencies in the Department of Transportation before state and local government groups, accelerating the delivery of grant programs, coordinating the cooperation of our varied agencies and helping field elements work together more smoothly. It looked like an exciting and interesting challenge and I was glad to do this pilot program.

The Department of Transportation was different from other major federal agencies. Each of the departments within Transportation had their own regional director. These included the Federal Highway Administration, Federal Railway Administration, Urban Mass Transit Administration, Federal Aviation Administration, National Highway Traffic Safety Administration, U.S. Coast Guard, and St. Lawrence Seaway Administration. The Regional Directors of these departments were very apprehensive that I was going to try to take over their jobs, working as a spy for the Secretary, and would start swinging my weight around in their shop.

Of course this was not true and I reassured them at every opportunity. I was there to help, not to hinder. My regional states were Oregon, Idaho, Washington and Alaska. During the two years I was located there I was able to get to know these States, their Governors, and Mayors and their problems with the Federal Government very well.

As a member of the Federal Regional Council, my role as Regional Representative of the Secretary of Transportation consisted of attending weekly meetings of the Regional Directors of the Departments of HEW, HUD, Dept. of Labor and the Office of Equal Opportunity. The goal was to coordinate information and grant programs for the cities and states.

When I first arrived at Seattle I officed with the Coast Guard. My typing assistant was a young corpsman from the U.S. Coast Guard who was formerly a school teacher. On one of my regular monthly trips to Washington D.C., Frank Turner, who was the director of the Federal Highway Administration, mentioned to me that his Northwest Regional Director was going to hold public hearings on the location and design of an extension of Interstate 90 that was to be routed into the business district of Seattle. The route was very controversial. It crossed Lake Washington to pass through Mount Baker which had a large black community. The public hearings were to be held at Seattle Center, an auditorium on the grounds of the former World Fair.

The Federal Highway Administrator asked me to attend. The group was very emotional. They used the microphone and utilized every advantage to make their point of opposition. Predictions were made that blood would run in the streets and that it would be looked upon as a purposeful effort by the federal establishment to get rid of the housing of the black community. The three night hearing ran into seven nights of hearings. I was surprised at the participation of University of Washington students in the hearing process, although I probably shouldn't have been since those were the days of campus activists.

The power structure in Seattle, as in every city that size, consisted of about ten professional business and community leaders who made things work in an understated and anonymous manner. I knew this and was acquainted with the full-time director of the group. I sensed the antagonism which surfaced at the hearings and decided to have a chat with the Director. I called him and asked for a breakfast appointment. We met and I described to him the great level of hostility I saw at the hearings. I told him of my fear that something might erupt which could be avoided if certain things were done to alleviate the situation. I suggested the movers and shakers consult with some of the ethnic leadership in the community in a very quiet and unobtrusive way. This should not be in a publicity minded atmosphere, but rather in a very behind the scenes way in which a rapport was built with them. This was done and conflict in Seattle was avoided.

The Seattle offices of the regional council were in a renovated department store building. One of the most interesting and challenging states in our portfolio was Alaska. In a sense, Alaska was the "new kid on the block," having just recently been converted from a U.S. Territory to a State of the Union.

186

Major federal programs and money had been going into the Territory of Alaska since it was purchased from Russia and now was used to assist the economy and social problems for the State as distinguished from the territorial existence. Different rules applied. Construction of the pipeline had not yet begun but the pipe for the oil line was stacked all along the proposed route from Prudhoe Bay in the Arctic to its terminal south of Anchorage.

Environmental hearings were held and scientists consulted. They testified to the effect the hot crude oil in the line would have on the permafrost, caribou and the environment. Leaks of the oil line were predicted from earthquakes and other causes. After all the trauma predicted in these hearings, it has turned out to be a very good solution to the transportation problem.

The Bureau of Indian Affairs (BIA) in the Interior Department pretty well directed the social system of the state through their policy manuals. They had been doing this since Alaska was purchased from Russia. One of the results was that Eskimo and Native Indian children reaching high school level were sent to live-in schools in the lower 48 states and taught by professional teachers. One of these schools was a BIA institution in Oregon and the children were kept there until graduation. The BIA claimed that the experience in special schools was good for them since they would be able to ride on trains, see the big cities like San Francisco and Seattle, and learn a lot.

I totally disagreed with this conclusion. In my view this would almost insure that once the child had finished high school, there was almost no way he would return to his family and be satisfied with their way of living. Granted there is a fine train in Alaska which runs from Anchorage to Fairbanks, but that is used for cargo and a few passengers. The experiences of students in our lower 48 states is hardly to be replicated in the vast expanse of virgin country in the Alaskan wilderness.

An example of the psychology of the Federal officials who had been running Alaska for years was a so called "summit" meeting which was held while I was stationed in Seattle. The meeting was in Anchorage and included all the top officials of the Federal Government who had a stake in the decision process in Alaska.

We of the Federal Regional Council of Seattle were present. It was a day of lively discussion and the basis for better understanding of our mutual problems. During the course of the meeting I queried the absence of Eskimos and native Alaskans and Indians in the room. My inquiry "why they were not present" produced a strange quiet. Here we were in a discussion concerning the future of the Native population and they didn't have a chance to hear or speak.

Later in the afternoon over cocktails, I asked the Commissioner of Education why they had not been present. The answer was that they had not been invited. I asked why not and his response was, "They just aren't smart." I almost kicked him in the shins.

The Department of Housing and Urban Development in the previous administration had decided that it would be nice if Congress would authorize decent housing for the Eskimos. A good place for this would be an inlet from the sea on the west coast at Bethel, Alaska. A long deep ditch would be dug there from the sea to accommodate the fishing boats that came into the community from the sea and their houses could be built right there on the deepened inlet, referred to as the Venice of the North.

They must have gotten the idea from Peter the Great of Russia who built St. Petersburg. They proceeded with the work, building about 20 or more cottages with the most modern furnishings and layouts from the lower 48. One of the many problems was that the Natives really did not know how to use some of the modern equipment. They thought that toilets were to be used as washbowls for their feet. They did not like the double-bed arrangements which were not their sleeping style. They were used to the floor.

The kitchen cupboard and sink arrangements were not their custom. HUD had to devise a way to teach them through classes on how to live in a lower 48 house. This was insulting to them — how to live in a house. The sewer system was impossible because the pipe had to be insulated as they ran through the perma frost. The land was frozen for a good ways down. In their existing homes, the Eskimos kept a square wash tub at the door to store blubber from the walrus hunts. As they went by the tub they would knife off a hunk and eat the blubber. This was a very important part of their diet and an indication of the lack of understanding by HUD officials of Eskimo life.

HUD sold the houses to the Eskimos at a ridiculously low price base with a payoff over a long period of time. The Eskimos in turn sold the houses to people from the lower 48 at a greatly increased price. What a federal debacle.

One day in the fall of 1972 during the normal course of business, I entertained a young man on the planning staff of the State of Alaska at lunch in Seattle. We then went to my office and had a very productive conference during the afternoon. It was concluded about 5:30 p.m. and I walked the several blocks to the parking garage. Seattle had just gone off daylight savings time and it was dusk. My car was on an upper floor in the parking garage. The elevator had a wooden gate which must be raised before getting on. It was dark inside the elevator shaft. I lifted the gate up and walked into space. The door safety guard was not working and the elevator was absent. I fell straight down the elevator shaft and landed with all 235 pounds on my left heel and elbow.

It was a 15 foot drop. I remembered my experience with the National Paraplegia Foundation and checked if my spinal cord was involved. I tried to wiggle my toes and they moved. Thank God. I was in excruciating pain in my foot, leg, elbow, and from muscle spasms in my back. I yelled, "Help-Help!"

After a while a man came down the dark steps and asked if someone was down there. I responded with a "yes." He then asked how I had gotten down there. I said I had fallen down the elevator shaft. He asked what he should do. I suggested that he go to an adjacent building for a guard who had a flashlight. "Good idea," and off he went. They came back together and the person with the flashlight shined it in my face. He asked how I had gotten down there. Then the same question, what do we do now? I suggested that they call the police. "Good idea."

He left and gave the flashlight to his friend who kept it on my face while the other man was gone. Soon, but not soon enough, a police car arrived with spotlights. Same question. "How did you get down there?" Same answer. All the time the pain was getting more intense. Same question, "What should we do now?"

I groaned that they should call the fire station down on Elliot Avenue since they have ladders. "Good idea." The firemen arrived and asked the same questions. They put their ladders down in the hole along with a wire body-basket. Before they did that, one of my audience suggested that he should go up and bring the car elevator down. I vetoed that suggestion. I was relatively safe down there with the whiskey bottles and trash.

Meanwhile, two firemen had brought down the basket and were ready to load me into the basket. I cautioned them that I might have a spinal injury and to be careful handling me. This cautionary word made no impression at all on my handlers. They put me in the basket and lifted me up to the top edge of the hole, all the time complaining of how heavy I was. When they set me down in the alleyway they said, "What do we do now?"

I suggested that a trip to a hospital would be good.

"Which one? Are you in the Military?"

"Yes, I am a retired Colonel in the Army."

"Do you work for the Government?"

"Yes, I'm the Regional Representative of the Secretary of Transportation."

"I guess we had better call an ambulance."

The ambulance arrived with two attendants. Same question, "How did you get down there?" Same answer. They decided we should go to the Veterans Hospital and placed me in the back with an attendant. On the way to the hospital my thoughts were focused on what kind of care I was about to receive. To beat the odds on good care, I mentioned that I was formerly the Governor of Iowa.

This got the attention of my attendant. He was really impressed. He asked me what it was like to be Governor of Iowa and a number of other questions which had little to do with my problems. At hospital admissions, I asked them to call Jackie's brother, Dr. John Doran, in Ames, Iowa, because he was most likely to converse and understand medical terms since he was a practicing physician.

They filled out the admission papers on a clip board and asked me to sign it. Of course the GI ball point pen wouldn't work with the clip board upside down, so they tried with another pen which wouldn't work either. They waived the signature and sent me up to X-ray.

I was fully clothed in a suit and tie, except for my left shoe which had been taken off in the ambulance. A pretty young nurse came in the X-ray room. She told me to remove all clothes and put on the gown which she handed to me. I was still in extreme pain in my back, arm, left foot and leg, which was beginning to swell up like a balloon. The pain was such that I didn't think it would be possible to accomplish this without help, but I did so anyway. That done, the nurse came back in and proceeded to take the necessary X-rays.

Then to a hospital room and some sedation for the pain. I asked if I could get a bed for Jackie in a nearby room and that elicited a flat NO. I said that President Eisenhower had a nearby room for Mamie when he was in the hospital. That didn't move them at all, even though Jackie had arrived on a plane from Chicago soon after the accident.

The next day the doctor, an orthopedic surgeon-professor from Washington University Medical School came in with his students. I asked him when they were going to operate and he responded that they don't operate on a crushed heel. They just wrap the foot, heel and leg with an Ace bandage. The foot had, by this time, reacted to the trauma by producing very large (6 inch by 3 inch) blood-blisters across the instep and around the back of the heel. The doctor said that this was sometimes seen in agricultural areas when the farmers fall down a silo.

After a stay in the hospital and recuperating, first at Seattle and then in Arlington Heights, I was able to go back to work, first with crutches and then with a cane. While living in Seattle I had looked around the city for a place to live. My Coast Guard compadres asked if I was a retired reserve officer and of course I thought this could be a solution to my housing problem. I went out to Fort Lawton, an Army post north of the business district overlooking Puget Sound. Inquiry disclosed that I could indeed have quarters in the Bachelor Officer Quarters. For $60 per month, my bachelor pad consisted of a living room, bedroom and bath, with linen and maid service. I had the freedom of the post meaning that I could eat in the mess, use the library, the Post Exchange and other facilities.

This was ideal for me and at a reasonable price. The maid service for the room was not exactly the best but I could put up with that. Before my accident the post changed the person who did the maid service and the new one, whoever she was, was very good. I felt that this should be recognized so I wrote a note to the Post Commander advising him of the excellent work which was being done by the new maid.

Alas, I did not know there was a different Post Commander on

Board who was unaware of my presence at Fort Lawton. While in the hospital I received a letter from the new Commander that I would have to move out of my quarters within thirty days. That got my attention real quick. I was still recuperating from the fall and still on crutches.

I expected to be transferred to the Chicago post from Seattle within a short while so that could be a solution to my problem. I picked a good day to call on the new post Commander and found his office to be on the second floor of a World War I barracks building. I hoped that this long string of steps leading up to his office would instill in him a bit of sympathy for my condition of being on crutches and change his decision. My optimism rose as I walked into his office and noted that he was wearing the Second Infantry Division Indianhead Patch on the shoulder of his uniform.

We reminisced for several minutes about the Division. We were brothers-in-arms from the same outfit and then got down to business about my problem, or rather his problem. He said that he didn't know that I was on the post until he had received my letter. He then started research of Army Regulations to see if I could legally stay on the post. He found nothing and sent his aide to Fort Lewis to use their library where he also found nothing. So he checked with the Department of Defense and, bingo, he found something that said I couldn't be there.

I just about told him he shouldn't have tried so hard. In the end, I stayed there as long as was necessary to transfer to Chicago.

Before leaving Seattle, I made one last trip to Alaska. The General Manager of the Alaskan Railroad asked me if I would like to take the train from Anchorage to Fairbanks, Alaska. The Railroad was owned by the U.S. Government through the Department of Transportation. He said to be at the Railroad Station at 7:30 a.m. for one of their regular trips with cargo and passengers up to Fairbanks.

They attached the observation car onto the end of the ten car train and we were off. The Alaskan Railroad is also known as the "Moose Gooser" since in the winter time the moose like to get on the railroad right-of-way because it is easier walking through the snow. The engine then has to goose the moose along with the front of the engine to persuade them to get out of the way. This was sometimes not successful.

There was available in the Alaskan jewelry stores a pendant for a charm bracelet which depicts an old fashioned railroad engine goosing a protesting moose. This is in gold and a welcome trinket to epitomize Alaska. I purchased one to take home to Jackie since she also had the privilege of riding on that trip to Fairbanks. The train stopped at cabins along the route when the occupants wanted the train to pick up baggage or people.

It was a wonderful ride through the wilds of Alaska. We frequently sighted wild animals. The General Manager asked if I had ever "driven" a train and I replied in the negative. He then said the magic words, "Would you like to?" He stopped the train and we walked together to the diesel engine and climbed aboard. He asked the engineer to give me his seat. The engineer showed me what to do and how to do it and we were off.

What an experience to handle the power in those diesel engines. It was not too different from how it felt when running up a B-17's four engines to full throttle in preparation to take off on a mission with full fuel and bomb load. Both machines similarly shivered and shook with power until they got underway. I drove the train for about a half-hour and enjoyed every minute of it. It was a happier trip on the train than it had been on the B-17. There were no flak or fighters and the two railroad rails to keep me on the path.

Fairbanks, Alaska, is a fine city nestled in the prairie area of Central Alaska. The temperature in the summer was not unlike that of Iowa. It is located on the Tanana River a number of miles from its junction with the Yukon River, the principal river of Alaska. It is the home of the University of Alaska.

Of special interest to me was that it was also the home of a herd of musk oxen, a strange and unusual breed of animal. We enjoyed seeing them. We then boarded the DC 3 FAA aircraft for the trip to the Arctic Ocean. On the way we stopped at an Eskimo village which was located on the caribou migration path as they went through the pass in the Brooks mountain range every spring and fall. The village was located at Anaktuvik Pass in the mountain range.

When we landed, the native men came running out to the plane for the mail and other supplies and their wives and children came also. A mist had developed so we stood under the wings of the plane and visited with them.

It was time to take off so we flew on our way to Prudhoe Bay on the Arctic Ocean. The oil exploration process was well underway to the extent that a small refinery was set up to provide gasoline and fuel for the operation there. This saved the expense and time which would have been needed to ship the fuel up from the lower 48 states.

Nearby Prudhoe Bay was the Naval Arctic Research Station which conducts research on Arctic animals. The animals included wolves, polar bear and wolverines as well as others. Some of the research on polar bears involved putting a radio collar on the polar bears and then releasing them so their path could be tracked by radio signal to a satellite which would then send the signal down to a receiver at Baltimore. Their wolf research consisted in part in studying the behavior of the wolves in packs. Although I am aware that this information was valuable to someone, I'm not sure of its relationship to the operation of the U.S. Navy. We also saw the 10 year old daughter of the manager leading a wolverine on a leash—that seemed a bit dangerous!

We then flew to the airport at Barrow, Alaska. As we taxied up to the operations office and terminal which was a tin shed, we saw the front portion of a caribou that someone had shot. It was lying on the ground, dressed out for the butcher or his customer. We went to our hotel to get settled for the night. The hotel consisted of a frame house with about seven bedrooms, each with an iron army cot. The keys to the rooms hung on a keyboard at the entrance to the house. Prospective roomers simply walked in and picked up their key. Shortly before midnight, sunset came.

The water heater for the showers and shaving was more limited than we expected. Jackie arose early to take a shower and apparently stayed in too long, depleting the entire supply of hot water. None of us knew of this limitation at the time and the men had to shave with cold water.

Then to the cafe at a nearby building where we had breakfast. The owner of the cafe was present. He was one of those who went out to Wainwright, Alaska, on August 15, 1953, after Will Rogers and Wiley Post, his navigator, left and subsequently crashed, killing them both. It was from there that this news was radioed to the world. They had announced that they were to undertake a flying trip around the world. They only made it to Alaska. Several pieces of the plane wreckage were displayed on the walls of the restaurant.

Departing, we observed the long sandy beach as well as the apparent junkyard that is Barrow, Alaska. There was no garbage disposal system. Trash was merely discarded on the land along with non-working snowmobiles and other junk. The shallow water of the port seemed to stretch out to the sea for miles. This necessitated the anchoring of scores of ships which were bringing provisions and cargo to Barrow and bringing cargo into Barrow by shallow draft lighters.

Then on to Kotzebue on the western edge of Alaska. Passengers were met at the airport with a huge sign billing it as the Polar Bear Capitol of the world. It was also the center of a considerable trade in jade since a huge deposit of jade was nearby in a mountain. In front of a jade shop was a piece of jade which was about three feet square and six feet long. It had been ordered by Juan L. Peron when he was in power as President of Argentina. It was to be a statue of his wife, Evita. The only problem was that he died before it could be shipped to Argentina to be carved into the Evita figure. And there it rested, waiting for another admirer of jade art work.

The next town on the supply mission for the FAA was Nome, Alaska. Nome is the largest city or town on the western edge of Alaska. It was also the base used by our Air Force during the war to transfer ownership of planes going to Russia to fight the Germans. The Russian pilots picked up their planes there and ferried them to the front.

As we flew in to the blacktop landing strip at Nome, we saw a three-story gold dredge which was located in the water near the end of the runway. Apparently it had been used a great deal back in the gold rush days before the gold petered out. It had been abandoned where it was.

After the war the city fathers decided that they would replace the boardwalks with surfaced sidewalks. Imagine their surprise when they discovered that gold dust was recovered in the dirt underneath the sidewalks. There was a new gold rush.

Since they had not yet gotten a grant from the United States Government to install a sewage disposal system in the city, they used honey buckets which were reached through doors in the sides of the houses. It was said that the mayor of Nome spent more time in Washington D.C., than he did in Nome in his endeavors to obtain Federal funds for the improvement of his city.

The next town on our route was Bethel, Alaska, the so-called Venice of the North.

King Salmon was also on the coast of Alaska and lived up to its name as a major fishing port for salmon. The trip back into Anchorage was a beautiful sight over the mountains which were snow covered and stunning. Along the way we flew over a recreation camp on a beautiful lake owned and operated by the Armed Forces of the U.S.

Sixteen: Federal Service, Continued: The Highest Appointed Federal Officer In The Great Lakes States

The Federal Regional Council concept had been in being for several years and it was felt that it should be formalized by an administrative order from the White House. The Office of Management & Budget and the White House asked me to come down to Washington and serve on a committee to formalize procedures and guidelines for the operation of all of the Regional Councils in each of the ten regions. I did so and enjoyed the opportunity to provide input into how the system should operate.

Shortly after the completion of that task, I was appointed by President Nixon to the post of Chairman of the Federal Regional Council of Region V at Chicago. The Chairman was the highest ranking, non-elective administrative officer of the Federal Government in the six state region.

We chairmen of the Federal Regional Councils were invited to come to Washington once a month to meet at the White House with the President for discussion of our progress in the Federal Regional Council program. It was a demonstration of the personal interest by the President in this new concept.

It was with just a little regret that I left Seattle and headquartered in Chicago. Alaska is beautiful country and if I were to be starting out in a career and knew about the Northwest, I would have been very contented to have established my family in Seattle. If one is in government, however, it is a great distance from the power center of Washington D.C. But at that time in my life I looked forward to being stationed in Chicago for work in the Midwest Region as well as being back "home" with Jackie in Arlington Heights, Illinois.

There were six states in the Region V area of responsibility: Illinois, Wisconsin, Minnesota, Michigan, Ohio and Indiana. The region, bordering on the Great Lakes, was characterized as being the most populous of the ten regions in the United States. It had more cities with a population over 100,000 than any other Region in the Country. This meant that they used more of the government programs in more different ways than any other region. I was responsible for assuring the effectiveness of the delivery of these federal funding programs and resolving conflict and difficulties which arose between these agencies of the Council. The administrators and executive officers with whom I worked were more knowledgeable about these programs because they worked with them all the time. I felt at home in the work since it was not unlike my post as Governor of Iowa. I provided direction and relied on persuasion to get the job done. I had fine professional assistance in George Bardahl and Harold Wieland, both from the Federal Highway Administraation.

Several situations are indicative of my work with the council. One of these was persistent problems with the City of East St. Louis, Illinois, a "bedroom community" with many of its citizens working in other places. It has practically no home industry or employer. They had been recipients of federal grants from almost all of the grant making agencies in Washington. They consistently ran out of money or failed to keep records, or waited at our door to get more money.

Most of the time we almost ducked when we heard that there was someone coming from East St. Louis to talk about the finances of that community. I felt that it might help if I would go down there with a staff member or two to see for myself if it was as bad as I had been told.

We fixed a date. The Mayor was the chief administrative officer of East St. Louis. We had a conference in his office at City Hall, talking primarily about the unemployed and the poor economic straits of the city. When it was time for lunch, my host took me to the luncheon place of their choice and I realized to my surprise that it was not in the City of East St. Louis. I joshed the Mayor a little bit, asking if we couldn't eat in a cafe in East St. Louis. He responded that there weren't any worthwhile restaurants in the whole city.

I'm not sure that this visit on site was productive. It did satisfy my need to see if it was really as bad as described, and satisfied their request that we should come down to see for ourselves. I don't think it did a bit of good. In 1995, they installed a gambling casino boat as a solution to some of their financial problems.

We had another situation in Green Bay, Wisconsin. There was a band instrument repair business operated by the Wisconsin Chippewa

Indians with a major grant from the OEO administration. There had been complaints that they were not productive with their funds and that there was not the proper accountability for the grants which they received.

I went up to Green Bay to see for myself and ascertain what the trouble was. On arrival I was taken to a metal building about 40 by 100 feet in size. Inside I noted that the inner walls were lined with wooden shelves filled with band instruments in various stages of repair. I queried the manager about their method of advertising as well as their competence in this field, the volume of instruments which they received, the locations from which they came for repair, and what system they used for organizing the repair process.

It was a most deflating exercise. Although I found it very interesting to observe the finished instruments and the workshop in general, I didn't see any employees who were working on the instruments. I wondered about this at the time. I asked him about scheduling and other problems which they had. The employees apparently took their responsibilities very lightly when it came to work in the shop. He said when the blueberry season was on, there were a large number of unexcused absences because of the blueberry harvest. In fact, most absences were unexcused.

It seemed to me that this operation could be one with a great deal of potential for a viable business if they would use some management methods. I expect that by now they too have shifted their attention to a casino operation.

Gary, Indiana, was another city which seemed to have more troubles with their bookkeeping and accountability.

Indianapolis was a very interesting place to visit. They were in the process of merging their city and county into a Metro Government under the leadership of Mayor Lugar who later became a U.S. Senator. This was one of the few cities where this process was successfully implemented. It was always refreshing to see how they were getting it done.

The problems in Detroit were always complex and took a great deal of time for the Regional Council to resolve.

The Federal Regional Council chairmen met in the White House Roosevelt Room about every six weeks. President Nixon usually came in for a few minutes, assuring us of his interest in the system and his support, as did President Gerald Ford when he took over. The membership of the Federal Regional Council had jumped from its original five members to ten members, probably because some of the original non-member agencies wanted to be sure they weren't missing out on something.

My office, as Chairman of the Regional Council, was the fastest paper shuffling headquarters in Chicago. Each agency felt that they had to have multiple copies of what we were doing. Our copy machine was kicking out copies continually. Fortunately, I had an understanding assistant, Dennis Judycki. He was an engineer from Massachusetts who had been with the Federal Highway Administration since graduating from college He joined me from his last post in California and I lost him when he was promoted to headquarters of the Federal Highway Administration in Washington, DC. His career has been enhanced by successive responsibilities in the Washington office, all of which he earned.

Chicago was quite a different assignment than was Seattle. The late Mayor Daley described it as "The city that works," and he was right. It was a very dynamic metropolitan area. I rode a commuter train to the Loop every day and had the impression the transportation system in Chicago was superb. Not so, however.

I soon learned that the commuter trains and buses, which fanned out in all directions from the Loop, did not communicate with the operators of the feeder lines in the suburbs and were not giving the service which their thousands of customers desired.

Representatives told me of the dilemma they had in working with the commuter railroads which extended into Wisconsin and Indiana as well as the Illinois suburbs. I had several conferences with the representatives of the commuter railroads and as a result of these contacts, carried out a summit meeting of the movers and shakers of the communities in the suburbs along with the executives of the commuter rail lines and bus routes.

They had never sat down face to face and discuss their problems. We set up a meeting at the Bismarck Hotel for October 13, 1971, for about 300 of those working in and /or interested in metro transportation. I suggested that I, the new kid on the block representing Washington

By virtue of the authority vested in me as President of the United States
I do designate

Norman Erbe

of the

Department of Transportation

as Chairman of the Federal Regional Council for Region Five with headquarters
at   Chicago, Illinois   authorizing him to do and perform
all such matters and things as to the said office do appertain during the pleasure of
the President of the United States for the time being.

The White House
July 1, 1973

Richard Nixon

By virtue of the authority vested in me as President of the United States
I do designate

Norman A. Erbe

of the

Department of Transportation

as Chairman of the Federal Regional Council for Region Five with headquarters
at   Chicago, Illinois   authorizing him to do and perform
all such matters and things as to the said office do appertain during the pleasure of
the President of the United States for the time being.

The White House
July 1, 1976

Richard Nixon

D.C., hoped to gather them, the community leaders and decision makers from each of the entities, for a discussion on cooperation.

I presented a speech, part of which said,

> *This is the first time ever that persons with your common interest in transportation problems have met together representing such a broad-based geographical background. I suggest that you cooperate with other districts and the CTA, as well as with the State Department of Transportation and the Regional Transportation and Planning Board, so as to produce mutually acceptable goals and means of reaching those goals.*
>
> *I know this can be done: your State mass transportation program was produced by agreement of the most intractable organizations of all, the two major political parties.*
>
> *I am not here to impose a solution on you, but to suggest how you all can and should solve your problems yourselves. I will go so far as to suggest the obvious way of achieving meetings of the minds—regular meetings of the persons interested in solving the same general problem. Perhaps you will want to select one of your trustees from other districts and a CTA representative at some "neutral" ground, to discuss your mutual concerns, problems and possible course of action.*
>
> *If requested, my office can act as a go-between to initiate this activity. And while you are presently powerless to decree or initiate changes in highway plans, you are certainly not without conviction as to the desirability of, or preferential route for, a proposed new highway; your voices should be heard in the highway councils as well.*
>
> *Progress in public multi-modal transportation is indeed your decision. That's what democracy is all about.*

The Regional Transportation Authority of Chicago, the RTA, was born that day and is successfully operating now. Interestingly, the same situation existed in Seattle with the ferries which plied Puget Sound. Now the buses meet the ferries and even operate free on short routes in the downtown area from the docks.

While we were in Arlington Heights, Illinois, in the early and middle seventies Jackie heard of the Northwestern University archeology program which was involved in a significant native American spot near Kampville, Illinois. It was a site which had been used many times for camping by the Hopewell Indians. This site promised a great learning and training experience for students at the University and Jackie decided that she wanted to join the effort if the professor would allow her to do so. She made an appointment to interview him and recounted to him the many years she had been engaged as an amateur in walking the plowed fields successfully searching for evidence of Indian occupation. The professor agreed to admit her to the class of students and I delivered her to the Kampville site for education and training in archeology. I returned to work in Chicago and felt that it was just like delivering one of our girls to a summer camp. Jackie said, she felt the same way although this time she was the girl. The camp was great, she learned a lot and I was later to serve as a volunteer tour guide for the hundreds of interested people from all over the world who stopped in to see the evidence of the American Indian life. The National Geographic carried a major article on the work at Kampville and Jackie later participated in comparable "digs" along the Red River in Oklahoma and Texas.

One of the modes of transportation with which I had little familiarity was that of barge traffic on the inland waterways. I attended a Midwest conference in St. Paul where the attendees were representing the barge and tugboat operators on the Mississippi and Ohio rivers and other waterways in the central United States. It was a very interesting conference and I learned a lot about the process and the problems of these operators.

One of the tugboat operators asked me if I had ever been on a tug boat. I replied that not only had I not been on one, but I had never seen a tugboat up close. He asked me if I would like to ride on a tugboat. I responded that I would if my wife could join me on such a ride. He said that would be possible and if I would like to do so, he would call me in the spring at an appropriate time we would ride from St. Louis to New Orleans.

The following spring I did get that call. Jackie and I went to St. Louis to join him on the tugboat. In the hotel, both of us were a little apprehensive about the conditions we would encounter. About the only thing we had to relate to was an old movie we had seen which featured Marie Dressler, "Tugboat Annie," which pictured a life on the boat among barrels of oil and tar covered hawsers with generally primitive conditions.

We met our host about 10:30 at night at the docks in St Louis and took a boat out to our tugboat. Our taxi boat fit the description of Marie Dressler's craft. However, once we arrived at the tugboat everything changed.

We stepped aboard and found that we had shag carpet throughout the living quarters, along with two Barcaloungers, twin beds, and a TV set as well as our own private bathroom. We were very pleasantly surprised. It was bedtime so we retired after our host told us the times when breakfast would be served. The next morning we joined our host and the 14 members of the crew at the breakfast table where the two cooks had prepared almost everything any person could want for breakfast.

This was true of all of the meals we had on board. The cooks were southern ladies, so as can be imagined, the cooking was southern style. The crew were also mostly from the southern states. At first I expected that the cooks would be unhappy if I didn't try to eat something of everything. I very soon found out that that simply would not do at all if I expected to hold my weight down on this trip. I became very selective. The noon and evening meals were just as generous in quantity and quality as was the breakfast. The refrigerator and freezer were open and available around the clock.

During the course of the trip, I expected that we would stop to take on provisions as well as fuel. Wrong. The cooks had an order form with fine print for the various foods used. They filled out the quantities needed of each item and used the radio telephone to call ahead with this order.

When we arrived at Memphis, a supply boat tied alongside our tugboat and placed the provisions on board as we continued our trip down the river. The same method was used when resupplying our fuel for the giant diesel engines.

On completing our first breakfast on the boat, Jackie and I discovered what kind of boat we were on. Our tour took us first to the pilot's bridge where the direction and operation of the boat was carried on. The captain held forth there with his large wheel. He was a Native American who had been on the river for more that 23 years. His assistant had spent about ten years on the river. The tugboat was pushing five barges wide and seven barges long, each of them tied together with a large steel hawser. These thirty-five barges were loaded with soybeans, corn, coal and other cargo.

Piloting tugboat on the Mississippi, 1974

Sometimes we stopped to drop off a barge or to pick up one or more barges. It was a very impressive sight to look out into the distance and see all of those 35 barges being pushed ahead of us around the bends in the river.

The captain placed a call every morning to his company headquarters in St Paul, Minnesota. He received directions on pick-ups or drop-offs of barges as well as any special messages which might be necessary for the load. There were no locks to pass through on the route between St. Louis and New Orleans so the load did not have to be divided. Nor was there any waiting for other barges to be locked through, like above St. Louis where the dams of the Mississippi are located.

There were many curves and turns on the Mississippi as we pushed our way south. The captain or pilot guides the barge load by aiming at huge billboard-sized markers which are colored a brilliant green and located at the various turns. He aims at one green board until he gets close to it, and then aims at the next one. This gives him a sense of direction for his load as well as helps him avoid the many sandbars in the river. They were also marked on the river chart which he had at hand in the pilot house.

The captain mentioned that one of the problems he had with novices in the pilot house was that they complain that they can't see that little blue light at night which is mounted on the first barge in the load, way out ahead. The captain said it was too bright and the novices said it looked too dim.

The principal duties of the crew is to continually monitor the steel cables which tie the whole load together. They are required to continually walk out on the barges to check the cables. They must

Tugboat on the Mississippi, 1974

wear life jackets at all times that they are on the barges.

The assistant captain was a man about 38 years of age. A few years before, he was out checking cables and fell into the river in the gap between the barges and tumbled over and over underneath the barges as they moved along. He finally was able to pop up between two barges to be rescued. He was very lucky to be alive. Most of the time, a person does not survive such an experience.

Although we had a beautiful trip down the river, I can imagine how difficult it must be in the dead of the night with a violent gale blowing sideways to the bow, trying to keep the load together and save it all from going aground and splitting up. That is known as severe trauma for the captain, almost as bad as flying a B-17 through a carpet of flak over Berlin.

Jackie and I spent a good deal of time on the bridge visiting with the captain and our host. We enjoyed the beautiful scenery along the river and the sights as we passed cities and towns. We had a thoroughly laid back and enjoyable time. When Jackie had a tough time sleeping, she would go up to the bridge and sit with the captain. He would direct his searchlight on the shores of the river so she could see the animals coming down to drink from the river.

As we neared Carville, Louisiana, I remembered from my high school days reading about the leper colony which had been established there. Now I would see it from the tugboat. In 1993 it was scheduled to celebrate its one hundredth anniversary of service to humanity and hopefully, a cure which modern medicine would have provided for the patients.

The Captain asked me if I had ever navigated or piloted a tugboat. It was obvious that I had not done so and my answer was in the negative. He asked if I would like to do so. This was like asking if I would like to drive a diesel engine on a train or fly a B-17 Flying Fortress. Of course the answer was yes.

I moved over to the pilot's seat and he stood at my shoulder as I aimed for the green billboard signs. I piloted the tugboat and its load of 35 barges for about a half-hour past the hospital at Carville. What a wonderful experience.

As we continued on under the much more capable hands of the experienced captain, we approached the industrial river area of Baton Rouge, filled with refineries and processing companies which made

Five barges wide and seven long = 35

use of the river water in their manufacturing processes. It was a real disappointment to see these insults to the environment choking up the river.

We also observed the access to the inland waterway which provides a water route from about this point to the Houston industrial area. I didn't know that this existed. From there on the route became more congested with commerce. Finally our orientation tour of the Mississippi was concluded at New Orleans.

Our tugboat trip was one of the greatest experiences Jackie and I were to have. That wonderful slow boat down the Mississippi River for a week of rest and relaxation gave us wonderful memories.

Then it was back to work again to call on the governors, mayors, bureaucrats and VIPs in the populous midwest region. Meanwhile, President Nixon was having his troubles and my heart sank each morning as I picked up the paper to read the latest bad news.

After he had been defeated by John Kennedy, he asked me to come out to California to discuss his pending decision to run for Governor of California in 1962. I had a long discussion with him and suggested that it would not be a good idea. Of course, he did not follow my advice.

Following his re-election as President in an unprecedented action, he requested the resignations of all of his cabinet officers including that of John Volpe, our Transportation Secretary. He offered John the post of Ambassador to Italy with thirty minutes to decide. Volpe accepted and President Nixon replaced him with Claude Brineger of California. He also requested my resignation but he did not accept it so I stayed on.

The Department conducted an awards ceremony in the auditorium of the Justice Department building and I was to be one of the honorees.

Secretary Brinegar of the Transportation Department presented me with the Department's Silver Medal, his award for Meritorious Achievement. "For his exceptional performance as the first secretarial Representative and for his leadership in the Federal Regional Council in Chicago on behalf of the Secretary of Transportation." I value this medal just as much, if not more, than I do the Distinguished Flying Cross and the four Air Medals.

Secretary Brinegar asked me to represent the Department in attending the International Conference on Transportation to be held at the United Nations in Geneva, Switzerland. It was principally devoted to the problems of transfer of cargo and goods between countries, and the related difficulties with language, customs, duties, processing facilities and insurance of cargo crossing national boundary lines. It was an extremely interesting session.

I was distressed to observe that the least developed countries held up their consent to proposals until they received promises of financial aid from the developed countries, which would assist them in upgrading their facilities. In effect, each agreement was predicated on the fact that they would vote "yes" if someone would give them a financial grant. That seemed to me to be blackmail. And there were 53 countries doing it.

Since we were in Geneva, we took the opportunity to do some traveling on the weekends. This included the beautiful Alps as well as Milan, Italy, and Germany and other countries.

We became friends with an attache at the American Embassy in Geneva and found that life as a foreign Service Officer in the Department of State is not all that one might envy. His wife needed health care where it is only available in the U.S. and the State Department would not approve her return for treatment.

They had always looked forward to getting posted to Geneva and now that they were, they discovered that with the high rate of exchange they couldn't afford to live there. They also mentioned the difficulty of stateside residence for a foreign Service Officer. Because they have no home in the States, they must rely on staying with relatives which gets old, or lease of high cost quarters depending on the definition of the term 'temporary.' And, of course, this is difficult for the children and their education.

After the National Election in 1972 when Jimmy Carter was elected President, I expected to get my letter from the President advising me that my services were no longer needed in the federal government. I held my position as a Presidential Appointee until April of the following year when they found me. That's when I received the ax.

THE WHITE HOUSE

WASHINGTON

February 10, 1972

Dear Norman:

Today I signed an Executive Order strengthening the Federal
Regional Council System and providing that Council Chairmen
will be designated by the President of the United States.

You have been recommended by Secretary Volpe and nominated
by the Under Secretaries' Group for Field Operations to serve
as Chairman of the Regional Council for Region V. I am pleased
to inform you that I am hereby designating you as Chairman for
that Region.

Your professional record shows that you are sensitive to the vital
role played by Councils in the effort to strengthen coordination of
Federal program activities in the field. Confident that you will
appreciate the high responsibility which you assume in accepting
this designation, I am sure you will also understand that this
recognition is an indication of the respect you have earned through
your distinguished service to your fellow citizens.

This initial designation will be effective immediately and will
terminate on February 28, 1973, or before that date if required
by administrative considerations.

With my best wishes for every success in this important endeavor,

Sincerely,

Richard Nixon

The Honorable Norman A. Erbe
Secretarial Representative
Department of Transportation
3166 Des Plaines Avenue
Des Plaines, Illinois 60018

THE WHITE HOUSE

WASHINGTON

June 13, 1973

Dear Governor Erbe:

As you know, a key element of my domestic program has been
the continued strengthening of the Regional Councils as the
cutting edge of the New Federalism. I will be taking a
number of actions this year to further strengthen the capacity of the Councils to coordinate Federal programs in the
field and to increase the potential for intergovernmental
cooperation. One such step is the selection of the most
effective leadership available to guide the work of each
Council.

To this end, you have been recommended by Secretary Brinegar
and nominated by the Under Secretaries Group for Regional
Operations to continue to serve as Chairman of the Federal
Regional Council for Region V. I am pleased to inform you
that I am hereby designating you to continue as Chairman
for the coming fiscal year. This designation will be effective July 1 and will terminate on June 30, 1974, or before
that date if required by administrative considerations.

Your professional record shows that you are sensitive to the
vital role your Council plays in coordinating the delivery
of Federal services with State and local governments, and
that you are well qualified for the high responsibility of
this Chairmanship. This recognition is an indication of the
respect you have earned through your distinguished service
to your fellow citizens. My congratulations and best wishes
in your new assignment.

Sincerely,

Richard Nixon

Governor Norman Erbe
Regional Representative of the
Secretary of Transportation
300 South Wacker Drive
Chicago, Illinois 60606

THE WHITE HOUSE

WASHINGTON

November 8, 1972

Dear Norman:

Your term as Chairman of the Federal
Regional Council in Chicago has been distinguished by the successful implementation of
a number of initiatives, and I want to congratulate you on your outstanding leadership.
The productive meetings you have had with
Governors and Mayors are a special tribute
to your skill and encouraging signs that the
new partnership of federal, state and local
officials is gaining momentum under very
capable direction.

With my appreciation and best wishes,

Sincerely,

Richard Nixon

Honorable Norman A. Erbe
Chairman
Federal Regional Council
300 South Wacker Drive
Chicago, Illinois 60606

THE WHITE HOUSE

WASHINGTON

June 30, 1974

Dear Norman:

I am pleased to inform you that I am designating you
to continue as Chairman of the Federal Regional Council
for Region V. You have been recommended by Secretary
Brinegar and nominated by the Under Secretaries Group
for Regional Operations. This designation will be effective July 1 and will terminate June 30, 1975, or before
that date if required by administrative considerations.

Federal Regional Councils are continuing to play an
increasingly significant role in fostering interagency
program coordination and improving intergovernmental
relations. Moreover, the capacity to deliver unique
services in response to special problem situations is
critical in demonstrating Federal responsiveness to
regional needs. This ability was successfully tested
in the recent energy crisis coordination. FY 1975
should be an especially challenging year as strengthening the FRC system is one of the highest priorities
of New Federalism.

Selection of effective leadership is paramount if FRCs
are to continue at this high level of activity. Your
performance in Council matters shows that you are well
qualified for handling the demands and responsibilities
of this Chairmanship. Congratulations on your continuing
assignment.

Sincerely,

Richard Nixon

The Honorable Norman A. Erbe
Regional Representative of the
Secretary of Transportation
300 South Wacker Drive
Chicago, Illinois 60606

THE DEPUTY SECRETARY OF TRANSPORTATION
WASHINGTON, D.C. 20590

January 20, 1977

Mr. Norman Erbe
Secretarial Representative
U.S. Department of Transportation
17th Floor
300 S. Wacker Drive
Chicago, Illinois 60606

Dear Norm:

I am pleased to be sending you herewith the Secretary's Award. You
have already received the Secretary's Award for Meritorious Achievement,
the Silver Medal. We have been following the practice of not sending
duplicate medals, so this certificate is in lieu of a second Silver
Medal, but I assure you that the contributions you have made to DOT
would otherwise warrant another medal. I have always felt that our
affairs in the critical Chicago region have been in the most competent
of hands, and I am personally grateful to you for your willingness to
continue chairing the FRC. You are recognized unanimously by all
Departments and agencies as the most capable representative in that
region, and I do not feel that your effectiveness as Sec Rep was
diminished in any way by the other demands on your time.

Bill Coleman and I have submitted to Brock Adams our recommendation
for reorganization of DOT and its programs, and I will see to it that
you receive a copy when it is ready for public distribution. You will
note that we recommend focussing the work of the Sec Rep more on
intergovernmental relationships and strengthening the whole role of the
Department in that area. I hope you will have the opportunity to stay
on to fulfill that role.

In any event you have my best wishes for continued success and my
sincere thanks for the great job you have done.

Sincerely,

John W. Barnum

Enclosure

DEPARTMENT OF TRANSPORTATION

SECRETARY'S AWARD

Presented in Grateful Appreciation to

Norman Erbe

January 1977
Date

William T. Coleman Jr.
Secretary

Roy Ash, OMB Director presenting commission to Norm Erbe in Roosevelt Room, White House, 1974.

THE WHITE HOUSE
WASHINGTON

December 9, 1974

Dear Governor Erbe:

I want to express my appreciation to you and the members of the Region V Federal Regional Council for your efforts in improving the way in which the Federal Government conducts its business.

The proper functioning of government requires the development of closer working relationships between State and local governments and the Federal grantmaking agencies. It requires that improved coordination be achieved among the Federal programs. It requires that better communication be achieved with the citizens we serve so that trust and faith in government are strengthened and maintained.

The Federal Regional Council, through the efforts of yourself and the other agency Regional Directors, has made significant efforts to achieve these goals. Your Council has demonstrated strong initiative over the years in promoting improved intergovernmental relations in Region V. Your efforts to develop a coordinated Federal and intergovernmental strategy to address shoreland damage problems along the Great Lakes are noteworthy. Of comparable significance are the efforts of the Council to work with State and local governments in identifying ways in which Federal requirements can be simplified to promote greater responsiveness by all levels of government.

I look to the Federal Regional Council to continue to provide assistance in our efforts to reform and make government more responsive, to decentralize and coordinate Federal activities and to increase State and local government participation in the Federal decisionmaking process.

You and your fellow Regional Council members have my full support in your efforts to make our governmental system work more efficiently.

Sincerely,

Gerald R. Ford

The Honorable Norman A. Erbe
Chairman
Federal Regional Council
300 South Wacker Drive
Chicago, Illinois 60606

Jackie and Norm Erbe with John Barnum, Undersecretary of Dept. of Transportation. Presentation of Silver Medal.

Secretary of State George Schultz presenting commission to Norm Erbe in Roosevelt Room, White House, 1974.

SEVENTEEN: BACK TO OUR ROOTS IN BOONE

After leaving the Federal Government, I held an executive position with a construction industry association which was going through a transition period. Then Jackie and I decided to move back to our roots in Boone, Iowa.

On our return to Boone from Arlington Heights, Illinois, we purchased a home formerly owned by Mr. and Mrs. Bert Holst. It was a 1906 vintage house which had been remodeled a number of times to reflect various eclectic needs and desires. Holsts were world travelers and had been most of their married lives.

As the story goes, Bert Holst got tired of his wife asking him for money to continually modernize the house. He gave her a 640 acre section of his land in Kossuth County and said, "Here is some land for you. Use the income from this to work on the house." Bert's father was the publisher of an encyclopedia and in his lifetime had accumulated a large collection of books of every kind. The 3,000 volumes were located in the extensive library which was part of the remodeling, and there they were when we purchased the house.

One day Jackie was leafing through a book and found an insert between the pages. There was a pressed rose in tissue paper and a message which said, "Jackie Doran and Norm Erbe's wedding - September 27, 1942." Jackie's mother had asked Lillian Holst to help with our wedding back then. It was obviously meant to be that we purchase and live in that house forty years later.

One of the many real pleasures on our return to Boone was the opportunity to teach at the Des Moines Area Community College at Boone. The students ranged in age from 22 to 70 years and were dedicated, interested and motivated to be in the classroom. My subjects included State and Local Government, National Government, American History, The Opening of The Frontier History.

Teaching these courses was a challenging and fascinating experience, relating to the students and sharing with them my years in government and the history of our country. A need was expressed a little later on for establishing a course and curriculum in International Trade. I took over some research and lesson-planning on this project at the Ankeny Campus of the Des Moines Area Community College.

But we soon discovered that there were not enough people interested in the International Courses to make the pursuit worthwhile.

It was a pleasure to have the opportunity to teach in the classroom again after the experience I had enjoyed teaching the young men in the Iowa National Guard at the Military Academy. While driving home from my class duties one day in August of 1986 I turned on the Boone radio station and heard the announcer in a message that there was a crisis on the Boone and Scenic Valley Railroad arising from a train wreck.

As a volunteer tour guide on the railroad for all of the tourists riding the train, I knew that information must be incorrect since there was only one track and only one train on the track at a time. Thus there was nothing that could cause a collision and train wreck.

I drove to the station and discovered that the report was true. There was indeed a train consisting of the diesel engine and three open cars and three closed cars, each of them full of people, which at about this time was crossing the Des Moines River Bridge. The facts were that two volunteers at the station had been working on a railroad passenger car at that station and had forgotten to set the brake on the car. The car started to move out of the station, volunteers tried to stop the car, but were unable to do it. So they jumped off the car as it picked up speed and rolled down the track. The track makes a one degree grade downhill for five miles from the station to the Des Moines River Bridge. Since there was no one to stop it, it swept along down the hill, picking up speed as it rolled along. A collision was inevitable with consequent injuries to the passengers and possible loss of life. What to do? Fortunately the engineer in the cab of the diesel engine had a radio which was tied in to the radio at the station back in Boone. The manager at the station called the engineer on the train and advised him of the pending catastrophe and made some suggestions about preparing to avoid the collision. By this time the lone car was picking up speed estimated to be more that 40 miles an hour. Ambulances were alerted and asked to race down to the road intersection nearest the river. Several school buses were alerted to proceed to the intersection, to bring the railroad passengers back to Boone in the event that the train was disabled from the impending crash. Meanwhile the diesel engineer who was on his return trip to Boone decided to increase his speed until he could see the approaching vagrant car. He then stopped the train, reversed directions and picked up speed so that he was going about the same speed as the loose car. This worked! They then came together with a slight bump and few, if any, passengers knew that they had been in the midst of a headline grabbing accident. The train with its volunteer addition then stopped at the gravel road intersection where the emergency vehicles were waiting, and the passengers who wished were transferred to buses and brought back to Boone. Only one lady had to be treated for bruises from the potential accident.

About this time Jackie thought it would be a good idea for me to direct my attention to a genealogical report on the Doran clan. This had never been done for her branch of the Doran side. I worked at it through the mail and with telephone calls. I found that I could indeed get into it and that there were a number of people who were interested in the results and also interested in helping me put the names and dates together.

Since her ancestors came from Ireland and we were going over there on a pleasure trip, we decided to combine the two and see if we could find out anything. We did get the right county, Carlow, but spent some fruitless hours trying to find the right cemetery. We located a Protestant cemetery and couldn't find the name Doran anywhere.

We also went to the genealogical office in Dublin Castle and tried to get information, but that was no help. Our trip around that lovely isle was over too soon.

Further investigation at home disclosed that we had gone to the wrong place. We should have been looking in a Catholic cemetery instead of a Protestant cemetery, and we should have called on the Catholic priest who in many cases has the records.

When we were in Ireland again a year later we were better advised and much smarter. We set out to find the place where her ancestors came from, meeting some of their descendants for a chat. Our host insisted I had to have two fingers of Irish Whiskey neat, which I did not really enjoy but felt I had to do it since they might be insulted if I didn't. Jackie would never have whiskey so I had to drink hers also. And all this at ten in the morning.

At any rate we found the right place, went with them to a nearby cemetery alongside a church where her ancestors probably worshiped, called on the priest who filled some gaps in the heritage, and left Ireland this time satisfied that we had found all that we could find about the Dorans. It was great fun and productive in the preparation of that green covered genealogy book which set it all out.

Of course, one thing led to another and the result of all of this was a family reunion of the Doran clan on the farm at Beaver, Iowa, with 124 attending. There are 752 names in the genealogy, 456 descendants of the originators from whom the blood flows, Patrick and Ellen Doran. Patrick was born in 1809. Although this did not go back very far in lineage, it did accomplish the goal sought, and that was to find out the names and addresses and relationship of all the descendants.

Since that was completed and I now knew how to go about it, I decided to take on the subject of the genealogy of the Erbe and Erck clan—Erck being the maiden name of my grandmother on my father's side.

When my father passed away we found amid his records an address book containing, among other names, the addresses of about 13 people by the name of Erck, and most of them residing in Germany. My parents had been over in Germany in 1925 and at that time had called on some of our Erck relatives. They returned to Germany in 1930 and carried on a correspondence with some of them through the years.

Since I was going to be in Germany in 1984 on a pleasure trip, I used my father's address book and extracted every name found in Germany. I wrote a letter telling the recipient that I was going to be in Eisenach, giving the date. The letter was translated into German and I sent copies to thirteen Erck addresses. I hoped that I would get a reply from one of the thirteen.

I got a response only from Willy Erck. He lived in Eisenach and would be pleased to meet me. It was January of 1984, and I got the necessary visas to get me through the checkpoints into East Germany. The train was stopped at the border which separated East and West Germany. I was very thoroughly searched by the authorities. I was intrigued by the fact that they were extremely professional and very businesslike in the search, confiscating my Time Magazine and New York Herald Tribune. They then turned around and tried to sell me some Bach medals. They were celebrating his anniversary that year.

At any rate, the train proceeded on and about fifteen minutes later arrived at the railroad station at Eisenach. Meeting me at the bottom of the train steps was Willy Erck and his wife and son. Willy showed me a passport picture of my parents who, had visited them in 1925. This was, of course, a sure means of identification.

I spent two and a half days there with them and we had a very wonderful time. Willy was to die of prostate cancer in a year but he was sturdy and well while I was there. They took me down to the village where the ancestors had lived and we sat in the church where they worshiped. I admired the organ and furnishings of the small church. It was built in the 1500s, about the time of the thirty years war.

Later, Jackie, her friend, Kay Anderson, and I, went to England and were touring the countryside. We wanted to spend the night at a bed & breakfast near Peterborough. It was about 9:00 p.m. which was a bit late to knock on a door. Stopping at one that had a beautiful garden of flowers, I went to the door to inquire. The hostess was Miss Bryan, a retired teacher, who stated she had no room for the three of us. In the fading dusk I returned to the car and asked the ladies to get out and come look at the garden. Miss Bryan was apparently convinced by our appearance and sensitivity and decided that she could put us up if one of us slept on the lounge on the front porch. We took it and she called the local pub at 9:30 p.m. to prepare dinner for us. The next morning she served a delicious English breakfast.

Our conversation turned to the war and she was sullen and somewhat remote. She stated she was put out that we hadn't joined the war. I protested that we did join the war. She said, "Not soon enough."

We went to see my old air base at Glatton. I knew the general area where it was located but could find no trace of it. We stopped at a hardware shop in a small village at about closing time and asked about the base. The man knew where it was and gave directions. He was a German POW, captured in one of the battles in Africa and sent to a U.S. POW camp. At the end of the war he was temporarily detained in England before returning home. He met and married a British girl whose father owned the store. This man had been detained at Glatton Air Base on his return to Germany from the POW camp in the U.S.

We drove to its location and the only thing that remained was the principal runway I had used so much on my missions to the continent. Nothing would do but for me to drive down that weedy, unkempt relic one more time in my rental car and relive the experience. A rabbit joined me in a race this time.

It was a great and productive trip. Upon our return, I completed the genealogy of the Erck family. Nothing would do but that we would have a family reunion in Boone, Iowa, in the summer of 1984. A family headed by Willy's son Helmut, his wife and son came over from Germany for the reunion. The shindig was attended by 65 descendants.

My grandfather on my father's side had come over from Germany as a small boy of seven. From their home at Gemunden, a small village about 60 miles northwest of Frankfurt an der Main. He married grandmother Erck whose family we had called on in Germany. The descendants of the Erbes whom we met in Gemünden happened to be professional genealogists and had traced their lineage to our joint ancestors in 1639. They too attended the reunion.

The genealogy book I prepared of the Erbe/Erck clan consisted of 172 pages, and contained 407 blood descendants who, along with their spouses, comprised 647 people scattered all over the world. I expect that somewhere down the line, one or more of our descendants might want to follow up on this research and bring it up to date. At least they now have a good start on the process.

It was time to celebrate our Fortieth Wedding Anniversary in 1982. We decided that the only way to do it properly was to take a trip on the Orient Express, the train leaving London, through Paris, and ending up in Venice, Italy. This was the first season the train was operating again and we had some difficulty getting tickets, but it was soon arranged. We had outstanding service and accommodations on the train. Jackie and I had become train "buffs" as result of our many trips to and around Europe and we thoroughly enjoyed the experience.

When we settled in our own hometown where both of us were born and raised, we became involved in a number of civic causes and enterprises. One of them which just seemed to come naturally to us was joining the Boone County Historical Society. We had belonged to it for years while absent from Boone, but now we could actively participate in its work.

This was a logical follow-up to the interest both of us had in antiques and older things which we had collected for years. That was one of our very enjoyable interests while we lived in Arlington Heights. We could jump in the car and be at a new and different antique show or antique shop within thirty minutes, to see and learn about antique French Baccarat glass, cut glass, or old furniture in need of restoring, or needing new cane seats.

Boone County Cultural Center and Historical Society

We re-joined the Society in Boone and took an active part in its activities. The only problem was that it had no home other than the Board Room of the Boone Chamber of Commerce. It seated about ten people around the table and this was about the attendance of the Board of Directors of the Boone County Historical Society. We met periodically and tried to solve the problem of where and how to get a permanent home for the society in Boone, and what to do with the artifacts which the people of Boone County would be donating to the Society for safekeeping.

This quest had gone on for years and the problem was growing. Our city library was a two story structure with the second story devoted to a "grandma's attic of artifacts" which went back to the town's beginnings.

As a child I went to see all these old things, which were getting dusty even then, and they had not improved with time. Admission by school children and adults had been prohibited and the Library Board had plans for remodeling the structure. Something must be done with all the artifacts stored in their attic. The County Historical Society agreed they must be saved, but where and how?

I took on the responsibility of finding a site or building to house this great collection. We investigated all possible buildings in Boone, climbed through attics, checked roofs and basements, examined deeds and mortgages, and were offered vacant land out at the airport grounds and other locations or temporary quarters. But none of them would fit our needs.

Finally, it was whispered that the three story, limestone and brick Masonic Building at the entrance to the business district might be available because of decreasing membership in the lodge. Built in

1907, it had an elevator and was designed by Proudfoot and Bird, noted Des Moines architects. There was 30,000 square feet of usable space that had been well cared for during its entire existence. The location was outstanding and it could be purchased for $41,000.

We had no money. Some of our board members felt that this would keep us from acquiring it. I felt that it was essential that it be saved and offered to be the fund-raiser to get the needed money for the purchase.

Funds were raised within two months and we took possession of the building. Then we began the cleanup process and adaptation to its new use as a cultural center and museum. Cleaning, painting, tossing rugs, and scraping floors followed, with me, Jackie and other members of the Board doing the work.

I was elected president of the Boone County Historical Society as well as elected to the Board of Directors of the State Historical Society. Our work of preparing our building coincided almost with the move of the State Historical Society from its own building into new quarters. It has been a real asset to the City of Boone to have the Cultural Center and Museum in our community. Since it opened in 1990, more than 35,000 people have visited the building to experience the changing displays and activities. New windows have been installed and the new heating and air-conditioning system provides constant temperatures year round. New dining furniture has converted it to a multi-purpose facility for the community. Its operation had been overseen by a professionally trained museum manager, Charles Irwin. He has been supported by many volunteers, Mr. and Mrs. Don Schoof, Mr. and Mrs. Roland York, Owen Fitzsimmons, Mrs. Charles Irwin, Mr. & Mrs. Jack Shelley, Mr. & Mrs. Rueben Sansgaard, Nancy Jacobsen, Mike Overton, Mr. & Mrs. Bill Lees, and other members of the board. The Boone County Museum has come a long way since the Board of the Historical Society sat around the Chamber of Commerce table and wondered where we were going to go and what we were going to do.

When I was elected to the office of President of the State Historical Society we secured a seed-money grant of $10,000 for a program to prepare a history book of the State of Iowa, intended to be taught at the sixth grade level in all the schools of the state. Included with the program was the training of teachers.

The seed-money grant was received from the Iowa Centennial

Memorial Foundation, who administer funds obtained from the sale of Iowa Centennial 50-cent pieces in 1946. As a former governor, I served on the Board of Directors of the Foundation and chair the Scholarship Committee which dispenses $70,000 each year to needy Iowa college students. I also chair The Iowa Award Committee which every four years recommends the recipient of the Iowa Award to a deserving Iowan. Past winners included: 1951-President Herbert Hoover; 1955-Jay N. (Ding) Darling, Cartoonist, Conservationist, Pulitzer Prize Winner; 1961-Dr. Frank Spedding, Educator, Physicist, worked on the first atomic bomb; 1962-Dr. James Van Allen, Educator, Physicist, rocket and space exploration; 1966-Henry A. Wallace, U.S. Secretary of Agriculture, Vice President of U.S.; 1970-Mamie Eisenhower; 1975-Dr. Karl King, composer, bandmaster; 1978-Dr. Norman Borlaug, crop geneticist, worked to end world hunger, Nobel Peace Prize Winner; 1980-Monsignor Luigi Ligutti, Director of National Catholic Rural Life Conference; 1984-George Gallup, founder of the Gallup Poll; 1988-Meredith Willson, composer, musician; 1992-Carrie Lane Chapman Catt, leader in sufferage movement and for world peace; 1996-Simon Estes, bass baritone concert and opera singer.

In the summer of 1992, I was invited along with President Ronald Reagan to speak at the rededication of the enlarged Herbert Hoover Library. I was invited since I was the only surviving speaker from the original dedication of this West Branch, Iowa, Presidential Library in 1962. It brought back painful memories. My failure to be re-elected as governor was something that I had never quite gotten out of my system.

It was a hot, sweltering day with close to 5,000 in attendance. We all braved the brutal afternoon to pay homage to one of our greatest presidents. I personally put Mr. Hoover among the finest men I had ever met. It was sad that he was not alive to witness this honor.

My career had provided me the good fortune to meet and visit with all of the presidents since Roosevelt, with the exception of Jimmy Carter and FDR. Human nature seems to dictate that we remember the 'not so proud' parts to a person's accomplishments, weighing these sometimes unfairly with the truly great things that were done. Kennedy's womanizing and Nixon's Watergate mess are examples. But none was so unfortunate as Herbert Hoover during his one term as president.

President Hoover at dedication of Hoover Library, 1962

He had his humble beginnings in West Branch, rising to become a multimillionaire in the mining business. What brought him to world greatness was his famine relief efforts after both world wars. Many disliked him because he did not take "no" for an answer. If someone tried to block his efforts to get food to starving war-torn areas, he went around them to get the job done.

He was elected in 1928. Unfortunately, he took office just before the crash of Wall Street and the Great Depression. He never took a dime in payment from the Government during his entire public life. No man was more dedicated to his country.

Yet the Depression wasn't the only factor in his political demise. His four-year term had also been during Prohibition. The illegality of liquor consumption in the U.S. contributed greatly to his downfall.

He had set up an investigative commission to analyze the liquor problem. The results stated that Prohibition was widely disapproved of and often openly defied. Prohibition also contributed to brutal criminal activities such as those of Al Capone, and no tax revenues were being received by the government on the unregulated sale of illegal alcohol. The commission recommended a repeal of the Fourteenth Amendment.

With the disastrous financial problems facing the country, Hoover chose to set aside the commission's work. He therefore found himself to be a very unpopular president. When he opened the baseball season by throwing out the first bal, he was booed from the stadium by the chant, "We Want Beer! We Want Beer!" Those who knew him, though, continued to praise him, even at the derision of their peers. Harry Young remembers when he worked for Hoover's re-election campaign in 1932 as a high school student in California. "They threw tomatoes at me. I always believed in him. He was a high quality man."

During the dedication, when I was seated on stage and hearing the profuse praise of Hoover, it finally dawned on me. He and I had more in common than just being raised in the same state. President Hoover, man whom I admired, whose portrait I had hung over my desk while governor, had made a grave error in his political life. I had not learned from his historical mistake. I was a preacher's son, yet I had committed the same cardinal sin. Neither of us had listened to the electorate. Politics and the business of running the government was a remote concept to the taxpayer. We had considered the liquor problem minor in the overall picture, but it was a major issue among the voters. Freedom of choice to hoist a drink was a personal right. Both of us had missed that point, and both of us had found out the hard way.

President Hoover at dedication of Hoover Library, 1962

President Truman at dedica- tion of Hoover Library, 1962

Somehow that revelation has made a difference. If a great man like Herbert Hoover can make a mistake like that, Norman Erbe has good company.

So maybe life hasn't been so bad after all. Maybe more has been accomplished through my efforts than I believed. After all, many things were fixed that needed fixing and I had the great privilege to meet, visit and get to know many leaders of the free world during times of significant world events. My ancestors who landed in America a short generation ago would be astonished to know that I knew such world leaders as President Herbert Hoover, President Harry Truman, President Dwight Eisenhower, President John F. Kennedy, President Lyndon Johnson, President Richard Nixon, President Gerald Ford, President Ronald Reagan, and President George Bush. The circumstances of meeting with them and their families have provided lasting impressions and memories which are etched in my mind. My colleague, Nelson Rockefeller and his brother, David, as well as Margaret Thatcher and Nikita Kruschev, also occupied the world stage in my personal notebook of great memories. The hundreds of wonderful men and women whom

I have had the privilege to know during these short 75 years have made invaluable contributions to me and to my family (through their counsel, guidance and assistance.)

I am further blessed to have a wonderful wife who has the stamina to tolerate my faults, three terrific daughters and five grandchildren of whom I'm extremely proud, many friends, and relatives whom I have

To Norm Erbe
with best wishes

Gg Bush

To Jackie Erbe
with best wishes

Gg Bush

From L To R: Iowa Governors
Norman A. Erbe,
Robert D. Fulton, Robert D. Ray
and Terry E. Branstad.

Photo by KC Borchert,
Bondurant, Iowa.

227

ADDENDUM

STATE OF IOWA
1961
INAUGURAL ADDRESS
AND
BUDGET MESSAGE
OF
NORMAN A. ERBE
GOVERNOR OF IOWA
TO THE
FIFTY-NINTH GENERAL ASSEMBLY
IN JOINT SESSIONS
DES MOINES, IOWA

JANUARY 12, 1961
AND
FEBRUARY 2, 1961

known down through the years. I am grateful for each and all. Who could ask for more?

MR. PRESIDENT, MR. SPEAKER, MR. CHIEF JUSTICE, SENATORS AND REPRESENTATIVES, STATE OFFICIALS, DISTINGUISHED GUESTS, LADIES AND GENTLEMEN:

Today, probably more than in any recent decade, we stand at the threshold of a legislative session with unlimited opportunities to solve and resolve the problems and issues facing Iowa. Because of our unique great natural assets in this state, our people, and the fertile land upon which we live, we must strive to continue to make good the dream of greatness which we hope to pass on to our children.

This challenge is ours, and I say "ours" purposefully. It is neither yours alone, as members of the legislative body, nor is it mine alone, as the chief executive of this state. It is a cooperative effort on the part of both of us working together for the good of the State of Iowa. If we are to successfully adopt and carry out a program of progress for this great state that we love, it can be accomplished only if the members of the legislative branch and the executive branch of our government operate in an atmosphere of mutual respect, confidence, and true partnership.

First, I want to congratulate you upon your willingness to spend so much of your time in the cause of good government by serving in our legislative body, in most cases at great financial hardship to each of you, and I pledge to each one of you that I am dedicated to assist you in any way that I may during the coming months of your deliberations in the legislative session. I hope that I may be of help.

It is my belief that the people of Iowa expect, deserve, and must have as efficient and economical a government as it is humanly possible to provide. We join in recognizing the many urgent needs of our state, and it is our responsibility during this session to resolve these needs through the process of debate and passage of legislation so that we may fully discharge this responsibility to our constituents and ourselves for a better Iowa. In this message, it is impossible to consider all the facets of state government that will demand our attention, however, I will discuss with you the most pressing needs of the state. It is with this philosophy in mind and in accord with a true spirit of cooperation that I respectfully submit to you, our lawmakers who will provide the course for our ship of state in the next biennium, a number of recommendations for the path which I hope we may chart.

The voters of our state, under the right given them by the framers of our Constitution, in their wisdom decided that the work of amending our Constitution should be done through our regular legislative process by you, their elected legislators, selected from among them to perform this function. The interest of our people in the enacting of vital changes in our Constitution is not diminished by their selection of your body as the means to effect that change, but rather is a vote of assurance and confidence that you will meet the problems of constitutional amendment and fully discharge that obligation in a representative manner. Reapportionment of the General Assembly was given thorough consideration during the Fifty-eighth General Assembly. I join Iowans throughout the state in the hope that this vital issue will be favorably resolved at an early stage in your proceedings on the federal basis of providing one house on area and one house on population with district representation in those counties with multiple legislators in the population house. Automatic reapportionment every ten years would, of course, continue to provide fair representation for those who follow us in government and should be included in the amendment.

You wisely took the first step in the constitutional amending process of the judiciary branch through the passage of SJR 7 in the last session of the Legislature. I urge your favorable action on the second step of this process during this session so that this issue of modernization of our court system can be presented to the electorate for its consideration.

I commend you for your legislation during the Fifty-eighth General Assembly enabling most county officers to serve terms of four years. This good government decision of yours did not, however, extend to county attorneys who are constitutional officers. I not only urge your favorable consideration of lengthening the term of county attorneys but I also invite your attention to the archaic method of compensation of these law enforcement officials who now, by law, must depend for a portion of their salaries on fines levied by the courts against violators of the law. This method of compensation of public law enforcement officials is completely contrary to modern principles of government and should be abolished. Perhaps in connection with this review of the status of our county attorneys you could profitably consider the desirability of adopting a system of district attorneys elected to serve the judicial district for four-year terms with adequate compensation for fulltime work.

Your recognition of the need for four-year terms for county officials indicates the even greater desirability of four-year terms for elective state officials in order to provide stability and efficiency in the administration of state government. In the interest of good government, I urge your favorable consideration of a constitutional amendment to provide four-year terms for state elective officials as well as your consideration of annual sessions of the Legislature, limited as to time, with one session each biennium devoted to fiscal affairs.

I submit for your careful consideration and approval the proposition of lowering the minimum voting age requirement to 18 in Iowa. The young men and women of Iowa are sufficiently mature at 18 to become a valuable part of the electorate and this fact has been recognized by President Eisenhower in his recommendations as well as by two of our sister states.

I have been informed officially that the Iowa representation in the United States House of Representatives commencing with the Eighty-eighth Congress will be reduced from its present eight-member delegation to seven representatives. I am confident that you will wisely redistrict the counties of the State of Iowa so that our total population will have equal representation in the national Congress.

Our youngsters constitute our most valuable asset in the Iowa of tomorrow and it is our obligation to them to continue to provide for them the best in education so that they may be better prepared to meet the challenge of the future. You have recognized this obligation by requiring reorganization of school districts and consolidation of teaching services so that they may receive the best in education. However, this has, in many cases, thrown a disproportionate financial load on the property owner. I am sure that you share with me the conviction that some means must be provided in this session of the Legislature for property tax relief through increased agricultural land tax credit payments and a program of increased state aid for schools.

Iowa's three state institutions of higher learning are among the leaders in the nation in their respective fields. Everything possible must be done to insure that each maintains its ranking. The recently-completed interim study "Resources and Needs for Higher Education in Iowa" provides you with an authoritative report upon which to base legislative action during this session. I especially invite your attention to the need for legislative approval and commitment to a long-range building program for the Board of Regents institutions so that capital planning can be carried on now for the future needs of our students in the fields of higher education. The severe statutory limitation of alumni representation on the Board of Regents also merits your inquiry as to its usefulness. I recommend authorization for greater representation by alumni on that important agency.

I suggest a re-examination of the report of the interim study committee on election and election practices headed by your very able colleague and public servant, the late Clark McNeal, and the enactment of legislation which will prevent inequities in our voting laws and preserve for every citizen this most valuable of his rights in our governmental system.

Iowa's highways have been properly called her "lifeline." The report of the Iowa Highway Study Committee created by you during the Fifty-eighth General Assembly points out the many problems facing our primary, secondary and urban road and street systems in the next twenty years. The allocation of funds will properly receive serious consideration by your body and, I am sure, will result in a distribution which will be in the best interests of the people of Iowa. Continued progress in the improvement and construction of our secondary, urban, primary and interstate systems is, of course, mandatory and expected by all Iowans. Prompt removal of curbings from our narrow primary roads is a project which I am confident our highway commission will carry out in the interests of safety for the traveling public.

I invite your attention to a re-examination of the requirement of the last session of your body that speed limits on secondary roads should be effective only upon posting by the Board of Supervisors. Experience has demonstrated that enforcement has been rendered more difficult because of the problem of proof of existence of speed signs and the lack of uniformity. Additionally, the counties have been required to assume a substantial increased financial burden as a result of the requirement of posting.

Those of us who drive upon the roads of our state are, in judgment, entitled to protection from the drinking driver. I urge the adoption of an implied consent law as well as a manslaughter by motor vehicle provision to protect us from the driver who endangers our life and property.

In these days of the shorter work week, the outboard motor and the vacation trailer, the responsibility of our State Conservation Commission becomes greater, not only to provide better recreational areas so that Iowans will enjoy their free time in Iowa, but also to acquaint our fellow Iowans and tourists from other states with the many fine vacation spots in our state. A balanced conservation program designed to fit the needs and desires of all Iowans is vital if we are to continue to attract industry and its people from without our state.

Great strides have been made in recent years in caring for our less fortunate ones who suffer from mental illness. I commend you for your passage of enabling legislation authorizing the establishment of local mental health centers which have done such an outstanding job in the field of treatment and care at the local level. We must continue the program of local and state care and treatment so that these patients may be restored to the status of useful members of our society.

Our senior citizens who provided for us the heritage which we enjoy today are greater in per-capita numbers than any other state in the nation with the exception of Vermont, and we, in Iowa have done less than our best in properly discharging our obligations to them in the golden years of their lives. Confusing regulations administered by agencies with overlapping powers have hampered the wonderful work which private and church organizations have done and are doing in this most important field. It is my hope that you as members of the Fifty-ninth General Assembly will arrive at a program which will combine the best resources of government, private enterprise and the groups providing health care, to solve the housing and economic problems of domiciliary and health care for the aged in Iowa. Such a program should include enabling legislation authorizing participation by this state in the provisions of the Kerr-Mills Bill granting medical care for the aged as well as legislation permitting local political subdivisions, following an election by its citizens, to provide nursing homes and homes for the aged in their communities if they do so desire.

Historically, Iowa's economy has been termed "agricultural" in nature. The first half of the twentieth century has seen a healthy evolution of the partnership between agriculture and industry in our state. Today we have an ideal and fertile climate for the greater promotion of our state in the vital area of industry. Favorable tax laws coupled with a plentiful labor supply of excellent quality and our ideal location in the heartland of our continent present conditions which are attractive not only to our existing industry but also to those companies seeking new locations.

It is not, however, sufficient for us to say that we have what it takes for promotion of these valuable assets. We must strive to do something about them. This necessitates an aggressive program of salesmanship for our state including promotion of Iowa as the land of opportunity for new industries, promotion of our existing industries, development of our outstanding labor supply, and last, and by no mean least the advancement of our basic industry, agriculture, all of which will provide a better future for our children.

This means a challenge for you and me, today, and not tomorrow, for the need is with us now to develop a better Iowa. We are all immensely proud of the outstanding achievements in their respective fields by Dr. Spedding at the Institute for Atomic Research at Iowa State University at Ames, and Dr. Van Allen of the Department of Physics at the State University of Iowa at Iowa City which chart for us the course of the future in technological and scientific development. In order that we may meet the challenge of today in the fields of agriculture, industry and scientific development, it is vital that we develop the proper climate here at home through our Iowa Development Commission and promote our many assets beyond our borders. It is not enough to say that one state department or agency should do this work since it is the obligation of all Iowans, whether a part of state government or not, to put their shoulder to the wheel and do their best to promote a greater Iowa.

You and I as elected officials of this great state have a deeper obligation which extends over the length and breadth of state government and that is, through the laws of this state as well as through it administration, to operate state government at the greatest peak of efficiency and economy that is possible. This should be true in any year but it is especially true in the coming biennium when our people are carrying an ever-increasing tax burden and are entitled to the best use of their tax dollar. I share with you the view that full and complete collection of the taxes now authorized by law must be effected by our tax commission and I pledge to you that I will do all in my power to assist in this vital task.

The budget hearings provided for me and your colleagues on the budget and financial control committee a unique opportunity to inquire into the operations of our state departments and agencies. As a result of these hearings and my studies and personal experiences in state government, I am convinced that the purchasing practices of state government should be drastically revised so that the lowest prices can be obtained for volume purchases.

Not only consolidation of purchases but consolidation of the many machine records operations at the seat of government will provide for the taxpayer the greatest return on his investment in government. The solution to a number of these problems can, I am sure, be obtained by administrative cooperation but it is possible that legislation may be required and if this is so, I shall confer with you during the course of the legislative session.

Additionally, the budget hearings disclosed a continuing complaint by agency heads of the competition provided by other states and the outside business world for their skilled employees. This problem can, in my opinion, be solved by the enactment of a civil service system which will provide open competition for employment, selection on the basis of ability, equal pay for equal work, and career employees who can and will give their best to government service in Iowa without fear of the results of the next election or the requirement of having to participate in a political campaign in order to insure their jobs.

You and I have the unique opportunity at the present time to complain as taxpayers about the cost of government and, best of all, the good fortune to be able, through appropriate legislation, to provide a more efficient government for ourselves and our constituents. The enactment of a civil service law, a restudy of the Brookings Report of the 1930's, a review of the Little Hoover Committee report and its recommendations, and the views of the recent Interim Tax Study Committee should be considered so that needed changes which provide economy and efficiency in government can be adopted at this session.

These problem, which I have discussed today, are most assuredly not all of the problems facing the people of Iowa. No doubt many of you can think of other problems which are also of great importance. Frankly, I would like to visit with your today about not only each of the issues which I have mentioned but also the many others which are of concern to Iowans. As you know the budget message of the executive will contain a discussion of the fiscal problems to be considered by you during this period. Suffice it to say that you and I will be counseling together many times during the course of the legislative session ahead concerning the problems and solutions for a greater Iowa.

As stated at the outset, it is my belief that the people of Iowa expect, deserve, and must have as efficient and economical a government as it is humanly possible to provide. It is likewise the right of our people to be fully informed concerning the operation of their state government, and it is my intention to provide this flow of information during the course of our administration to the best of my ability so that our friends and neighbors may know and take a greater interest in government, which is theirs.

During the months ahead, you, the elected legislators of Iowa, have an opportunity which is unparalleled to provide a legislative program of vision and progress for the people of our state. They are watching you with confidence that such a program will be the result of your efforts. In all humility I want you to know that I am proud to have the opportunity to be associated with you, the Fifty-ninth General Assembly, in the work which lies ahead. At any time that I can be of assistance to you in any way, either individually or collectively, my door will always be open. With the ever-present help of the Almighty, I am confident that the challenge will be met and that the work will be done.

BUDGET MESSAGE
February 1, 1961

MR. PRESIDENT, MR. SPEAKER, MEMBERS OF THE GENERAL ASSEMBLY, LADIES AND GENTLEMEN:

Chapter Eight of the code of Iowa required the Governor to present to the General Assemble a financial program for each year of the ensuing biennium. This message, comprising part one of the Budget, sets forth the present financial condition of the State Treasure, and the proposed fiscal program for the biennium beginning July 1, 1961.

Supplementary materials to be placed in your hands provide a more detailed statement of current and estimated balances in the General Fund of the State, and of recommended appropriations and sources of revenue, in accordance with the requirements set forth in section eight point twenty-two of the Code.

I would like to extend my personal thanks and appreciation to the members of the Budget and Financial Control Committee who generously gave of their time and effort to participate in the budget hearings this past December. The careful consideration and informed questioning by them at these hearings was a significant contribution to a better insight into the operations of our state agencies and departments and their askings.

Special thanks and appreciation are owing to Duane Wicker and the staff of the Office of State Comptroller for their outstanding work and long hours in preparing the way for this budget message.

BASIC CONSIDERATIONS

The welfare of each individual in the State of Iowa is vitally affected by a sound economical state government. It is important to all Iowans that a healthy economic climate be achieved. This means that it is incumbent upon the State Administration to have and to follow a sound fiscal program.

Iowans have traditionally adopted a wise course of living within our income and we must continue to pursue a policy which will preclude deficit financing. This is true not only of the State Government as a unit but also of each subdivision within our government. It is my considered judgment that budgets of state departments and agencies, as fixed by appropriations by you, should be strictly adhered to.

The executive practice previously followed of approving transfers of funds between departments has made a mockery of appropriation and budget limitations and must be stopped. A budget is meaningless if this practice is allowed to persist.

I am presenting to you a balanced budget which does not call for any tax increases. It is my belief that it will be possible to carry out the prevailing sentiment of our Iowa people regarding revenues and tax relief and still move ahead in all essential areas.

It must be kept in mind that only ten states in our nation levy more state and local taxes per $1,000 of personal income that Iowa. It would seem to me to be imperative to keep the tax structure on a basis that will not strangle the individual initiative of our Iowa citizens.

Recommended Expenditures

Total expenditures from the general fund of $378,861,700 are recommended for the biennium beginning July 1, 1961, and average of $189,430,850 per year.

This total investments in capital improvements, state aids to local schools and governments, and expenditures for the operation of state institutions, departments and agencies. It also is inclusive of estimated expenditures under standing limited and unlimited appropriations (such as Agriculture Land Tax Credits, Homestead Tax Credits and Tax Refunds), as well as those outlays requiring specific appropriations by the Fifty-ninth General Assembly.

The major components of average annual expenditures during the current biennium are compared with proposed annual average expenditures during the biennium beginning July 1, 1961, in the table below:

Type of Expenditures	Average Annual Expenditures Current Biennium	Proposed Average Annual Expenditures July 1, 1961-June 30, 1962
Capital Improvements	$ 12,358,242	$ 14,933,470
Current State Purposes	76,580,885	83,782,350
State Aids to Local Communities Including Schools	82,448,648	90,715,030
TOTAL	$171,387,775	$189,430,850

Average annual appropriations for the Fifty-Ninth biennium annual askings, and recommended annual appropriations for the Fifty-Ninth biennium beginning July 1, 1961, are shown in "Exhibit A" of the budget materials. You will note that the items in this exhibit are set up under major groups of related activities.

I would like to discuss, briefly, the major items in the proposed budget.

EDUCATIONAL EXPENDITURES

Annual expenditures of $92,816,630 are recommended for all types of education. This is an increase of nearly twelve million eight hundred thousand dollars per year over appropriations made by the Fifty-ninth General Assembly. With this proposed increase in expenditures, for educational purposes, state support of education accounts for forty-nine percent of the total budget during the coming biennium. This, I feel, is where we must place the bulk of our increased spending. The cliché is over-used but it is still applicable that the future of our state depends upon our youth; that future will be bright only if we give our your people that best education possible. We cannot afford to slight either the higher educational institutions, the elementary, or the secondary educational programs. If we fail to provide as much state assistance to education as is humanly possible, we shall be failing the future generations and encouraging outward migration of our youth.

STATE AID FOR EDUCATION

In order to give some measure of property tax relief an increase of almost twenty-five percent in aid to public schools is recommended over the appropriations of the last biennium. The 1961 fiscal year appropriation amounted to $24,151,148 as contrasted with the 1962 fiscal year proposal of $30,131,530. This is an increase of $5,980,382.

Average annual direct aid of the fifty-eighth biennium was $590,000 as contrasted with the annual recommendation for the fifty-ninth biennium of $645,000.

The Agriculture Land Tax Credits payments during the last biennium amounted to $10,500,000 each year. Under the present law this appropriation paid only 44 percent of all claims filed on a proportionate basis.

It is my belief that some new formula must be found for payment of the Agriculture Land Tax Credit. Under the present budget that I recommend to you, I suggest payment of all Agriculture Tax Credits between 15 and 20 mills in those school districts that levy taxes above 15 mills.

To pay this formula during the two years of the next biennium, I recommend an average appropriation of $11,250,000. The appropriation recommended calls for an increase of nearly 7 percent over the present expenditure.

This amount which I recommend to you is not as much as I would like. However, under our present revenues and considering the total state aid to school program, this is as much as may be allocated.

HIGHER EDUCATION

The Fifty-eighth General Assembly appropriated an average $36,577,822 for salaries, support and maintenance of the educational institutions under the Board of Regents. The annual recommendation for these institutions that is submitted to the Fifty-ninth General Assembly is slightly more that ten percent above the previous appropriation and totals $40,373,000. In order to begin a long range building program necessary to meet the demands for capital improvements at our institutions of higher education, I recommend a total of $20,834,200 for Board of Regents institutions. This is an increase of over twenty-six percent above the previous appropriations which actually constituted the capital programs for four years 1956-60.

It should be noted that different recommendations are made for each of the two years in the biennium. This has been done at the request of the Board of Regents. It is my belief that this may well be a procedure that should be followed in all appropriations in the future. It is, however, a poor substitute for annual appropriations made if the General Assembly were to meet each year.

While I regret that it is impossible to grant as much capital improvements as has been requested, I do believe that with this excellent beginning the long range program proposed by the Board of Regents can be completed by 1973. It is vital to the welfare of our educational institutions for the next fifty years that we plan now for the buildings that will be needed for the enrollments of our institutions of higher learning in the last half of this decade and the decade of the seventies. All of us realize that is impossible under our Constitution and laws for one legislature to bind another, but it is imperative that we assure the Board of Regents of a continuing source of income for capital improvements.

It is my contention that the capital improvements can and must come from the surplus that has been accumulating in our State Treasury. It is not the purpose of government to accumulate a surplus. I do not subscribe to the practice of exacting excessive taxes from the taxpayer so that we may have a surplus in the State Treasury for future use. I do believe we must be on a pay-as-you-go basis on current recurring expenditures but can in good conscience utilize the surplus to "catch up" on our overdue capital improvement programs.

BOARD OF CONTROL INSTITUTIONS

Total annual appropriations of $24,922,640 are recommended for salary, support and maintenance, and capital improvements at institutions under the State Board of Control. This is an increase of $2,689,493 per year over the appropriations during the current biennium. Salaries, support and maintenance accounts for $21,674,820 of the annual appropriations to the Board of Control, an increase of 10.30 percent over the present annual rate of appropriations. A careful examination of the recommendations for the fourteen institutions governed by the Board and a comparison with the askings will reveal that the recommendations of the administrative agency have been followed as closely as possible. All of the institutions under the Board are important, particularly those dealing with the problems of our mentally ill. However, I do not believe we should slight one type of institution at the expense of others under the same administrative group.

The sum proposed for capital improvements at Board of Control Institutions is nearly 25.8 percent greater than that given by the Fifty-eighth General Assembly which again was in reality a four-year capital improvement. Thus, I believe we will be able to make genuine progress toward a realistic building plan.

Although not as essential as in the Board of Regents situation, a long-range program of capital improvements should be established.

Department Of Public Safety

The last session of the Iowa General Assembly appropriated annually $4,863,800 for the operation of the Department of Public Safety. My recommendation for this most important agency of state government is 12.6 percent above this annual appropriation for an annual total of $5,477,460.

This sum should permit the present programs to continue on a high level. If it is thought necessary to add personnel to the Iowa Highway Patrol, additional money will have to be provided to meet this increased expenditure. An obvious source, should the added personnel be allowed, is to increase the cost of the Iowa Drivers License. This has been utilized in the past but should be carefully studied before action is followed merely because "that's the way it's been done before."

Our Department of Public Safety compares favorably with those of our surrounding states and I believe the proposed recommendations will allow this agency to continue in an excellent comparable position.

Administrative Departments

An increase of slightly more than eleven percent above the fifty-eighth biennium is recommended for Administrative Departments of State Government. The appropriation recommended totals $8,309,285.

It should be noted that this figure amounts to only 4.3 percent of the total budget. The appropriation should allow most departments to give their employees at least a one step increase in pay during the two-year period.

During the budget hearings, many of the Administrative Departments indicated a desire to create new positions. These new posts have been carefully studied and in most instances they have not been included in my recommended appropriation. It is my belief that only in unusual circumstances should new jobs be allowed during this biennium. I am concerned about the number of administrative personnel that are leaving state employment and believe that two steps should be taken to curb this exodus. First, as suggested in the inaugural message, a civil service system established to assure career opportunities in State Government and, second, salary increases should be authorized to the efficient personnel now employed in State Government.

Miscellaneous State Aids To Local Communities

I am recommending virtually the same appropriation that was made by the Fifty-eighth General Assembly for state aid to the agriculture societies (county fairs), state soil conservation commission, and the state participation in county mental care activities. The present annual appropriation is $1,262,500 and I recommend $1,260,000 for each year of the coming biennium.

Homestead Credits

The Homestead Tax Credit is paid under a standing unlimited appropriation, therefore it is impossible to determine the exact amount that will be disbursed during the coming biennium. The estimate on the basis of recent trends in Homestead Tax Credit claims, for the coming biennium, calls for an expenditure of $29,165,000 in each year. This is an increase of $965,000 over the present annual appropriation.

Social Welfare Department Programs

It is recommended that the total appropriations for the State's share of Social Welfare programs be made in the amount of $18,908,500 per year during the coming Biennium. This represents an increase of $573,500 each year over the current appropriation or an increase of 3.12 percent. This will allow some adjustments to be made in the present Social Welfare programs. A corollary recommendation concerning the state's participation in the federal program of medical care for our senior citizens is presented elsewhere in this budget message.

Medical Care For The Aged

In my inaugural message, I indicated my hope that you would give serious consideration to an enabling act that would allow Iowa to participate in the federal program of medical assistance to our senior citizens. You will note that I have not assigned an appropriation for this program. The estimates of the cost to the State of Iowa for participation range from one and one-half million to four million dollars.

I would suggest that legislation allowing Iowa to participate provide that the surplus of money procured for payment of the Korean bonus be utilized for the initial phase of participation in the medical are for the aged program. Not only will this appropriation help to discharge our obligation to our senior citizens, but additionally enabling legislation in this field by your body during this session may serve to retard the announced goal of the National Administration to include these benefits within the structure of the Social Security system and the inevitable final result of socialized medicine. Developments in this field will, I believe, be stabilized by 1963 so that the Sixtieth General Assembly may then intelligently provide for a continuing program in this field.

TOTAL NON-EDUCATIONAL STATE AIDS

The recommendations for non-educational forms of state aid to local communities total $49,333,500. This is an increase of $1,536,000 over the present appropriations of $47,797,500. This increase in non-educational aids to local communities accounts for eight and one-half percent of the total budget increases recommended for the next biennium.

MISCELLANEOUS SERVICES

The sum recommended for miscellaneous services, including State Conservation Commission, Iowa Development Commission, District Court Judges, Iowa State Fair Board, the State Historical Society, Hoover Birthplace Society, National and State Guard, Civil Defense Administration, the Reciprocity Board, and the Mississippi Parkway Planning Commission, totals $7,172,785. This category no longer contains the Teachers Retirement Allowance, which has been transferred to the Standing Appropriations. The Conservation Commission recommendation is ten percent above the amount appropriated by the Fifty-eight General Assembly and represents $641,850 each year of the total in this category. The increase proposed for the Iowa Development Commission is about twelve and one-half percent above the current appropriation. The recommended figure is $237,900, plus $25,000 for Municipal Planning Assistance. An appropriation of $942,900 is recommended for the National Guard and State Guard activities. The largest percentage increase is recommended for the Reciprocity Board which received $30,750 from the Fifty-eighth General Assembly; an appropriation of $40,470 is recommended to help get this new agency on a firm operating basis.

An eleven percent increase is recommended for the Iowa State Historical Society bringing their recommended appropriation to $104,500, while $12,000 is suggested for the Hoover Birthplace Society.

The District Court Judges appropriation of $900,665 is relatively inflexible and that total requested is recommended.

TOTAL CAPITAL IMPROVEMENTS APPROPRIATIONS

Total capital appropriations of $29,866,940 are recommended for the fifty-ninth biennium, equivalent to $14,933,470 for each year. It is my recommendation that this money be appropriated from the Treasury surplus, since it is regarded as a non-recurring appropriation.

Of the total capital appropriations of nearly thirty million dollars for the biennium, $20,834,200 would be allocated to the Board of Regents Institutions, and $6,495,640 for improvements at institutions under the Board of Control.

Miscellaneous capital improvements appropriation recommendations total $2,537,100. This amount includes $1,960,600 for the Conservation Commission's capital needs, and increase of $442,950 over that appropriated by the Fifty-eighth General Assembly. A total of $234,650 is recommended for the State Fair Board, $226,250 for National Guard Armories and Armory construction and $115,600 for the capital improvements needed by the Department of Public Buildings and Grounds during the two-year period. These recommendations for the miscellaneous capital improvement appropriations represent a decrease of $259,300 annually from the appropriations of the current biennium.

SUMMARY OF PROPOSED EXPENDITURES

The budget as submitted is the result of careful analysis of the department and agency requests, as filed with State Comptroller's Office. Each unit was given full opportunity to explain their requests in the budget hearings held in December.

I am sure that you are aware that the budget requests totaled a great deal more than I have found it possible to recommended. The requests amounted to $259,821,508, as contrasted with the recommended expenditures of $189,430,850.

No doubt, in your collective judgment, you will decide to appropriated amounts in some instances greater than recommended and in others less than suggested in the executive's budget. This is your right as the policy making, representative body of our sovereign state. I have presented to you a budget which in my judgment, after many hours of study, will provide for all essential services and a capital program that will help us gain in many areas where we have lagged.

RECOMMENDED SOURCES OF REVENUE

Under existing statutes general revenue appropriable receipts during the next biennium will total $348,994,760. Of this amount, $172,298,515 will be received during the first year of the biennium and $176,696,245 in the second, an average of $174,497,380. The unencumbered balance June 30, 1961, is estimated at $45,898,788.37.

It is my belief that the steady growth in revenue will continue during the coming biennium. The estimate figures are computed with a conservative economic growth rate factor of four percent per year in the four major tax revenue areas, sales, use, individual income and corporation income tax.

This budget is so constructed that the recurring appropriation will be met by the current annual income, thus avoiding deficit spending in the recurring appropriation areas. The proposals for the regular operating expenditures during the biennium are: (1) For current state purposes, $83,782,350, and (2) Current state aid to local communities, $90,715,030, for a total of $174,497,380, which is the equivalent of the average estimated annual current revenue. Capital improvements recommended total an average annually, $14,933,470.

This amount I recommend be taken from the Treasury balance presently on hand. If this program outlined is followed, the estimated Treasury balance on June 30, 1963, will be $16,031,848.37.

I am confident that this program can be carried out, providing the 10 percent of the sales tax can be transferred to the road use tax in the last three months of each fiscal year. This will allow for a lower working balance than has been previously needed.

Legislation allowing this transfer in the final quarter of each year will be introduced. I urge you to give it favorable consideration.

I have purposely refrained from trying to project an estimate of additional funds available from such sources as more efficient and complete tax collection procedures, consolidation of some of our myriad costly inspection services, centralization of state purchasing procedures, coordination of machine records operations at the seat of government and greater budgetary control by the executive, all of which, in my opinion, will provide for the taxpayer better and more economical government for his tax dollar. I am dedicated to the view that these reforms and changes must be accomplished and I hope to have your support and assistance in those areas where legislation is required.

SUMMARY

The people of our state have been justifiably proud of the great heritage of our forefathers of fiscal conservation and this has been reflected in past sessions of your body by appropriations based on a pay-as-you-go basis. This has resulted in the sound economy which has made the State of Iowa one of the bright spots in the nation in-so-far as a stable and healthy fiscal climate is concerned, and I am sure, has been a persuading influence for the relocation of many of the industries to our state from other areas. I congratulate you for achieving and maintaining this climate.

During the last year in our travels about the state you and I heard from many of our fellow citizens their justified expressions of concern regarding the ever-increasing property tax load which we are carrying. The budget as presented today purposes to provide tax relief in this area. Some will say that it is not enough. To those of our constituents who desire more, I would respond that additional tax relief for property invites the answers to certain questions from our neighbors back home.

1. Have they in the past and will they in the future attend and influence the budget hearing of the local tax levying bodies who in the first instance determine the rate of local property taxes?

2. Do they want more from their government, both state and national, and, most importantly, are they ready and willing to pay higher taxes into government in order to get more from their government?

3. Are they ready to face the challenge of the future by providing better education of our youth and willing now to pay the price in increased taxes?

4. Do they want and will they demand a reversal of this trend toward centralized government and can they continue to afford this monster of state and national government which grows larger with each succeeding year thus placing a heavier tax burden on our people?

5. Do they still believe that government was created by them to do only those things which they could not do themselves, or are we to become a welfare state looking to government for all our needs and paying the inevitable high price for those things which we receive?

6. Do they want a reduction in the number of state boards, commissions and agencies with a resultant lower cost or are they apathetic about the use of their tax dollar?

7. Is our state to be the master of our people with our every move controlled and directed by government or shall government be the servant of man, held in check and controlled by him?

My friends, all of Iowa looks to you during this session of the legislature to determine the answers to these questions. Simple arithmetic clearly shows that existing revenues and taxes will provide the program of appropriations which I have outlined. The burden now rests with our constituents to tell you whether this is adequate and, if it is not, whether they are ready and willing to pay the price for more. I hope and pray that they will call upon you, counsel with you and advise you and that you will be guided by their views in reaching your conclusions.

"CHICAGO AREA TRANSPORTATION... PUTTING IT ALL TOGETHER"

REMARKS BY THE
HONORABLE
NORMAN A. ERBE

REGIONAL
REPRESENTIVE
OF THE
U.S. SECRETARY
OF TRANSPORTATION

BISMARK HOTEL - CHICAGO
OCTOBER 13, 1971

Reprinted with the permission of Gov. Erbe
by Chicago and North Western Railway Co.

Presented at a Meeting of
Community Leaders of the
Eight-County Metropolitan area
of Northeastern Illinois and
Northwestern Indiana

I am indeed pleased to have such distinguished group of transportation people present here this evening. I understand from Mr. Davenport, and others, that collectively you represent transit interest in the six northeastern counties in Illinois, and two northwestern counties of Indiana, and the great city of Chicago. I also understand this is the first time, ever, that persons with your common interest in transportation problems have met together, either formally or informally, representing such a broad-base geographical background.

In terms of what I shall say tonight, this coming together of persons like yourselves is indeed a significant event. I commend the six commuter railroads for their initiative in calling this meeting, I thank you for the courtesy of your attendance.

The general invitation that brought us together tonight has much relevance to what I have to say to each of you. I don't know whether you noticed it or not—but the general invitation said I would talk tonight about what *you* might do to help solve a transit problem that exists in this area. When you read your invitation, I hope you sensed the implication of personal involvement written into that piece of paper. In case you missed it, it was there; it was intentional; and was intended to convey my message for the evening.

Folks—if you remember nothing else about these remarks, please take this one thought home with you because it is basic to everything I have to say:

The future of mass transportation in the eight county area you collectively represent—the direction it will take—lies in *your* hands, and in the hands of the people you represent.

Disregard your responsibilities; ignore what is before you to be seen; and the movement of people and goods in the Chicago metropolitan area is in for hard times.

Accept the challenge of personal involvement; open up the channels of public awareness and concern and there is no limit to the regional benefits that will follow.

I would like to expand on these thoughts now, but before I do, let me answer a question I am sure is running through all of your minds.

Rightfully, you may ask—How can Norm Erbe, a man from Boone, IA stand there with so much assurance about what he claims is our problem.

As the Regional Representative of the Secretary of Transportation, I am charged with the job of assisting the Secretary in discharging his duties for the Chicago Region, and I take it as my responsibility to do all I can to clarify the Chicago transportation picture for him, and to encourage and promote multi-modal transportation planning and execution.

I will be the first to admit I am not quite the expert in these matters which the boldness in my comments might imply, but things have happen in mass transportation in the past few years which don't require that much technical learning to document and then articulate

First—the evidence is in, all over the country, that mass transit operators generally cannot survive on fare box revenues alone, and cannot depend on them to pay their operating costs and have enough left over to buy transit equipment they need to give the quality of service their patrons should have.

Secondly—the debate about whether subsidies are wise, or not is over. Public subsidies are a fact. The question now are "Where should these subsidies be applied?" "How should they be used?" "How can we avoid operators but not others?" and most important of all, "Who should makes these decisions?"

Thirdly—transportation thinking, both at the Federal level and elsewhere, has ripened to one point of hard fact about Mass transit subsidies that cannot be ignored. The fact is that transit subsidies and how they are used, should be a matter of *local* governmental concern. Secretary Volpe has stated, "Our policy is that the decision as to what type of public transportation to utilize is a local decision." And President Nixon recently said, " The hard fact is that the best mixture of transportation modes is not something that remote officials in Washington can determine in advance for all cities, of all sizes and descriptions, in all parts of the country.

In other words, under Federal government grant procedures, there is a *deliberate* and *intended* requirement of *local government involvement* as a prerequisite for a grant. This requirement cannot be foisted off on transit operators. It must be recognized. It's philosophy must be accepted if mass transit is to survive in most urban areas.

If you would permit me, I would like to document this point by reading very briefly from a pamphlet just published by the Department of

Transportation called, " Statement on National Transportation Policy."
On pages 35 and 36 of the document, the following observation is made:

"The social and environmental fruits of past transportation projects, carried our according to a centrally directed design with little or no effort to secure the advice or consent of those affected, have frequently been bitter. The lesson of this experience is another objective must be added to transportation's policy-making process—*that of securing maximum public participation in the process of itself.* This participation must include not only the highly visible elected officials, *but also the interested, informed and affected citizenry,* and it must be secured in a fashion designed to make good use of the products of that participation. Such an objective is essential to the development of sound transportation policy, facilities and services at all levels, and is compatible with the policy of decentralizing governmental power. Thus, to the original list of four principal objectives must be added the fifth: *to facilitate the process of local determination by decentralizing decision making and fostering citizen participation.*

Now, what does all this mean to you?

It means, first of all, that private mass transit operators who have helped this area to become the transit envy of cities all over the country, can no longer be expected, nor required, either directly or indirectly, to make or finance mass transit policy in large urban areas.

In the foreseeable future, mass transit policy must be a public function, a planned response to need, and not a by-product of private enterprise interests, strengths or weaknesses. Concerned members of the public, like yourselves, must recognize this shift in the burden of transit responsibilities to translate this concept to those you represent.

As a more practical matter, this new notion of public responsibilities for transit policy also means that, for the first time in transit history, private operators must seek an alliance, or accommodation with public bodies, in order to survive. Most cannot survive without public subsidies. The unsubsidized operator cannot compete with those that are subsidized. All need, in some manner or form, to become tied to public transit body. You should help them in this alliance-seeking effort.

The private operators in this area are well aware of these transit facts of life, and are reacting predictably, and with a great deal of foresight and energy.

In the Department of Transportation, we know about the activities so some private operators in this area to encourage the formation of transit districts under the Illinois statutes. We also know that some carriers in the area are strongly working to create a single operating authority for the entire six-eight county area. These initiatives are to be commended. It is your job and mine to understand them with the context of what is happening nationally in mass transit. It is your job and mine to correctly interpret these activities to the people we represent so they are not viewed with suspicion or mistrust.

Sometimes I am asked whether these two activities are compatible with each other. Quite frankly, I think they are. For both have as their basic premise a recognition that there is a need, in the years to come, for an affiliation with a responsible public body that can qualify for public subsidies, and, at the same time, provide the public with an acceptable vehicle by which it can become involved in transit matters.

Which is the best method?

I suppose the answer to that turns on the theme that underlies these remarks. This is a policy decision that rightfully lies in the public domain of the region you represent.

If the responsible leaders and citizenry of the eight county area are content with segmented and uncoordinated mass transit, with no common transit philosophy for the area, with no machinery to meet area-wide transit emergencies, with no method for providing the means for the efficient transfer of people from one segment of mass transit to the other, with no area-wide concern about relationship and function of highways and airports to mass transit, then a decision of mullet— public transit agencies, acting completely independent of each other, probably will be the end result.

Quite frankly, a financial penalty follows that kind of decision. For the policy of Congress, as it is expressed in the Urban Mass Transportation Act of 1964, is to provide areas which followed this philosophy with some financial assistance, but not all the assistance that might otherwise be available. Such areas can qualify for 50 percent Federal capitol grant assistance, however the balance of capital needs on an area following that kind of policy must come from fares charged the public. And as we have seen here, and elsewhere, that decision has its own problems.

On the other hand, if is the policy decision of an urban area like ours to be concerned about mass transit on a regular basis; if the informed transit leadership of such an area collectively sees mass transit as a unitary system involving highways, airports, and rail lines and bus lines, each bearing a relationship to the other that extends across the city and county lines and indeed across state lines; if the leadership of such an area is concerned as a region about strengths and weaknesses of its private carriers as a group; if it's leadership thinks there should be a regional philosophy about environmental matters, such air and noise pollution, and that enemy that plagues us all—traffic pollution, and understands that solutions to such problems defy small area capabilities for financing, then the leaders of that area must sit down together and work out these problems on an area-wide basis.

If they do, area-wide need can be identified. Area-wide priorities can be developed. And the product will be a plan of local design, and decision, that quite likely could qualify the area for maximum participation in Federal assistance.

Secretary Volpe has said, " the final analysis it is up to the local community to decide what sort of public transportation will work best." I do not tell you what is best for your area.. As the Secretary stated, the policy of Federal law is to leave that to you. The purpose of my remarks tonight is merely to bring to your attention that there is a need in this eight county area for making a public decision about how transportation problems should be addressed.

Should transit problems be treated on an eight-county basis, or should they not?

Your position as a transit operator, or as a Transit District Trustee, or as an officer of State or local government, or as a newspaper reporter, can be a springboard for creating public awareness of the fact that there is a need in the eight-county area you represent for a public decision as to whether transportation needs and problems should be handled on a area-wide basis, or in a sub area basis.

Perhaps your decision will be to work for decision making in the area on a frontal basis, as some suggest, by pushing immediately for adoption of an area-wide authority.

Perhaps your decision will be to work for unification of decision making on a developmental basis, pooling the talents and strengths of existing Transit Districts as means to that end.

Maybe your decision will be to accept what you have and make the best of it. Again *this is your decision.* My hope is that transit opinion molders, like yourselves will develop the organizational means by which the area can answer the public question before, in a rational and informed manner, rather than let it go undecided, or be decided by default.

In the past few weeks, you probably have read in local press about the problems we have experienced in certifying this area as one qualifying for full capital grant assistance rather than the lower - level 50 percent assistance. At the heart of this problem is the very thing I am talking about, namely, the dilemma our administrators face in deciding whether or not the area has made a collective decision of planned public involvement in mass transit matters *as a region.*

You are fortunate that the Illinois Legislature has authorized the creation of Mass Transit Districts: they necessarily involve the local government, which must pass an ordinance, and the local populace, which is heard in public meeting before the ordinance is acted upon. Then, the local government must appoint a Trustee to the Mass Transit District, and he or she (and I am glad to see several women Trustees in our audience) must be responsible to the community which made the appointment. This is involvement at the most grassroots of levels, and can produce the very type of citizen contribution to problem solving that President Nixon and Secretary Volpe have been talking about. A multi-community mass transit district, and there are four such districts (North, Northwest, South, and West) represented here tonight, must also resolve intercommunity differences to perform effectively. We thereby obtain a limited form of regional cooperation. I say "limited" just because the Mass Transit Districts up to this time have not established any continuing form of intercommunication, nor are the Districts themselves all-inclusive. But a start has been made, and we should not lose the advantages we have while searching for the "perfect" form.

The possibility of solution, I submit, through your involvement may lie in the very center of our national experience dating from barnraisings, quilting bees, and the like: mutual cooperative effort.

I call for your involvement in public multi-modal transportation problem solving to transcend the geographical boundaries of your particular Districts, just as your communities have joined with others to form multi-community Districts.

I suggest that you cooperate with other Districts and the CTA, as well as with the State Department of Transportation and the Regional Transportation and Planning Board, so as to produce mutually acceptable goals and means of reaching those goals.

I know this can be done: your State mass transportation program was produced by agreement of the most intractable organizations of all, the two major political parties.

I am not here to impose a solution on you, but to suggest how you can, and should solve your problems yourselves. I will go so far as to suggest the obvious means of achieving meetings of minds: regular meetings of persons interested in solving the same general problem. Perhaps you will want to select one of your Trustees or representatives of your group to meet with other Trustees or Representatives from other Districts and a CTA representatives at some "neutral" ground to discuss your mutual concerns, problems, and possible course of action.

If requested, my office can act as your go-between to initiate this activity. And while you are presently powerless to decree or initiate changes in highway plans, your are certainly not without conviction as to the desirability of, or preferential route for, a proposed new highway; your voices should be heard in the highway councils as well.

Progress in public mullet-modal transportation is indeed your decision. That's what democracy is all about.

GENEALOGY

It was a slow, perilous voyage across the North Sea and the Atlantic Ocean to New York harbor in the year 1854, a destination in the New World known only to a few of the occupants of the creaking sailing vessel. Among the passengers was a brave wondering girl from Horn, Lippe-Hanover, Germany, 18 years of age, known as Sophie Droste, the second daughter of Wilhelm and Julia Droste. This dangerous voyage to an unknown land was brought about by a professional book binder, Fredrick Carl Festner, 48, who had written his relatives requesting a "nice German girl to marry." They were married after the ship docked in 1854 in Brooklyn, New York.

Their union resulted in six children of whom my mother, Louise Festner, was the youngest. Fredrick Festner became a Captain in the Civil War, leaving his position as Treasurer of Madison, Wisconsin, to lead his company in the Union Army of Tennessee. At the time of his death from pneumonia in 1890 at age 74, he owned the only German language newspaper west of the Mississippi, in Omaha, Nebraska. His wife Sophie lived until 1924. She died at the age of 88 and is buried beside her husband and children in Prospect Hill Cemetery in Omaha.

Conrad Erbe was born in 1846 at Gemunden, Germany, near Limburg an Der Lan. He came to the New World under sail with his widowed father and older brother when he was seven. Together they braved the waves of the North Sea, Atlantic Ocean, and the Gulf of Mexico on their way to New Orleans; then they traveled by river barge up the Mississippi River to St. Louis in 1857.

My wife Jackie, with daughters, Kevin, Jennifer & DeElda. Photo was taken about 1959.

Conrad served in the Union army in 1864. He married his second wife, Bertha Erck, in 1874. They had seven children, three of whom survived to adulthood. My father, Otto, was the oldest. Conrad was a printer by trade, and superintendent of the printing department of Concordia Publishing House in St. Louis, at the time of his death from diabetes and gangrene in 1902. He and his wife, who died in 1940 at 86, are buried in Concordia Cemetery in St. Louis, Missouri.

Otto Erbe and Louise Festner were married in Omaha in 1902 where he was serving as pastor of the German Lutheran Church. They moved to Boone, Iowa, in 1906, spending the next 40 years of his pastorate and raising six children. This was where I fit in, born October 25, 1919, the sixth and last child. My father died in 1960 at age 83. My mother died in 1963 at age 88. They are buried in the family plot at Linwood Park Cemetery in Boone, Iowa, along with my brothers and sisters.

Norm & Jackie Golden Wedding Anniversary, 1992.

Jackie and and our daughter DeElda Wittmack, 1992.

Charlie Wittmack, Grandson, DeElda's son.

Ellen Wittmack, Grandaughter

Jennifer Wilson & Justine Beriker, 1996

Justine & Timur Beriker, 1996

Kevin & Edward Sisson, 1996

Jacqueline & Henry Sisson, 1996

INDEX